SURVEILLANCE IN GREECE

FROM ANTICOMMUNIST TO CONSUMER SURVEILLANCE

Surveillance in Greece

FROM ANTICOMMUNIST TO CONSUMER SURVEILLANCE

Minas Samatas

ΡΕLLΔ
PELLA PUBLISHING COMPANY, INC.
New York, NY 10018-6401
2004

Surveillance in Greece:
From Anticommunist to
Consumer Surveillance

© Copyright 2004
by MINAS SAMATAS

Library of Congress Control Number 2004195203

ISBN 0-918618-90-4

PRINTED IN THE UNITED STATES OF AMERICA
BY
ATHENS PRINTING COMPANY
337 West 36th Street
New York, NY 10018-6401

To the memory of
my father, *Michael Samatas*
and *Aspasia Lydaki*, my godmother

TABLE OF CONTENTS

Part IV
The Galaxy of Nonstate Surveillance

Part V
Ineffective Legal and Institutional Privacy Protection

Part VI
Surveillance and Democracy in Greece:
The Legacy of Mass Repressive Surveillance

PREFACE AND ACKNOWLEDGEMENTS

A FTER LIVING ALMOST 12 years for studies in New York City, and returning to Greece in 1987, long before the 9/11/2001 tragic events, throughout all these years, I have been teaching and researching political sociology issues at the Sociology Department of the University of Crete. At the same time, I have been a participant observer of the liberalization, modernization, and "Europeanization" of Greek post-dictatorial statism, after Greece's full membership in the European Union and the European passport-free Schengen zone. As a Greek and European citizen, parent, and consumer, I had the opportunity to experience not only the modernization of Greek state surveillance but also "Euro-surveillance," and market surveillance as well. Without these new surveillance experiences in Greece , my surveillance study would be limited and outmoded.

My first interest in the issue of surveillance emerged with my post graduate studies in political sociology at the Graduate Faculty of the New School for Social Research, in N.Y.C. I had focused then on the analysis of Greek statism, from the establishment of the Greek state in 1830 until the early PASOK administration in the 1980s. The issue of state surveillance recording in police files of the entire Greek population's political beliefs and activities was a central issue in my dissertation analysis, "Greek Bureaucratism: A system of sociopolitical control" (1986).

Political control surveillance was also the issue of my first post doctoral publications in the *Journal of Hellenic Diaspora*: a. "Greek McCarthyism" (1986b) and b. "The populist phase of an underdeveloped surveillance society"(1993). The research materials for all these writings could have been adequate to publish a book on the Greek state's surveillance ten years ago. Such an early publication however, would be mostly focused on the Greek state's political control surveillance, without any serious reference to the new types of surveillance for mainly market and profit purposes, which then were not developed in Greece.

Thus, after I have tried to study the whole range of "panopticism" in Greece, i.e., all types of state and private surveillance, I can , finally, publish this book. Therefore, this delayed publication is a challenging and ambitious attempt, not to record every type and case of the various surveillance and data collection practices in contemporary Greece, but to sociopolitically analyze the whole phenomenon of "Surveillance in Greece: from anti-communist to consumer surveillance," comparing the new "soft" surveillance with the traditional "hard" one.

Since the first two chapters of this book go back to my Ph.D. dissertation, I wish to thank again my teachers in the Graduate Faculty of the New School University, Professors Jeffrey Goldfarb, Andrew Arato, and Adamantia Pollis , who encouraged me to study "Greek Bureaucratism." I also have to acknowledge the valuable theoretical and empirical inspiration I have received from the wonderful websites of the "Surveillance Project" and the electronic journal *Surveillance and Society*, directed by the Canadian sociologist Prof. David Lyon, an international expert on the sociology of surveillance. I would like also to thank the Greek press, from which I have got most of my information and exhibits; also the *Statewatch Group* and *Privacy International* for their valuable help via their websites to substantiate several issues of this study, especially those on "Euro-surveillance." I would like to thank Dr. Stefanos Stavros, a jurist and lawyer at the Secreteriat of the European Commission of Human Rights, who kindly has sent me several applications of the law and judgments by the European Court of Human Rights against Greece. I find the opportunity to thank all my dear friends and relatives in NYC, especially my cousin George and Kiki Spanos's family, and Lygnos Brothers Shipping, who have supported me during my long studies there. I wish to give my profuse thanks to my dear friend Melinda J. Scott, who generously has spent so much of her time to edit my original work, and my close friend Nick Patouris, who still continues to provide me with American articles and books. My dear brother Marinos, who has shipped valuable Greek literature and documents to me in NYC, also continues to bring pertinent materials to my attention. Nicole Lachanas has worked hard to edit the new chapters; my 14-year-old daughter Maria has eagerly scanned the photo exhibits, and my wife Angeliki has spent long hours in computing and has helped me in countless ways to complete this project. This book is finally published thanks to my publisher Leandros Papathanasiou, who was patient enough to wait for me for so long.

This book is dedicated first to the memory of my father, Michael Samatas, who passed away three years ago; he, like thousands of other Greeks, used to be very proud of his police surveillance dossier, despite its serious negative impact on his and his whole family's life chances. It is also dedicated to the memory of a school teacher, Aspasia Lydaki, a tragic victim of the Greek repressive parastate back in the 1950s, who was my godmother.

Rethymnon, Crete, December 2003
M.S.

INTRODUCTION

S URVEILLANCE IS AN INTERESTING feature of contemporary infor- mation market societies; various sociological approaches empha- size different dimensions of surveillance (Lyon, D. 1988 & Webster, Fr. 1995). In our sociopolitical view, *surveillance reflects both moderniza- tion and democratization of a state and society;* aside technological advance and determinism, *surveillance function, impact, and control reflect the power relations in a given society.* Hence, this book is not about spies and technology, but *surveillance and democracy in Greece* throughout the last 50 years. Our study begins with the post-Civil War era, marked by the repressive anticommunist state surveillance, and ends with the present time of booming consumer, market surveillance. Starting with the 1950s post-Civil War period, and a reference to the interwar origins and foundations of anticommunist surveillance in the 1920s, we study surveillance in Greece in close relation to the sociopolitical processes of the Greek state and society, following up until the preparation for the Athens 2004 Olympic Games.

Over the past 50 years, Greece has been transformed from a post-Civil War developing society with an authoritarian police state and a "guided democracy" to a democratic market society and a full mem- ber of the European Union (EU), enjoying the most liberal period of its modern history. This liberalization and modernization is also reflected in the fact that Greece has ceased to be an oppressive surveil- lance society; the traditional police surveillance of Greek citizens' political convictions and activities, and its sociopolitical impact on their life chances, has formally ended in 1974 after the collapse of the military dictatorship. Democratization of Greece has been directly related to the end of institutionalized anticommunism, political con- trol by state surveillance, and the sorting of and discrimination toward Greek citizens, as well as by the constitutional guarantee of civil liber-

1

ties and freedom of expression. Surveillance has ceased to be a monopoly of the Greek state, and the basic mechanism for sociopolitical control. Traditionally surveillance was an exclusive privilege of the repressive police state, which has used the notorious police paper files, or dossiers, (*fakeloi*) to enforce loyalty to the regime and to discriminate against all those stigmatized as Greek leftists or dissenters. In contemporary Greece, many different types of electronic surveillance are applied daily for multiple purposes and by various powers to affect and control citizens. Like in every developed western society, this new type of extensive, routine, institutional surveillance is used almost everywhere in Greece through the use of cameras, closed-circuit television (CCTV), computer systems, databanks, and even satellites. Surveillance is conducted on the street, at work, at shopping centers, at banks, on various modes of transportation, at play, at home, and on the Internet, and for various purposes, reflecting the remarkable socioeconomic, political, and cultural changes in the Greek state and society, in relation to the European integration processes and a globalized information capitalist market.

Although Greek people still react against state, police surveillance due to the authoritarian past, most Greek consumers easily consent to their market surveillance, and a large Greek TV audience enjoys to watch and participate in "Big Brother" reality TV shows. The new Hellenic Data Protection Authority (HDPA) has been established in Greece as a requirement of the country's membership in the Schengen Agreement. In brief, the modernization, democratization, and Europeanization of the Greek state and society is also reflected in the technological, legislative, and institutional modernization of surveillance in Greece. From the "ugly" repressive, anticommunist, political control state/police monopoly surveillance in the past, the Greek people are now surveillance subjects of a galaxy of multiple electronic surveillance by the state and suprastates, institutions and individuals, public and private, with and without consent, for legitimate and illegitimate purposes, for security and profit, and even for entertainment and self-monitoring.

DEVELOPED AND UNDERDEVELOPED
SURVEILLANCE SOCIETIES

Academic inquiry and privacy advocates argue that information societies—dependent on information exchange through the use of computers and telecommunication devices—are becoming "surveillance societies" (Flaherty, D.H. 1989: 409, Castells 1996, 1997, Lyon 1994, 2001). Information technologies have immensely increased the technical ability of both modern governments and corporations to collect detailed personal information on their populations, either for legitimate purposes, such as security, law enforcement, revenue collection, welfare programs, licensing, registration, traffic control, etc., or for illegitimate purposes, such as sociopolitical control, discrimination, and other expediencies.

In our information and surveillance age, it is quite possible for any developing authoritarian society to use advanced surveillance technology for illegitimate purposes without any control and respect to civil liberties. Yet, regardless of the level of surveillance technology, real *advanced* or "developed surveillance societies," are only the truly *democratic* societies, which: 1) have advanced technical ability for legitimate surveillance, using it basically for lawful purposes, and 2) have installed effective institutional and legislative control mechanisms that satisfactorily safeguard the privacy and civil liberties of their citizens, holding accountable all those who exploit surveillance. On the other hand, we consider "underdeveloped surveillance societies" those which, regardless of their sociopolitical system, economic development, and technological surveillance ability, use surveillance for basically illegitimate purposes, without any substantial legal protection or respect for personal and civil liberties, openness, social control, and accountability. In other words, "surveillance development" or "underdevelopment" is reflected not simply by the technical surveillance apparatus, but mainly by the fact of whether or not societies have established effective safeguards to protect their citizens' rights. In democratic market societies, there is a policy of serious control, openness, and accountability of all those who collect private information by par-

liamentary and independent agencies and by civil society organizations, despite legislative inefficiency and the imbalance of power
between surveillance powers and surveillance subjects (Foucault
1976). The European Union officially promotes such institutional and
legislative controls against intrusive surveillance, however problematic
can be their implementation and the actual enforcement, as is argued
in our pertinent chapter on "Euro-surveillance" in Greece.

Hence, for example, if Sweden—with a highly computerized civil
service and a very efficient state apparatus, has institutionalized legitimate surveillance, which is accepted by its powerful civil society
mainly due to bureaucratic accountability and informed trust between
the state and its citizens—can be considered as a model of an advanced
surveillance society,[1] post-Civil War Greece, according to our analysis,
was definitely an oppressive surveillance state and an underdeveloped
surveillance society. Even before entering the information age and
without using informatics at that time, the Greek state organized mass
surveillance of its entire population as a basic anticommunist sociopolitical control mechanism, in order to enforce mass loyalty (Samatas
1986). Post-dictatorial Greece, 20 years after the fall of the dictatorship, still remained an underdeveloped surveillance society, due to the
authoritarian remnants in the state apparatus and the insecurity of
"Machiavellian" populist leaderships. Ever since, however, in the mid-
1990s, after entering the European Monetary Union and the Schengen
Information System, Greece has joined the developed European surveillance societies, facing new problems and challenges.

It must be added that the above distinction between surveillance
"development" or "underdevelopment" disregards technological
determinism and applies primarily to formal democratic states and
parliamentary democracies with formally established constitutional

[1]Sweden is undoubtedly the model of a developed surveillance society in the capitalist world because of: 1) its high degree of automation, 2) the pervasiveness of the
"Personal Identification Number" (PIN) for record linkages and data transfers
between the public and private sectors, and 3) a complex legal structure, dominated
by "the principle of openness" expressed in its famous Freedom of the Press Act, that
makes available to third parties a wide range of identifiable personal data normally
kept confidential in other countries. (Flaherty, D. H. 1989: 143-155).

freedoms. This is because in authoritarian and totalitarian regimes, surveillance is always supplemented by open or disguised mass violence and terror against citizens' rights (Giddens 1987:303-304, Clive, Th. 1984: 88-92). Therefore, in our analysis we are not interested in the surveillance technology used by brutal dictatorial, nondemocratic regimes, such as the Greek military dictatorship of 1967-1974.

Thus, by studying surveillance in Greece in the whole postwar period up to the present, we don't focus on the introduction of new surveillance technology, but rather on the modernization of the Greek sociopolitical control system vis-à-vis civil liberties and democracy. *Our surveillance analysis is not technocentric but sociopolitical.* That is, we don't analyze surveillance technology and every type of high-tech sophisticated monitoring and data collection method as determinant of social change and as an omnipotent "Big Brother" type of power; *instead, our analysis is sociopolitical, with a historical and a comparative dimension, relating surveillance to the power relations in Greek society, critically exploring contradictions and resistance.* Thus, the goal of this study is to analyze "Greek panopticism," i.e., a variety of various surveillance systems in Greek society, from a sociopolitical control perspective, that is, as a mechanism of the sociopolitical control system, by which the various power elite and institutions monitor and classify Greek citizens for security and profit, control and influence, creating new inclusions and exclusions, favors and discriminations.

TRADITIONAL AND NEW SURVEILLANCE IN GREECE

The sociopolitical study of surveillance in contemporary societies interrelates the expanding trend of "panopticism" with the changing role of the nation-state in a globalized capitalist market, and the impact of all those who use new electronic surveillance technologies to affect and control individual subjects. That is why regardless who is watching whom, and the legitimacy of the surveillance motives, the fact that a range of surveillance either by the state or by private individuals and firms can have a discriminatory impact on personal choices and life chances, producing a new social sorting of exclusion and inclusion, gives political dimensions to the new surveillance, even to the market, consumer surveillance. Hence, the dichotomy of "traditional" and "new surveillance," is preferred to the political or non political, not only on technological criteria but on qualitative ones. In the Greek case, we preferably refer to the traditional surveillance, mainly the anticommunist surveillance that was conducted by the authoritarian Greek state for sociopolitical control, perpetuated with some post-dictatorial remnants until the 1980s vis-à-vis the new surveillance, which since the mid-1990s is not directly used for political control, but for security, marketing, and profit purposes, including state and private surveillance. Thus, the most characteristic of traditional surveillance in Greece was the anticommunist surveillance, while the most characteristic type of new surveillance is the consumer surveillance, gradually developed since the 1990s. This is not an evolutionary process but a democratization and modernization process of the Greek state and society; from authoritarian statism in the postwar and post-Civil War period, to the present democratic market society, integrated in the European Union in the post-dictatorial period.

Both traditional and new surveillance in Greece have always worked as a mechanism of sociopolitical sorting, classifying people with various criteria for inclusion or exclusion, raising sociopolitical and ethical questions. If traditional state surveillance in postwar Greece has always sorted people into sociopolitical categories of loyal and disloyal citizens to the regime, seriously affecting their life chances, new surveillance in contemporary Greece, like in every democratic information society, by the use of the new surveillance technologies either by the state or by the market, has broadened the classification criteria beyond strictly political behavior to create all sorts of citizens' profiles. These include consumer, genetic, driving, credit, and more profiles, and affect not just personal privacy but democracy and social justice (Lyon D. 2003). Although the new surveillance is more legitimated and not repressive, both traditional and new surveillance in Greece maintain an ethically and politically discriminatory character.

SURVEILLANCE VERSUS PRIVACY

Although surveillance usually violates privacy and raises the issue of privacy protection, our analysis is not limited to the surveillance impact on individual freedom. This is because firstly privacy is not a right, but a market commodity in informational capitalism; hence the end of privacy growing literature (Etzioni, A. 1999, Berman J. & Bruening P. 2001, Kateb G. 2001, Sykes Ch. 1999); secondly, because privacy protection can be treated as a personal issue based upon individual responsibility; and thirdly because of the absence of the concept of privacy in Greek traditional society and culture (Pollis 1977, 1988). Unlike personal privacy protection as an individual issue, surveillance is a part of the social power system, closely related with state, corporate, and symbolic power and manipulation. To limit and control the concentration of state, corporate, and symbolic power in our democracies, the power of people as citizens, consumers, and Internet users must be enhanced in general. Instead of blaming weak or irresponsible individuals, who are unable to protect, and occasionally even sell out, their privacy, there must be strict mechanisms to enforce institutional accountability of all those whose power is enhanced by unchecked surveillance and privacy intrusions (Stalder F. 2002). That is why the current ever-expanding globally and locally electronic "panopticism," i.e., the multiple daily electronic surveillance of citizens by various watchers and data collectors on behalf of state/political, corporate/economic, and symbolic/cultural power holders, is an exciting new social research field.

THE IMPACT OF TERRORISM

Another significant factor that has been taken into consideration in our analysis of new surveillance is that of terrorism; because in our times terrorism reinforces and legitimizes state and supra-state surveillance against human rights and civil liberties. In our early writings about Greek anticommunist surveillance, we had used the term

"Greek McCarthyism" (Samatas 1986) to point out the contribution of the Americans and the similarities of McCarthyism with Greek anti-communist surveillance and repression. Unfortunately, after the 9/11 terrorist attacks, we observe trends of "neo-McCarthyism" in the United States, which affect civil liberties in that country, but also in all American allies' countries and beyond. It is indeed ironic the fact that in this early 21st-century period, after the Soviet block has collapsed and the Cold War has ended, surveillance and a neo-McCarthyite-style of thought control is reviving, not only in the United States but also in the European Union, and subsequently in societies with an authoritarian past, such as Greece. In the name of security and the war against terrorism, state and supra-state surveillance is again legitimated and human rights are again at risk. Panopticism is now legitimated to face not the communist threat, but the terrorism of fanatics from abroad and within; EU suprastate surveillance has also been reinforced to face the overall border threats from illegal immigration. Market and other private surveillance are integrated in the service of a super state panopticism in a globalized network society (Castells 1997, Norris & Amstrong 1999, Lyon 2001:142ff). In Greece, the inefficiency of police to arrest the November 17 terrorist group has invited the antiterrorist surveillance of Americans and British (see Chapter 5).

FOUR SURVEILLANCE PERIODS IN GREECE

Although institutional anticommunism was formally banned in Greece after the end of the dictatorship and the legalization of the Greek Communist Party (KKE) in 1974, there were surviving anti-communist remnants and generally direct political surveillance until the mid-1980s, even after the Panhellenic Socialist Movement (PASOK) came to power. Hence, although traditional state surveillance in Greece, which basically monitored citizens' political beliefs and activities, seriously affecting their life chances, was formally abolished in 1974 and more substantially in 1981 by PASOK, it survived in Greece well into 1996; until then the police and security apparatus was not qualitatively changed, and was targeting the political opponents of each regime. Even if electronic surveillance has been eventually adopted by the Greek state since the 1980s, we consider that the new surveillance period in Greece actually begins in 1996, when the populist PASOK leader Andreas Papandreou was succeeded by the modernizer Costas Simitis, and Greece was fully integrated in the European Union, prescribing new legislation and institutions for personal data protection. Traditional anticommunist surveillance functioned until 1974 and its remnants until 1989. New electronic state, suprastate, and private market surveillance grew in the 1990s, and has flourished in the current period, which is the last under examination. Since new EU institutions and legislation are enforced for privacy protection, however efficient they can be, and also due to the Athens 2004 Olympic Games surveillance requirements, Greece has joined the advanced surveillance states.

Therefore, considering surveillance, either by the state or by the market, as a basic sociopolitical control mechanism, we examine four surveillance periods in Greece; these periods reflect the changing sociopolitical control system from post-Civil War Greece up to the present before the Athens 2004 Olympic Games. These periods are:

a. repressive anticommunist surveillance, until the end of military dictatorship, 1950-1974;
b. post-dictatorial state political control surveillance, 1974-1981;
c. populist and "Machiavellian" surveillance, during the first PASOK administration of 1981-1989, including also the second PASOK administration of 1993-1996 under Andreas Papandreou, and the New Democracy neo-liberal parenthesis during 1989-1993;
d. the current modernization and Europeanization period, 1996 to the present (2003).

During this last period with Costas Simitis's premiership, Greece became a full member of the European Monetary Union as well as had signed the Schengen Agreement, implementing the Schengen Information System (SIS), the Hellenic Data Protection Authority (HDPA) and modernizing the Greek police and security apparatus in anticipation of the Athens 2004 Olympic Games antiterrorist challenge, particularly in light of the tragic events of 9/11/2001 in the United States. Greece during this last period, as a fully integrated European Union member state, has been developed as both a democratic market society and an advanced surveillance society.

THE ORGANIZATION OF THE BOOK

In the following first part of the book, we examine the most characteristic "traditional surveillance" in Greece, i.e., the anticommunist repressive surveillance of the post-Civil War state from 1950 until the end of the military dictatorship in 1974. We don't particularly analyze the dictatorial surveillance, which was supplemented by naked violence and open repression. Based on our research and the Greek bibliography, we present the interwar origins and foundations of anticommunist surveillance by the liberal Prime Minister Eleftherios Venizelos, during 1910-1920. We also present the significant American contribution after the Truman Doctrine, by the dictation of specific anticommunist legislation and persecutions, during the entire post-Civil War period until the fall of the military dictatorship, which have led us to call it in a previous study "Greek McCarthyism," emphasizing the similarities to McCarthyism in the United States. Traditional anticommunist surveillance had taken totalitarian dimensions in Greece; it was very efficient as a mechanism of the authoritarian sociopolitical control system, due to the efficiency of the Greek police state and its information network that suffocated the entire society. In the same part we also analyze anticommunist surveillance in the post-dictatorial period 1974-1981 as a remnant of the authoritarian past, reflecting how difficult the democratization process was in Greece, where the transition from dictatorship to democracy was not a revolutionary process but a peaceful transition that maintained the military and the security apparatus almost intact.

In the same first part we also include the 1981-1995 period dominated by the PASOK socialist movement, under the charismatic Andreas Papandreou premiership. The first PASOK administration during 1981-1989, despite the end of institutionalized anticommunism and the liberation of society from most remnants of the police state, proved its populistic character first by its negligence in fulfilling its promise to ban anticommunist surveillance entirely and burn the files of all Greek citizens used to exercise political control. In addition, the close associates of the PASOK leader continued a "Machiavellian" surveillance practice by wiretapping real and potential opponents, even his ministers. Populistic surveillance politics continued after the electoral loss of PASOK in 1989 to the neo-liberal New Democracy government of the veteran Prime Minister Costantine Mitsotakis. The burning of the obsolete anticommunist paper files in 1989 targeted Papandreou, who had not kept his promise to destroy them since 1984; Mitsotakis, after revealing Papandreou's wiretaps and trying to persecute him for that, also organized his own wiretapping secret system, which was subsequently revealed in 1994, when Andreas Papandreou came back to power. Mitsotakis's "Machiavellian" surveillance was on par with Papandreou's, and in a compromise move he was not persecuted. Papandreou had also resisted signing the Schengen Agreement due to national sovereignty concerns.

In part two, we start to analyze the new surveillance in Greece, related to the suprastate "Euro-surveillance," i.e., the Schengen Information System, and its implementation problems in Greece; we also look at the foreign antiterrorist surveillance in Greece by Americans and British intelligence. As we have mentioned, this new surveillance period actually begins in Greece in 1996 by the administration of modernizer Prime Minister Costas Simitis, who succeeded Andreas Papandreou in the PASOK leadership. After the Imia crisis with Turkey, Simitis signed the Schengen Agreement to make the disputed Greek Aegean borders the external borders of the European Union. He also started to officially cooperate with the Americans and the British to fight Greek and international terrorism in preparation for the 2004 Athens Olympic Games. This new period was also marked by the Greek fiasco of the Kurdish leader Abdullah Ocalan in February 1999, in which American satellites and ground intelligence, with the assistance of Israeli intelligence, played a significant surveillance role in tracking him down, arresting him in Kenya, and delivering him to the Turks. Next to the Imia crisis that pushed Greece into the Schengen Surveillance System, and the Ocalan arrest, which caused the modernization of Greek National Intelligence Service (EYP) and contributed to the improvment of the relations of Simitis government with Americans and eventually with Turks, the third significant surveillance event was the murder of British Military Attaché Stephen Saunders by the November 17 Greek terrorist group in June 2001. Saunders' murder officially invited the British Intelligence into Greece. Unlike the Americans who suspected several prominent PASOK members and intellectuals of being terrorists, the British actually contributed to the arrest and trial of the November 17 terrorist group, which was proved in the trial not to have any relation to PASOK or to the parliamentary leftist parties.

In part three we discuss the modernization of the Greek state surveillance and the Athens 2004 "Olympic panopticism." The Schengen Agreement, and the foreign antiterrorist battle in Greece have significantly contributed to the electronic, legislative and institutional modernization of Greek state surveillance. Yet, under the post-9/11 global security crisis, the security of the Athens 2004 Olympic Games has pushed forward the modernization of Greek security and surveillance apparatus. Americans, British, Israelis, and several other states and corporate intelligence and security services, even NATO, have undertaken the security of the Olympic Games together with the SAIC-Siemens private international security consortium. Hence, we naturally speak of "Olympic super transnational panopticism."

In part four we examine the flourishing new galaxy of private and market surveillance. Although we don't examine all technological surveillance applications, we focus on the most characteristic, such as: CCTV, consumer profiles, "Big Brother" TV, "Big Brother" schools, satellite surveillance such as GPS, mobile phones, banking credit surveillance, etc. We also mention the surveillance merging of state, suprastate, and private business in Greece.

Next, in part five, we discuss the ineffective institutional and legislative anti-surveillance protections, emphasizing the anti-surveillance and privacy protection decisions of the Hellenic Data Protection Authority. Then we present three indicative surveillance cases: a. the violation of freedom of expression of a Greek officer, who had revealed the surveillance of the Greek Army; b. surveillance against a member of Jehovah's Witness, and also c. the privacy violation (mail-opening) of a foreign detainee; all had won compensations in the European Court of Human Rights against Greece.

Instead of a conclusion, in part six, we close with a general correlation of surveillance to democracy in Greece. We also discuss the popular attitude of Greek people vis-à-vis surveillance, as a legacy of the coercive political control surveillance in the authoritarian past. The comparison of traditional with new surveillance in Greece, based on qualitative rather than technical features, helps our assessment for the prospects of a democratic anti-surveillance and privacy protection movement in Greece, such as in the United States, the United Kingdom, and other advanced surveillance societies.

In the Appendix, we present a variety of 30 documents representing both traditional political control surveillance and the new state, suprastate, and market surveillance.

Part I

TRADITIONAL, STATE SURVEILLANCE

Chapter 1

ANTICOMMUNIST REPRESSIVE SURVEILLANCE IN POSTWAR GREECE: A BASIC MECHANISM OF SOCIOPOLITICAL CONTROL

A. THE LIBERAL INTERWAR ORIGINS OF MASS POLITICAL SURVEILLANCE IN GREECE

MASS POLITICAL SURVEILLANCE of the entire Greek population as a significant mechanism of the Greek anticommunist state goes back to the liberal Prime Minister Eleftherios Venizelos's era in the first decades of the 20th century.[1]

Greek institutionalized anticommunism, not just as an ideological campaign but as an organized state policy of political repression, reflected in specific laws and actions, was based on mass political surveillance.[2] Its organization began much earlier than the post-Civil War period, during the decade 1910-1920, when, because of the impact of the October Revolution in Russia, the Greek Socialist Labor Party (SEKE) was founded in 1918, and in 1924 it was named the Communist Party of Greece (KKE). (Moskof, K. 1979:413-414).

As early as 1919, the first overtly anticommunist, repressive legislation, with its special administrative measures against the newly

[1]See Koundouros 1978, Lazarides 1979, Alivizatos 1983, and Samatas 1986, 1986b.

[2]Anticommunism is a defensive state overreaction based on the perception of a threat from below. It justifies gross discrimination against any person or any organization which, because of its politico-ideological beliefs, is perceived as presenting a fundamental challenge to existing power relationships or to key governmental policies. Goldstein, J. (1978) xvi.

17

organized Greek labor movement, was introduced and implemented by Venizelos. He also legalized the first "administrative deportations" in Greece for purely political reasons, based on police preventive surveillance of the suspects. In fact, Venizelos extended the brigandage law provisions used since 1871, to include every person *suspected* of disturbing the "public security" (Law 121 of 1913, Art. 2). Similarly, Venizelist Law 755 of August 18, 1917, extended compulsory preventive deportation, not only for every acknowledged spy but also for everyone *suspected* as dangerous to public order.[3]

The Venizelist anticommunist campaign was intensified during 1928-1932, when the rising Greek labor movement significantly increased its strike activity. Permanent police stations were established throughout the country, and in February, 1929, the Special Police Security Directorate was formed for more systematic surveillance and persecution of leftists and sympathizers.[4]

The landmark law of the Venizelist anticommunist armory was Law 4229 (July 25, 1929), the so-called *idionymo* law, enacting "measures for the security of the existing social regime." It introduced, in effect, the criminalization of communist ideology, without banning the Greek communist party, KKE. It prohibited not only specific political ideas and deeds, but also any idea or deed that could be presumed dangerous to the rulers. Named *idionymo* because it introduced a new crime (the "thought crime"), this law legalized state anticommunist repressive surveillance and oppression of every progressive idea from that time forward, and became the legal cornerstone of official Greek anticommunism until 1974 (Lazarides, J. 1979; Alivizatos, N. 1983: 360-374 and Koundouros, R. 1978: 81-94).

From 1935 on, however, this coercive anticommunist legislation and security surveillance apparatus backfired on its first imple-

[3]For details on this Venizelist legislation, see Alivizatos's *Political Institutions*, 342, 347-350. For the first prosecutions of Greek socialists under these laws, see A. Elefantis (1976), 46f. (Note: in Greek) see also Leon, G. B. (1976) 119f.

[4]Also during this Venizelist time the first disciplinary military concentration camp, used mainly for the incarceration of communist conscripts, was founded in Kalpaki. Koundouros 109f., Alivizatos 390, Moskof 460.

menters, the liberal Venizelists. The conservative monarcho-oligarchic regime was reestablished, and especially during the fascist-oriented Ioannis Metaxas dictatorship from 1936-1941, anticommunist legislation and security armory were used to persecute not only leftists but also anti-royalists and liberal Venizelists. (Linardatos, S. 1965; Alivizatos, N. 1983: 404-411). In fact, the Metaxas military dictatorship perfected the Venizelist anticommunist armory into a long-lived system of political control "technology," which included:

a. An overcentralized, bureaucratic security apparatus directed by the notorious underministry of public security, which supervised all state agencies and conducted systematic repressive surveillance of *the entire population*;

b. Use of the notorious "civic-mindedness certificates" (*pistopoiitika koinonikon fronimaton*) issued by local police, based upon the anticommunist classification surveillance records (files). These certificates, formally surviving until 1974, required for all state-citizen relations, were designed to reward loyal citizens and to punish dissidents who, without them, were excluded from all public jobs, permits, licenses, passports, benefits, etc. (see Exhibit 1);

c. Use of so-called "repentance declarations," (*dilosis metanoias*), also surviving until 1974, required to be signed for the release of those converted political prisoners, or of anyone wishing to be cleared of the communist stigma, either inherited by his family or ascribed;

d. The increase and extension of mass deportations, and the organization of specific anticommunist reconversion "laboratories," i.e., concentration camps, which used mixed physical and psychological terror against communists and other leftists;

e. The organization of most of the countryside (particularly the lengthy border areas) into militarized, "surveillance," or "prohibited" zones, targeting the "internal enemies." In these "defensive" areas, which included almost all of Northern Greece with its over one million inhabitants (in 1961), the security forces and the

militia (TEA) exercised total control, including physical and psychological repression, especially of ethnic minorities *related to
the neighbor Balkan states* (Alivizatos, N. 1983 420-433, Elefantis,
A. 1976; 256-262f., Koundouros R. 1978:106f., Linardatos, S.
1966).

All this pre-Second World War anticommunist "technology,"
based on mass political surveillance, restored and perfected during
and after the Greek Civil War of 1947-1949 by concrete US legislation
and political control technology, was perpetuated until the end of the
military dictatorship in 1974.

B. THE POST-CIVIL WAR GREEK ANTICOMMUNIST CRUSADE AND MASS REPRESSIVE SURVEILLANCE: "GREEK MCCARTHYISM"

The anticommunist winners of the Greek Civil War, with US guidance
and assistance, organized an oppressive anticommunist sociopolitical
control system, legitimated by a semi-parliamentary, "guided democracy." This elaborate state-organized sociopolitical control system
combined parliamentary and repressive control mechanisms to
impose *ethnikofrosyni,* i.e. national loyalty and conformity to the post-
Civil War regime (Samatas, M. 1986). The security police and military
surveillance network throughout the whole country, without the use
of computers and other electronic devices, systematically watched,
collected, stored, and updated information in special surveillance files.
Based on these surveillance records on sociopolitical ideology and
activity of every Greek citizen, group, and organization, they classified
them according to their "national loyalty" (*ethnikofrosyni*) criteria.
This bureaucratic surveillance procedure, expressed by the popular
Greek term *fakeloma* (literally, filing), was the basic mechanism of the
oppressive sociopolitical control system, which I have called "authoritarian bureaucratism" (Samatas 1986). It was used by the postwar anticommunist Greek state to enforce mass loyalty, classifying citizens

either as loyal, "healthy," nationally minded, *ethnikofrones*, or stigmatizing them as non-nationally minded "dirt," or *miasma*, a label applied not just to communists, leftists, or sympathizers, but also to anyone "disloyal"—not actively demonstrating conformity and obedience to the anticommunist regime (Samatas, M. 1986b).

US AND "GREEK McCARTHYISM"

The whole communist crusade in Greece was orchestrated by the United States; it took place under a liberal parliamentary camouflage that protected the Greek state's repressive policies from the American Congress and international scrutiny. The authoritarian policies and mass repression was targeted not only to Greek communists, who were considered Soviet agents, but also included the daily monitoring of the entire Greek population, especially a large segment of citizens who had been stigmatized as leftists or leftist sympathizers[5]Although US intervention in the Greek Civil War succeeded militarily, a need still existed to eliminate the ideological power of the communist-led National Liberation Front "*Ethniko Apeleftherotiko Metopo*" (EAM) and to void its effect on the Greek people. The ensuing ideological operation, rightly called "deEAMization," occurred not during an openly dictatorial regime, but during an apparently liberal parliamentary one.[6] The

[5]The post-Civil War liberal government stated bluntly in October 1949 when legalizing its "National Reformation Measures": "None of the (political) prisoners detained in prisons and (concentration) camps will return home unless they repent and subjugate themselves to the way of life which we insist on establishing in Greece with the ample aid and assistance of our trans-Atlantic allies." Quoted in the "Omicron Gamma Decree," published in the Government Gazette (Oct. 14, 1949).

[6]The liberal Prime Minister Themistoklis Sophoulis, a leader approved by the Americans, headed the post-Civil War, center-right coalition government, formed by the efforts of U.S. Ambassador John Peurifoy. He had to assure the United States that the main thrust of his program would be "wildly anti-communist." He agreed that his "individual ministers would be removed at the suggestion of the U.S. if they (were) uncooperative" (Wittner 1982: 134). The cosmetic presence in the Greek Cabinet of pro-US moderates and liberals with no substantial power helped enormously in establishing the domestic and international legitimacy of the Greek anticommunist state,

Americans in Greece projected the image of a great, united national struggle against the "heinous" Greek communists. The latter were portrayed as agents of Soviet expansion, not as indigenous Greeks who were political adversaries of Greek conservatives. (Tsoucalas, C. in Iatrides, J. 1981: 327. Vlanton, E. 1983: 76, and Wittner, L. 1982: 105f.).

In the United States during the early Cold War period in the 1950s, "McCarthyism" was popularly identified as a mass anticommunist crusade, and a repressive politico-ideological policy in which the U.S. government deliberately exercised political discrimination, thought control, surveillance, and invasion into private lives, as well as mass curtailment of civil liberties in order to eradicate communism and enforce mass loyalty (Tanner, W. R. et al. 1974).

Accordingly, I have used the term "Greek McCarthyism" to describe the Greek anticommunist crusade, organized by the United States in Greece after the Greek Civil War to eradicate any leftist influence of EAM, and to guarantee mass loyalty for the anticommunist regime (Samatas, M. 1986b). I have identified four basic similarities between US McCarthyism and the Greek postwar anticommunist campaign, which have led me to use the term "Greek McCarthyism":

1. both ideological anticommunist policies were state-organized, based upon the same repressive thought-control techniques;
2. both were related to the Truman Doctrine, which defended democracy against a perceived international communist conspiracy;
3. both operations have exploited a pre-existing institutional and conceptual anticommunist system;
4. American anticommunist legislation and political control techniques were exported to Greece in order to reinforce its anticommunist armory.

Of course there were significant differences in the US and Greek anticommunist crusades, such as the following:

which was assisted by the United States in accordance with the Truman Doctrine against an international communist conspiracy (Tsoucalas 1981: 327f).

1. While US McCarthyism was directed against an imaginary, domestic communist threat to support Cold War foreign policy, the Greek anticommunist state was the extension of a bloody Civil War, which was necessary to ensure mass loyalty and to consolidate the post-Civil War regime;
2. In contrast to the US anticommunist operation, which was successful for a short period of time but faded after 1955, the Greek counterpart was never successful and had to be *de jure* and *de facto* prolonged until 1974. Some remnants survived until 1982.
3. While McCarthyism can be seen as a repressive operation that affected a relatively small percentage of the US population, Greek McCarthyism, which was far more repressive, assumed totalitarian dimensions and affected the entire Greek population's private life and beliefs.

Let us briefly look at those basic similarities in the Greek anticommunist surveillance operations, modelled after the US McCarthyite ones, starting with some useful generalizations. Neither the US nor the Greek McCarthyism was a spontaneous ideological campaign, but rather a state-organized anticommunist policy employing similar "thought-control" repressive techniques. Both were repressive governmental crusades against a perceived communist threat. Each pursued the extirpation of communism from society "as a belief, as a teaching, as a plan of action, as a moral ideal." (Millis, W. 1968: 60). Both operations grew from the belief that people might potentially engage in "subversive activities" and might possibly *think* "incorrect thoughts, especially thoughts associated with the word 'communism." Also, both anticommunist crusades attempted to define nationalist thought and conduct with respect to orthodoxy and heresy in nationalistic politics. They tried to punish people for beliefs and associations, and to enforce their standards through special paraconstitutional legislation, frequently without due process. (Golstein, R. 1978: 391-392). They each tried to avoid using open physical violence; although that did not succeed in Greece, nevertheless the anticommunist objectives in both countries were pursued through mostly legal-bureaucratic repressive means.

Since American and Greek "mind-probers" could not actually read thoughts, they had to investigate all aspects of an individual's life. They searched not only for factual, documentable "wrong-doing," but also for any potential "wrong-thinking" that might result in *future* "wrong-doing." In fact, in the name of "national security," hundreds of American and thousands of Greek people were severely punished, not for who they were or what they had actually done, but rather for what authorities assumed they were or could potentially become. This "mind-probing" search in both countries included "the petitions one signed, the groups one joined, the books one read, the friendships one had, and the statements one made" (Golstein, R. 1978: 392; Millis, W. 1968:64).

Proof that thought control rather than real, concrete action was the target of anticommunist operations in both the United States and Greece is demonstrated by the fact that political repression in both countries was based primarily upon "preventive" law. "Preventive law" is executive, mostly "paraconstitutional" legislation, which deliberately uses vague terminology to violate constitutional rights, justifying repression on the grounds of national security. (O'Brien, J. L. 1955: 22). "Preventive" law legalizes many repressive measures, such as precautionary detention, or the precautionary exclusion of individuals or groups from certain employment or other activity on the grounds of potential harm to the "national interest" or to national security. These repressive measures are justified on the suspicion that the victims are "potential subversives" who, either implicitly or explicitly are "likely to commit some illegal overt act in the future even if (they) had not already done so." (Golstein, R. 1978:392). Because thought-control and "thought-crime" are difficult to legitimize (although not to legalize), "preventive law" employs paraconstitutional (and frequently illegal) techniques (surveillance, mail-opening, blacklists, etc.) which ignore civil liberties guaranteed by the constitutional protection of due process. Facilitating "preventive" law is the use of deliberately vague terminology: "disloyalty" instead of treason or sedition; and "lack of faith in the national ideals," or "belief in ideas aiming at the violent overthrow of the established sociopolitical order" instead of espionage or sabotage (Golstein, R. 1978: 392, Alivizatos, N. 1981: 224-227).

The basic goal of mass anticommunist repression in the United States and Greece was the protection of these countries from "ideological contamination" by communist (or other) ideas officially labelled "dangerous." Therefore repressive measures targeted not only "habitual wrong-thinkers" ("commies," "pinks," "fussy-minded liberals," etc.) but also all critical thinkers, including their own relatives and friends (Alivizatos, N. 1981, Catiforis, G., 1975: 62-63). The establishment of this "thought-crime," "guilt by association," and "collective responsibility" by US and Greek anticommunist states is reminiscent of the heresy-hunt and other ideological warfare methods of the 17th century (Millis, W. 1968: 66). The argument that political ideology itself was the major "thought-crime" (regardless of the commitment of an actual crime), is evidenced by the fact that "loyalty oaths" or the signing of "loyalty statements" were required for all Greeks like all US, state/federal employees. In Greece "repentance" or "recantation declarations" (*dilosis metanoias*) also had to be signed by converted communists or by those suspected of subversive beliefs and associations. The local press then published these "loyalty statements," which were also read in the church's Sunday service (Harper, A. D. 1969; Barth, A. 1952; 1955; Tsoucalas, C. 1981:328; Alivizatos, N. 1981: 227, and Catiforis, G. 1975: 63f). In the United States, many persons of questionable loyalty, including many teachers and academics, were dismissed from government employment either because they objected to taking anticommunist oaths on principle or because they appealed to the First and Fifth Amendments. By 1956, such oaths were required in 42 states and more than 2,000 county and municipal entities.[7] In Greece, communists sentenced to death could often save their lives just before execution by renouncing their ideas and their past politics. Political prisoners and deportees could be freed as soon as they had signed the

---

[7]"The swearing of loyalty oaths was also required to obtain fishing permits in New York City, to sell insurance or pianos in Washington, D.C., to obtain unemployment compensation in Ohio, to box ... to barber, to sell junk in Indiana ...," etc. (Bontecue, E. 1953: 101-156, and Goldstein, R. J. 1978: 302-4, 351-2).

"declarations of repentance," or "recantation statements," renouncing their ideology and declaring their loyalty to the regime (Alivizatos, N. 1983:226-227).

Another repressive dimension of Greek McCarthyism was guilt by association, or collective family responsibility, so that charges frequently involved associations with mothers, fathers, wives, brothers, and sisters (Alivizatos, N. 1981; Samatas1986b).

In Greece, this institutionalization of the collective responsibility of an accused's entire family was accomplished through the use of the aforementioned "civic-mindedness certificates" (*pistopoiitika koinonikon fronimaton*) (see *Exhibit 1*). These certificates were issued by police only to "healthy thinking" or "nationally minded," "clean" citizens, the so-called *ethnikofrones*. They were denied to all other Greek citizens, who were then stigmatized as communists, fellow-travellers, sympathizers, i.e., the *non-ethnikofrones*. Civic-mindedness certificates based upon police surveillance records, documented in paper dossiers (*fakeloi*), were officially required until 1974 for any Greek who wanted a public job, professional permit, passport, driver's license, even a scholarship or university education. Significantly, these police certificates—and the attendant police dossiers, which, as documented below, were active until finally burnt in 1981-not only classified the "loyalty status" of a citizen based upon his/her personal ideas and activities, but also took into serious account the convictions and behavior of the entire family, going back to the Second World War. Collective responsibility was heavily applied to Greek communists" close relatives, and many, irrespective of their own ideas and politics, had their property seized and were exiled or forcibly detained in special camps for "reconversion and rehabilitation"[8] (Tsoucalas, C. 1981:328; Vergopoulos, C. 1981; Alivizatos, N. 1983: 225; Diamandouros, N. 1983: 52; Samatas, M. 1986: 168-169).

---

[8]In Leros island, a camp, under the auspices of Queen Frederika, functioned as a "Royal Occupation School."

US-MADE ANTICOMMUNIST LEGISLATION AND THOUGHT CONTROL TECHNIQUES ENFORCED IN POSTWAR GREECE

The term "McCarthyism" could characterize Greek post-Civil War anticommunist policy merely on the basis that this policy imported specific US-made anticommunist legislation and control techniques, used extensively during the Truman-McCarthy repressive era. In fact, at AMAG's (American Mission to Aid Greece) suggestion, Greece adopted US legislation and procedures to purge communists from civil service and to develop an anti-subversive security apparatus modelled on the US version. (Alivizatos N. 1983:477-487, 566-578). Greece also adopted US ideological warfare technology and indoctrination techniques (Iatrides, J. 1980: 66-67).

In fact, Greek "emergency" Laws 512 and 516 (1948), plus a similar Law 1540 (1950), restated almost verbatim the basic civil service loyalty-security provisions of concrete US laws,[9] but prescribed harsher penalties.

These US laws were incorporated into Greek legislation, which introduced the fundamental concepts of "loyalty" *(nomimofrosyni)* and "disloyalty." This legislation became the legal justification for "thought-control" investigations of civil servants, which were eventually extended to all Greek citizens. The criterion of "loyalty" as a qualification for public employment in postwar Greece legitimized a repressive apparatus which judged an employee's current loyalty on

[9]a. the "Hatch Act" of August 2, 1939, which was passed to prevent "pernicious political activities" made illegal any civil servant's participation "in a party or organization which supported the overthrow of the U.S. constitutional political system." b. U.S. Civil Service Commission Circular 222 of June 20, 1940, which was issued in accordance with the Hatch Act and Smith Act. It defined as "illegal" any participation in or affiliation with "communist," "Nazi," or "fascist" parties or organizations. These acts permitted the immediate dismissal of participating civil servants and the rejection of any applicant for a public position who was found to be engaging in "illegal" activities. c. the aforementioned Loyalty Order of March 21, 1947 (Executive Order 9835), issued by President Truman. Based on the previous two acts, this Order initiated over 3 million loyalty investigations by both the House Un-American Activities Committee and Civil Service loyalty boards (Emerson, & al. 1967; Alivizatos, N. 1983: 481).

the basis of his previous associations, activities, and beliefs.[10] Without an explicit definition of "disloyalty," the executive order equated it with membership, affiliation or "sympathetic association" with certain types of groups. Thus was established in both countries the precedent for a crime of belief and association, rather than the punishment of actual deeds and activities.

The implementation of Greek "loyalty" laws was very similar to the US "Loyalty Order," which set up "loyalty boards" in all ministries and units of the public sector. Emergency Law 516 (1948), like the US loyalty program, gave Greek loyalty boards the authority to decide on all present or prospective government employees' loyalty based upon any written or oral information they received from any "pertinent available information source."[11] Unlike the US loyalty order, however, the Greek law did not establish any boards to hear testimony from the accused. Nor did it permit any appeals of its decisions to the courts. Furthermore, although the loyalty boards' decisions on "disloyalty" were final for the Civil Service Administration and therefore implied immediate dismissal, the decisions on *loyalty* were *not* binding on the Civil Service Administration.[12] Also, the same Greek loyalty law legalized the mass signing of "loyalty statements" by *all* public servants and agricultural cooperatives. "The refusal to sign such a statement constitutes proof of disloyalty for the employee" was stated explicitly in Article 4, paragraph 3 of Law 516 (Alivizatos, N. 1983: 486).

Two years after the conclusion of the Greek Civil War, but at the peak of the Korean and Cold Wars, the Greek military acted on a suggestion of AMAG by demanding adoption of the US Internal Security

[10]It is important to remember the sixth criterion of the Truman executive order Number 9835: "Membership in, affiliation with or sympathetic association with any foreign or domestic organization, association, movement, group or combination of persons, designated by the Attorney General as having adopted a policy of advocating or approving the commission of acts of force or violence to deny other persons their rights under the Constitution of the U.S. or as seeking to alter the form of government of the U.S. by unconstitutional means." Goldstein 1978: 300-301).

[11]Compare U.S. Loyalty Order 1st Part, Sect. 3 with Greek Law 516 Article 4, Paragraph 2 (Alivizatos, N. 1983: 484).

[12]Compare Article 2, Part II, of the U.S. Loyalty Order with Article 8 and Article 4, Paragraph 3, of Greek Law 516; Alivizatos, N. 1983: 484-486.

Act of September 23, 1950, which went far beyond the US loyalty program. This act had extended the US Espionage Act of 1917 by banning all communist activities, determining them a threat to US national security.[13] Thus Greek Law 1612 (December 31, 1950), in conformance with US law, reactivated the dictator Metaxas' Espionage Law 375 (1936). Law 1612 was implemented by martial law courts, which prosecuted communists and other leftists as spies of the Soviet Union. The accused were tried for crimes against both the national security of the state and of the Greek armed forces. As in the US, they received the death penalty in some cases.[14] Greek security apparatus was modelled on that of the United States and enjoyed direct US assistance, training, and technology. (Klare M. and C. Arnson, 1981: 42; Iatrides, J. 1980:67f.).[15]

The post-Civil War Greek Public Order Ministry organized a central political information databank similar to the FBI's security index list, which contained the names of all dissident, communist, or leftist citizens and "disloyal" fired, or "repentant" civil servants. Until 1974 this political information databank was used constantly and openly to blackmail citizens, and especially public employees, through occupational proscriptions and other repressive measures. This process reinforced mass conformity through civic-mindedness certificates, repentance statements, and loyalty oaths which required denials not

---

[13]As *ESTIA*, the arch-conservative and AMAG-influenced Greek daily, wrote on December 12, 1951: "For years the Greek governments consisting of villains and fellow-travelers have been repeatedly notified (obviously by AMAG) that they should not try the enemy agents during the ten months of the U.N. General Assembly's session; on the other hand they should take measures to prosecute them ... on espionage charges, considering that even in America the reds who are tried as spies are getting the most severe punishment without argument or protest" (parenthetical material inserted). (Cited in Alivizatos, N. 1983: 567).

[14]In the U.S. the only execution was the that of the Rosenbergs; in Greece in 1952 eight communists were sentenced to death. Four of them (including Nicos Mpeloyiannis) were executed on March 30, despite world outcry. The logic of all "espionage" trials in the 1950s and 1960s was, "Communism is spying; since you are communist therefore you are a Soviet spy." Alivizatos N. 1983: 575.

[15]M. Klare and C. Arnson, (1981): 42; Iatrides, J. 1981: 67f.

only of one's past but also of the activities, beliefs, and associations of one's relatives. (Koundouros, R. 1978:128; Catiforis, G. 1975:62; Alivizatos, N. 1983: 486-487).

Under the guidance of the American Military Mission to Greece, the Greek Central Intelligence Agency (KYP, modeled and named after the CIA) was established. KYP was the coordinator of the anticommunist, anti-subversion program, and became the official intelligence agency fighting the "internal enemy" (Iatrides, J. 1980: 66-67; Wittner, L. 1982:150-151). Just as the CIA and FBI used illegal tactics (Goldstein, R. 1978:338f.; Watters, P. and Gillers, S. 1973), so did KYP engage in large-scale surveillance, wiretapping, and mail-opening. By the mid-1950s, its monitoring extended to all vital government agencies, including the press and information departments of the Prime Minister's office (Iatrides, J. 1980: 67f.). Furthermore, the Greek contingency plan dealing with internal security was identical to the US plan for "detention of dangerous individuals at the time of emergency" (announced in August, 1948). It was drawn up by US security advisors and incorporated into the Greek war plan "Phoenix."[16]

AN EFFICIENT COUNTRY-WIDE NETWORK OF PRIVATE INFORMERS TO THE POLICE

Anticommunist surveillance apparatus was not staffed only by police, security and military agents; it was implemented by hundreds private

---

[16]Iatrides, J. 1980 and Roubatis, Y. 1979. Indicative of the anticommunist obsession that U.S. security officers tried to transplant to Greece is the comment of U.S. Acting Secretary of State J. Webb in May, 1950. Contending that the "major dangers confronting Greece now come from within," Webb warned the U.S. Embassy about the possible "recreation of commie org(anizations) and (the) capture of T(rade) U(nion)s and the municipal govts by disguised commies." Webb stressed that "reinforced police vigilance and careful screening of detainees before release" was essential, and that only by these methods would the Greeks "clearly understand (the) commie design and learn (to) recognize the commies and fellow travelers despite misleading labels." Wittner, L. 1982: 154 and Iatrides, J. 1981: 67).

informers to the police in every corner of Greek society. These informers (*hafiedes*), who numbered 60,000 on secret payrolls in 1962, (Tsoucalas, C. 1981: 328) were mostly ex-communists and lumpen
proletarians who purchased their personal freedom by spying against
fellow citizens and reporting to the police. Visceral anticommunism
and/or nationalist convictions (*ethnikosfrosyni*) proved by reporting to
the police *became* the keys for access to public funds, and to tax and
legal immunities for many new profiteers and former nazi-collabora-
tors, who never had been punished. (Vergopoulos, C. 1981: 311-315).

Poor postwar economic conditions, including high unemployment, created a pressing need among the Greek population for public
jobs and/or benefit assistance, and reinforced the overall power of the
state to impose mass loyalty. Public employment became a very significant socio-economic mechanism for upward mobility, and also provided a very effective mechanism of political control. Public
employment was particularly attractive to every educated, jobless person who, in return, had to agree to refrain from any disloyal activity,
reject any leftist relative or friend, and find other ways to demonstrate
his/her (and family's) clean national conviction (*ethnikosfrosyni*), by
collaborating with police. (Tsoucalas, C. 1981:322-323; Tsoucalas, C.
1986:82-136).

During the postwar reconstruction period, despite the constant
cleanups and purges of the leftist public employees, the Greek civil
service was inflated to unprecedented levels. In 1951, the total number
of civil servants was more than double the total number in 1944-45,
according to some estimates. Also, the high percentage of Greek civil
servants with university diplomas (42 percent in the late 1950s) reveals
the rapid formation of "organic," loyal intellectuals who were recruited
based on anticommunist criteria (Tsoucalas, C. 1986). By 1951, one-
third of the Greek population was completely or partially dependent
on public subsidies. This included large numbers of uprooted people
(over 700,000) who had been moved forcibly from battle zones to the
urban centers, especially those of Athens and Thessaloniki (Tsoucalas
C. 1986: 22-23). It thus becomes apparent that the distribution of public jobs and subsidies was, in essence, a form of blackmail/favors ren-

dered in exchange for loyalty and anticommunism. These impover-
ished people received public aid *only* if they were loyal to the regime.
For example, Art. 14, Par. 1 of Law 2963 (1954) organized a housing
agency for the homeless, which stipulated that houses should only be
provided to those with "healthy" political convictions. (Alivizatos, N.
1983: 592).

ENFORCED POLITICAL DESTIGMATIZATION

The civic-mindedness certificate was required for all state-citizen relationships and any request for public job, aid, scholarship, professional
permit-even for a passport to emigrate or to embark on the Greek
merchant marine boats. Thus, any candidate for public service, emi-
gration, or the merchant marine who himself (or any of his relatives)
was politically stigmatized as *non-ethnikofron*, had to be destigmatized
officially by going through the political "decolorization" or "destigma-
tization" procedure (*apochromatismos*) (Alivizatos, N. 1983: 592;
Samatas, M. 1986: 170-172). Political "decolorization" is a term based
on the fact that police used to underline with a red pen all critical personal data—true or false, it's irrelevant—in the files of all those citizens (and their relatives) who had been stigmatized as communist,
leftist, sympathizer, or "crypto." In fact, *apochromatismos* was required
not only of all "reconverted" ex-communists, but also of all who did
not have a recorded loyalty status by the police. They needed to establish such a loyalty status in order to gain access to public jobs and benefits. During the right-wing police state of 1952-63, and again during
the military dictatorship of 1967-1974, anyone who was not recorded
as a leftist could be stigmatized as crypto-communist or a communist
sympathizer if he had not been officially classified as *ethnikofron*. The
apochromatismos procedure clarified the loyalty status of those whose
political views were not clear to the authorities. Those who had never
publicly declared themselves either *ethnikofrones* or leftists were forced
to make public their loyalty (*ethnikofrosyni*) when applying for passports, driver's licenses, etc., with proper loyalty statements.

Apochromatismos also gave those who had been stigmatized as communists an opportunity to "return to the healthy nationalist family of *ethnikofrones*" by signing *repentance declarations* including loyalty statements and self-incrimination oaths. Also, everyone who had not voted in the 1946 elections (the Greek left parties abstained), or had voted United Democratic Left (EDA) in 1956, or had read the leftist daily *AVGI (The Dawn)*, or had associated with members of the leftist party EDA or the leftist youth organization "Lambrakis," was characterized as "crypto-communist" and could be "decolorized" if he/she signed a number of police repentance documents, declaring loyalty to the regime (Alivizatos, N. 1983:593-94). Like former communists, they were also required to publish a standard loyalty statement in one of the local daily papers. They were forced to renounce past politics, beliefs, and any friends or relatives, who had subversive records. All who were destigmatized through *apochromatismos* were then classified in the police files as second grade national-minded citizens (*ethnikofrones* of *second* grade, E2, rather than as original first grade, pure *ethnikofrones*, E1).[17]

GREEK ANTICOMMUNIST "APARTHEID" BASED ON SOCIOPOLITICAL SORTING

Where US political repression targeted a relatively tiny communist party and only a handful of "crypto" liberal sympathizers, state-organized Greek anticommunism extrapolated the Civil War schism to the *entire* Greek population. Greeks were deeply divided into two categories: "the healthy, clean, nationally minded" (*ethnikofrones*)—first-class citizens—and the rest. The "rest" were the sick, non-nationally minded *miasma*—the second-class—including not only communists, leftists, and sympathizers, but also anyone "disloyal," i.e., not actively demonstrating conformity and obedience to the anticommunist state

---

[17]On this political classification system of the Greek security apparatus, see Samatas, M. 1986: 400-401 and exhibits of repentance declarations at Samatas 1986b: 62-63.

(Alivizatos, N. 1981: 225-227; Tsoucalas, C. 1981: 328-330; Catiforis, G. 1975: 83-84; Koundouros, R. 1978: 140-143; Diamandouros, N. 1983: 52).

The post-Civil War Greek "Crowned Parliamentary Democracy" was simply a facade for an authoritarian police state. The 1952 constitutional charter protected, in effect, only the rights of *ethnikofrones*, those "nationally-minded" and "healthy thinking" citizens. It discriminated against the rest. Repressive Civil War emergency legislation (the so-called "paraconstitution") was enacted to deal with dissenters. A "constitutional dualism"—according to Alivizatos's (1981) terminology—evolved. There was a coexistence of the 1952 constitution nominally guaranteeing the civil liberties of the vanquished, with valid Civil War emergency measures that overruled that constitution. Thus a unique politico-juridical "apartheid" was sustained against the Greek leftists (Alivizatos, N. 1981: 227, Alivizatos, N. 1983: 526f; Catiforis, G.1975: 82). This politico-economic exclusion and discrimination was implemented by a large police bureaucracy, which kept political records (*fakeloi*) on all Greek citizens. Both the police files (*fakeloi*) and the police-issued civic-mindedness certificates implemented a brand of totalitarianism that entailed collective family responsibility and mass political surveillance, sorting the entire population according to the national loyalty (*ethnikosfrosyni*) criteria. (Tsoucalas C. 1981: 328-330).

Until 1974, all Greek citizens were categorized by the authorities either as: *ethnikofrones* of the first grade *(Epsilon one,* El), the second grade *(Epsilon two,* E2), "Alpha" leftists (A), "Beta" crypto-communists (B), "Gamma" dangerous communists(G), and "Chi," unknown (X) . (Samatas, M. 1986: 400-401). *Ethnikofrones* could easily lose their "clean" status and be stigmatized as leftist-sympathizers, and leftists could be destigmatized through the decolorization (*apochromatismos*) procedure we have discussed earlier.

Even in the Greek diaspora around the world, especially in the large Greek communities in Europe, the United States, Canada, and Australia, the Greek consulates kept close records for all Greek dissenters and suggested severe sanctions against them. For example, only

124 "undesirable" Greek citizens living abroad were deprived of their Greek citizenship during the 1948-1949 Civil War years, but 21,997 citizens were so deprived during the constitutional period 1952-1967. The zenith of citizenship deprivations—which was usually followed by the seizure of a citizen's property, thus imposing both "political and financial death"—occurred during the 1954-1959 period of the right-wing police state.[18]

THE DEFIANCE OF THE GREEK PEOPLE AND US DIRECT INTERVENTION

The post-Civil War anticommunist surveillance and repression and "Greek McCarthyism" in general did not succeed in rooting out from many Greeks the leftist ideology inspired by the EAM liberation movement. In fact, this failure of "Greek McCarthyism" is reflected in post-Civil War election results.

Despite political control repression and mass surveillance, shortly after the Civil War, the leftist "Democratic Array" garnered 163,800 votes (10 percent) and elected 18 deputies. This was remarkable in view of the 65,000 political prisoners in concentration camps and jails (3,000 of them under death sentence), and the parastate terrorism in the countryside.[19] Also, in the September 9, 1951, elections, peace/amnesty democratization themes of the leftist and centrist parties resulted in their winning 34 percent of the vote. This alarmed Americans. US Ambassador Peurifoy, who had a specific mission "to bring about the establishment of a powerful, stable, and uncompromisingly anticommunist Greek government," stated, "The Greek political situation must be clarified once and for all. The only existing way

---

[18]See detailed statistics in Alivizatos 1983, Table 7, 491 and 597-581; Koundouros 140-143; and Catiforis 83-84.

[19]The anticommunist rightist parties polled 38 percent of the vote, and the centrist liberals under General Plastiras polled 16.5 percent. See Linardatos 1977; N. Psyroukis 1975; and Meynaud, J. 1973.

is the election of a powerful government through the majority electoral system. For the Americans there is still the problem of ten deputies of EDA (United Democratic Left) who were elected by communist votes. No matter how old the zebra gets, he never loses his stripes" (*To Vima*, 19 August 1952).[20]

Many Greek communist accused of being Soviet "spies" were captured by the guidance of the US Embassy and Sixth Fleet surveillance. Several were executed. Among them was Nicos Mpelloyiannis, a prominent communist intellectual whose execution resulted in world outcry. Also, many Greek Navy and Air Force officers were tried as "red saboteurs"(Iatrides, J. 1981: 56; Wittner, L. 1982: 154). The US Embassy also contributed to the overwhelming victory of General Papagos' anticommunist Greek Rally Party in the November 16, 1952, elections. The US Embassy threatened a cut off of US aid if the proportional representation electoral system were not replaced by a "district-to-district plurality" system.

In spite of repressive surveillance and discriminations in the rigged elections of October 1961, of November 1963, and February 1964, the Center Union, a coalition of various liberal forces led by George Papandreou, won 53 percent of the vote and defeated right-wing ERE, which polled only 35 percent (Meynaud J. and Karanicolas, G. 1973; Koundouros, R. 1978: 140f.; Catiforis 1975: 83f.; Alivizatos, N. 1983: 597f.; Charalambis D. 1985: 120-126). This electoral resistance of the Greek people, and its defiance of the repressive, anticommunist surveillance also reflects the popular discontent and rising sociopolitical unrest and mobilization of the late 1950s and early 1960s. It is closely linked with the sharply uneven economic development of postwar Greece, which caused severe social inequalities and disruptions . (Mouzelis, N. 1978: 124). Yet this resistance is even more remarkable if we consider that increased dissent resulted in increased repression.

Most importantly, we must point out that although the bloody Civil War ended in 1949, it was legally prolonged until 1962 through a shrewd juridical construction. This was based upon the "theory of

[20]Quoted by Wittner 1982: 291, and Iatrides 1980: 69.

permanent Civil War," as Alivizatos calls it (1981: 227). In 1962, emergency legislation was formally abolished upon pressure from the European Economic Community (EEC), with which Greece had signed an accession agreement in 1961. That was the first positive EEC (the predecessor of the European Union, EU) intervention against repressive surveillance in postwar Greece, since as we will see later on, in Chapter 4, the EU through the Schengen Agreement plays a very significant, albeit dubious, role in surveillance issues in contemporary Greece as a full EU member/state.

Despite EEC intervention, even in 1962, when the last concentration camp had temporarily closed (until 1967), there were still 158 political prisoners who had been confined since the Civil War. In that same year, 176 political deportees were sent into domestic, guarded exile by security committees and courts. Also in 1962, 377 Greeks were deprived of their citizenship for political reasons. In 1963, that number was 398. Thus, no year in the entire pre-dictatorial parliamentary period (even from 1962 to 1967) was without political prisoners, however small their number (Alivizatos, N. 1981: 491, 579-581, tables 6,7).

All this anticommunist "technology" aimed to impose loyalty, based on repressive surveillance, was fully implemented and over-abused by the following military dictatorship (1967-1974). As we have already stated, in this book we do not focus on the heightened political repression that characterized the last military dictatorship. Anticommunist repression lost all its legitimacy when the military regime applied it indiscriminately against its opponents, including many non-leftists and traditional *ethnikofrones* who simply opposed the dictatorship. In this way the US-led "McCarthy-style" Greek anticommunist operation, covered by a parliamentary façade, was replaced by naked dictatorial violence without any parliamentary veil or legal restrictions. As a result, the persecution of all those who opposed the military regime—even political conservatives, royalists, and nationalists—resulted in totally discrediting not only the military junta but also the entire anticommunist operation.

Chapter 2

POST-DICTATORIAL SURVEILLANCE (1974-1981): THE ANTICOMMUNIST SURVEILLANCE REMNANTS

A FTER THE COLLAPSE of the military regime in 1974, Greece entered a period of democratization and Europeanization, undoubtedly the most liberal period in its modern history. The first post-dictatorial period has been marked by the abolition of the crown, the legalization of the Communist Party of Greece (KKE), the end of open US interference in Greek affairs, and the emergence of the Pan-hellenic Socialist Movement (PASOK), which, under Andreas Papandreou, promised socialist changes.

The post-dictatorial Greek state had inherited an overdeveloped, coercive security apparatus, which continued to restrict civil liberties and intrude into citizens' private lives, sorting them according to their political beliefs[1].This authoritarian proclivity was facilitated by the absence of any concept of the "autonomous individual" or the "right of privacy" in traditional Greek society and culture (Pollis, A. 1977, 1965; Campbell, J.K. 1983).[2]

Nevertheless, the 1975 Constitution, drafted after the military

---

[1]Even under the first years of the PASOK administration, KYP (Greek Central Intelligence Agency) had continued its political surveillance of leftists, despite efforts to reform it. Pertinent reports are found in *Ta Nea*, 23-26 Jan. 1984, and *Anti*, No. 253, 20 Jan. 1984, and Samatas 1993.

[2]For a discussion of the "right to privacy," issue as a limitation on publication and broadcast media ("to be let alone"); as the right to be free of surveillance by "Big Brother" (government) or "Little Brothers" (corporate/private); and as the right to make the basic personal decisions affecting one's own life without governmental interference, see Pilpel, H. F. (1968), Askin (1972), Gotlieb, C. (1996), and Clarke, R. (2000). See also Agre, Ph. Rotenberg, M. 1977 and Allen, A. 2001.

dictatorship, does make progress toward the protection of an individual's civil liberties, and it recognizes the rights of privacy and secrecy of communications according to Article 9, which states:

> "(1) Each person's home is inviolable. A person's individual and family life is inviolable. No house searches shall be made except when and as the law directs, and always in the presence of representatives of the judicial authorities. (2) Offenders against the foregoing provision shall be punished for forced entry into a private house and abuse of power, and shall be obliged to indemnity in full the injured party as the law provides.

(A constitutional amendment in 2001 that has strengthened the protection of personal information is discussed later in chapter 9: 133).

These constitutional provisions however do not guarantee the secrecy of written correspondence, or of any other communication, "in cases of national security reasons," thus continuing the policy of both the 1952 Constitution and the junta. The Greek security forces can legally inspect correspondence and can even use the Greek Telecommunications Organization (OTE) to wiretap telephone conversations on the grounds of national security. Since during that first post-dictatorial period communism and political radicalism in general were still considered by the security services to be a threat to national security, they continued to put leftist citizens and organizations under discrete surveillance, despite the legalization of the KKE.

The 1975 Constitution also prescribes preventive detention (and even preventive deportation) on the grounds of suspicion for future crimes "in cases of emergency and only to prevent the commitment of punishable acts" (Article 4, paragraph 4). This provision, which is similar to the US Internal Security Act, and legitimates preventive surveillance,[3] differs from previous dictatorial ones in that the suspicion of future illegal conduct must be determined by a court decision rather

---

[3]In the United States during 1956-1973, CIA agents examined over 28 million pieces of mail in New York City alone. They photographed 2.7 million envelopes and opened 215,820 pieces (Golstein 1878: 339).

than by a security committee. The Constitution also prohibits the "abusive exercise of rights" (Art. 25, paragraph 3). But since it does not indicate when the exercise of those rights is legal and when it is "abusive," interpretation is left to the arbitrary judgement of the administration, police, and courts.[4]

Under the pretext of dejuntaization and the cleaning up of the civil service from supporters of the dictatorship, leftists and communists were still excluded from public jobs. Civil Service Code Article 206 defines the most serious offense by a civil servant as being "lack of faith in the Fatherland, *lack of faith in national ideals,* as well as the violent subversion of the existing political and social regime *by acts or words*" (emphasis added). To check that faith in national ideals, Presidential Decree 670 (1974) established special loyalty councils in every ministry. In addition, Legislative Decree 64 (1974) enacted a "check of faith in the democratic system of the country of certain categories of public functionaries and civil servants," thus checking individual and family political convictions.[5]

Ultimately, under the auspices of the Minister of Defense, every Greek ministry had become involved in wide-ranging investigations of civil servants' entire lives. Civil servants should have a proper ethos, including "healthy social virtues." Post-dictatorial authorities did not recognize such "healthy virtues" in leftists, who were still characterized as non-nationalist-minded citizens. Presidential Decree 263 (1975) identified 27 major public corporations whose staff had to complete special questionnaires regarding their political beliefs. Although the required signing of loyalty statements declaring one's faith in the democratic system has so far been accepted as a matter of course, in the

[4]The discussion on the Greek constitutional provisions is based on the official Greek text of the 1975 constitution published in the Greek *Government Gazette* (June 10, 1975), and its English translation by the Greek House of Parliament, (Athens, 1975). Regarding human rights in constitutional provisions, see Manesis, A. (1979).

[5]This "faith" implies, as Alivizatos points out, not just respect but an "internal consensus" that goes far beyond the politically neutral position of civil servants dictated by constitutional Article 29, paragraph 3. See Alivizatos, N. 1983: 691. Also see Samatas, M. 1986: 288-293.

immediate post dictatorial period the authorities could use these statements to exclude from public employment all those who were considered as "non-democratic." Even PASOK followers were recorded as "extremists," and communists as "anarchists."[6]

In addition to the dictatorial legacy and surviving remnants of repressive legislation, political control and surveillance duties of the Greek police and military continued uninterrupted until 1981, simply because no substantial dejuntaization of the military and police occurred during the post-dictatorial period. Despite (or because of) the legalization of the Greek Communist Party (KKE) and the rise of new socialist forces, the police and military (under the auspices/protection of the conservative government) maintained total autonomy from parliamentary control and continued political control surveillance, as it was revealed by the first PASOK government (Samatas, M. 1986: 370-404; Alivizatos, N. 1983b). In fact, in the armed forces the 1980 military regulation echoed the 1968 dictatorial constitution (art. 129) in defining the mission of the armed forces: preserved among their military responsibilities was the defense of the political regime, and the legal established social system, "against any type of attack from external or *internal* enemies."[7] Further, "The security corps were used as a continuing anticommunist apparatus, even as a mechanism to prevent every progressive manifestation."[8] In addition, because of the Turkish occupation of northern Cyprus in July 1974 and the continuing Greco-Turkish conflict, a condition of state-of-alert remained silently in force until the mid-1990s, giving the military a Damoclean sword over civil liberties. Under the state-of-alert and mass conscription, all able-bodied citizens up to 50 years of age (i.e., the reserve

[6]Although no government accepts allegations that it makes occupation proscriptions for political reasons, the Greek press has frequently revealed such purges in the public enterprises: for a case in the Power Corporation during the New Democracy government; see Skiadopoulos, A. 1981; for alleged political purges under the PASOK 1986.

[7]"General Regulations regarding service in the Military," ratified by Presidential Decree 982/1980.

[8]Papakonstantis, G. (2003) cites a number of indicative secret police orders for surveillance during 1978-1979 of pure cultural events, like theater festivals, etc, (pp. 129-130, notes 58, 60, 61).

forces) were considered *ipso jure* conscripted. Civilian personnel were considered soldiers in civilian dress. This entitled the military to check the reservists' politics in order to exclude those who might not be trusted with confidential duties in the event of the emergency of war.[9]

Thus until 1981, the most significant political control function of the Greek military and police was covert mass political surveillance, i.e., discrete large-scale collection and documentation of private information on citizens' sociopolitical convictions and personal lives in general.[10] These paper files (fakeloi) with private sociopolitical information were unofficially used and updated until 1981; millions of such files had been gathered to be destroyed by the first PASOK government, but they were finally burnt as obsolete only in 1989, by the then national government, as we will see later (page 64; see also Samatas, M. 1986: 393-406).

Before 1981, information about the surveillance activities of police and military security services during the post-dictatorial period was revealed mainly by journalist reports. These reports resulted in protests by the opposition parties in parliament.[11] The conservative government had repeatedly refused to acknowledge the existence of the *fakeloma* system. But the Greek opposition press revealed how, in particular, the system of police identity cards and draft conscription have been used purely for political surveillance goals.[12] The complete picture and the totalitarian dimensions of the continuing *fakeloma*

[9]See Zouvelos, M. 1980, and his similar article in *Anti*, Nos. 211-212, 20-21 Nov. 1980.

[10]For similar mass surveillance electronic systems in the United States and the United Kingdom see Rule, J. B., (1974).

[11]See *Ta Nea*, 3 Jan. 1980.

[12]In April 1981, Colonel Vasilis Petropoulakis, temporary chief of the Conscripts Selection Council (SEO) had described to the Greek press in detail the military files procedures. Based on permanent orders, like Nos. 1-8/1978 and 1-21/1979, the military—with the cooperation of the police—opened files on all male Greeks from draft age (18 years old) and updated them through the end of their reserve status (50 years old). Petropoulakis stated that he himself created files on about 40,000 young Greeks, ages 16 to 18, during his tour of duty (Aug. 1978-May 1980). He estimated that in the period 1974-1976 files had to be created for 1.5 million Greeks, and that approx. 350,000 new files were added annually. *To Vima*, 12 April 1981. See also the Gregoriades case against military surveillance: 143-145.

*a*fter the fall of the dictatorship were officially revealed in 1984 by the PASOK government. As the following *Table 1* shows, surviving anti-communist apparatus under the supervision of the conservative governments created "a paper dossier society" of 41.2 million files for the total Greek population of 9.5 million. From these files, 25.5 million contained strictly citizens' personal political and ideological information. Thus, for most Greeks, there were multiple political control files.[13]

Although every state keeps files on its alleged enemies and criminals, the Greek state (like all authoritarian, police states) has kept files on every individual citizen, checking his/her political/ideological activities and affiliations. The surveillance legacy of Greek McCarthyism in post-dictatorial period is displayed in the Appendix, which contains a variety of surveillance documents *(Exhibits 1 to 7, plus Exhibit 9).*

These documents, published in the Greek press, exposed the surveillance system, its intrusion into private lives, and the inherent power of the Greek state to discriminate against its citizens accordingly. Under the impact of repressive, institutionalized anticommunism and its remnants in the post-dictatorial period in Greece, even well after the fall of the military dictatorship, the whole treatment, inclusion, or exclusion of any citizen and their family by the civil service, the police, and the military was basically depended upon the one's existing formal political documentation.

If institutionalized anticommunist surveillance in Greece frustrated national reconciliation for more than 30 years following the Civil War, its remnants and legacy inhibited social justice, democratization, and modernization of the post-dictatorial Greek state, politics, and society. Institutionalized Greek anticommunism sustained and perpetuated the rule of the Greek right until 1981, and finally con-

---

[13]The PASOK Minister of Public Order J. Skoularikis announced these data on March 7, 1984, with a promise to destroy all these files. However, destruction of the files was indefinitely postponed after the demands of the Left to return files to those marked citizens who requested them. Since February 1985 the PASOK government had also been promising a special bill banning any *fakeloma* activities by the authorities.

TABLE 1

Total individual citizens' files* kept by the police and security forces

SUBJECT

DEPARTMENT	Public Order	National Security**	Drivers License, Transit	Tourism	Market Control	Aliens	Currency Protection	Total Files	Space Occupied, Square Meters
Gendarmerie Headquarters	309,238	11,660,499	428,371	60,813	116,813	1,184,387		23,517,946	6,212
Urban Police Headquarters	309,238	11,660,499	428,271	5,871	146,067	520,642	30,938	13,099,636	3,326
National Security Service-YPEA		844,706				1,189,056		2,035,762	685
Department of Criminal Records								2,603,844	727
TOTAL	6,601,307	25,547,273	2,505,911	66,684	262,880	2,894,085	30,938	41,255,188	10,951

*Total Greek Population approximately 10 million; total files 41.2 million.

**This includes all records of socio-political beliefs information.

Source: PASOK Minister of Public Order announcement to the Greek Press, March 7, 1984

tributed to its fall. In contrast to US McCarthyism, which successfully reinforced the two-party system and undermined any attempt to launch a third liberal party, "Greek McCarthyism" was ultimately unable to curb the reincarnation of the Greek left and the emergence of new political forces in the post-dictatorial period. In fact, remnants of many repressive controls and discrimination against the left strengthened the opposition leftist forces; and these remnants contributed to the 1981 electoral victory of PASOK, which had promised the abolition of all political discrimination.[14]

Thus, as after the Civil War, when the Greek people had defied the repressive police state and brought into the Parliament the legal Greek leftist party EDA, again in 1981 the remnants of an obsolete police state did not inhibit the emergence to power of a radical leftist party, as PASOK was presented at that time.

[14]As we mention later on, even under the PASOK administration, KYP (Greek Central Intelligence Agency) has continued its political surveillance of leftists, despite efforts to reform it. Pertinent reports are found in *Ta Nea*, 23-26 Jan. 1984, and *Anti*, No. 253, 20 Jan. 1984.

Chapter 3

POPULIST SURVEILLANCE (1981-1995)

A. POPULIST POLITICS AND "MACHIAVELLIAN" POLITICAL SURVEILLANCE DURING THE FIRST PASOK ADMINISTRATION (1981-1989)

D ESPITE GOVERNMENTAL FAILURE in many other fields, the first government of the Panhellenic Socialist Movement (PASOK) put an official end to institutionalized anticommunism through: 1) the abolition of surviving Civil War anticommunist legislation; 2) the official recognition of the EAM/ELAS resistance movement; and 3) the unrestricted repatriation of Greek political refugees. The authoritarian proclivities of the state had not, however, ceased. In an effort to catch terrorists and prevent future troublemakers, potential scapegoats can always be found in certain stigmatized groups: political (e.g., extra-parliamentary, radical leftist groups—"anarcho-autonomists"); religious (e.g., Jehovah's Witnesses)[1]; sexual (e.g., homosexuals); and certain marginal dissenters (e.g., conscientious objectors).

Since PASOK's rise to power and the official banning of anticommunism, Greek police and security services, trained for years to fight communists and other "internal enemies," had been frustrated and confused about their reduced, non-political role. They had to focus on real criminal and terrorist acts, but due to their ideological confusion incurred by the "socialist" government and its clientelist politics they failed to do so. The security apparatus, on the one hand, as a prolonged

---

[1]Regarding legal discrimination against Greek Jehovah's Witnesses, see Konidaris, I. M. (1986): 34.5. See also Pollis, A. 1999.

instrument of the conservative governments, was not considered friendly, and it actually resisted the democratization policy of the PASOK government; while on the other hand, PASOK, instead of modernizing and democratizing the police and security corps, gave priority to controlling them by recruiting and promoting mainly party PASOK followers, establishing its own party-client police network to confront the conservative one. Without a substantial democratization policy in the police education and organization structures, PASOK clientelist policy contributed to the disorganization and inefficiency of the police and security corps.[2] This policy confused police organizational and ideological conditions, a confusion that was also reflected in the contradicting surveillance policy of this period.

Despite PASOK's preelection promises and some significant—albeit never implemented—antisurveillance legislation, political control surveillance was technically and qualitatively modernized to serve the objectives of a populist party, as PASOK soon proved to be after it came to power by its personalistic albeit charismatic leadership of Andreas Papandreou.[3] The over-centralized structures and populist ideological functions of the PASOK party were also reflected by the PASOK administration, which transformed the obsolete right-wing authoritarian "bureaucratism" into a modernized *populist "bureaucratism,"* that is a party and state-organized sociopolitical control system that served primarily the hegemonic objectives of the PASOK populist leadership. (Samatas, M. 1986, 1993).

From a sociopolitical control perspective, we consider political surveillance under the first PASOK administration not as accidental,

---

[2]See the documented analysis of Papakonstantis, G., *Greek Police: Organization, Politics and Ideology* (Sakkoula, Athens, 2003: 242-243, 139).

[3]There is little doubt that, with the PASOK rise to power, post-dictatorial Greece entered the phase of populism, since the Greek "underprivileged" people, liberated by the anticommunist, rightist state, were integrated and pacified by a proclaimed socialist party, dominated by a charismatic leader, who promised radical socialist change to mesmerize them and then "sent them back to their homes," as soon as he formed his own government (see Clogg, R., ed., 1993). For a faithful discourse on PASOK populist character, see Sotiropoulos, D. (1991, 1996). Also Lyrintzis, Ch. (1983), and Elefantis, A. (1991), Mouzelis, N. 1989 & 2001 & Papagaryfalou P. 2002.

but as an integral mechanism of the party's populist "bureaucratism," namely a mechanism of the organized efforts of the PASOK populist leadership to acquire, maintain, and impose the exclusive control of the state in order to safeguard power. We must point out that surveillance as a sociopolitical control mechanism gets more interesting when it is used not by authoritarian or conservative governments, but by proclaimed socialist governments and leaders, like in France by Francois Mitterrand and in Greece by Andreas Papandreou. In such cases we do have "Machiavellian" type of surveillance, which serves the hegemonic goals of the leader against all his real and perceived foes (Dandeker, C. 1990: 5-6, 204).

The following contradicting surveillance record of the first PASOK administration reveals its populist policy.

Populist promises and deeds

First, as the leading opposition party before it came to power in 1981, PASOK had repeatedly condemned the post dictatorial continuing surveillance filing of Greek citizens' political beliefs and actions by the military and security services. Whenever tangible surveillance records were exposed by the press, the then opposition leader, Andreas Papandreou, vividly condemned their existence, as he did on January 2, 1980, when he had stated that "over half of the Greeks, (according to) the police files that have been created (are considered as) nationally suspicious" (*Ta Nea*, Jan.3, 1980). Papandreou promised that PASOK would abolish all kinds of political surveillance immediately when it came to power.

Second, PASOK, almost three years after assuming power, was forced, by revelations of the press on continuing surveillance, to expose the totalitarian legacy of "Greek McCarthyism," which had created a discriminatory "dossier society." As we have already mentioned, for the total Greek population of approximately 9.5 million people, there were 41.2 million various files, kept by the police and security apparatus *(see Table 1)*. These figures were revealed on March 7, 1984 by the PASOK minister of public order, after reports in the Greek press accused the Greek Central Intelligence Agency (KYP) of continuing political surveillance of leftists even under the PASOK administration (*Ta Nea*, Jan. 23-24, 1984, and *Anti* #253, Jan. 20, 1984). Although the minister then promised to destroy all these files, this did not happen during the entire first PASOK administration.

Third, soon after it came to power, PASOK passed the first law (1291/82) to protect, according to the constitution, the privacy of telephone and other private conversations, making illegal telephone wiretapping and the opening of private mail. Not only was this not enforced, but the PASOK government was accused in the Greek Parliament by all opposition parties of wiretapping political rivals (Greek Parliament's Records of Sept. 20, 1989).

Fourth, the PASOK administration tried to establish, with Law 1599/1986, the following:

1) a computerized system of a Single Code Register Number (EKAM), for every citizen "to modernize Greek citizens' relations with the state" (Article 2).[4] This EKAM system, and the establishment by the same law of a new type of identification card, was not implemented, because of reactions by the leftist opposition, based on past experience with an authoritarian state. The fear was that EKAM could be the finest electronic totalitarian surveillance system.[5] Under the auspices of a self-called "socialist" government, such an electronic security apparatus, without any serious judicial or parliamentary control, could be far more dangerous in surveying citizens than the obso-

---

[4]The EKAM number would have replaced the numbers of I.D., passport, the election book, social security, the tax register number, the driver's license, municipal birth register number, etc. (Article 2, paragraph 4).

[5]The establishment of the EKAM system has actually caused more stormy reactions by religious and para-ecclesiastic organizations, which frequently demonstrate against the establishment of the new identification cards, which allegedly will also include the "666 Satanic number." Thus EKAM was never implemented during the PASOK administration, and the minister of interior of the National Unity Government stated that he had frozen all EKAM implementation procedures, / *Proti*, 1 Sept. 1989. See Pashos, G. (1986): 29-31; also Velitzelou, G. and Livada, E. (1987): 23-28.

lete and defamed anticommunist one. Also, the citizens' right to know the content of administrative documents never materialized, as it was neutralized by myriad exceptions prescribed by the same law—the authorities could refuse to show a document to a concerned citizen on the basis of general, police-state type of reasons, such as "the security of state and public order" (Article 16, paragraph 3) (Rowat, D.C. 1984).

In contrast to these generally positive legislative acts, the gap between words and deeds of the PASOK government is illustrated in the following surveillance practices:

1) military electronic "filing," (*fakeloma*), 2) "filing" of individual citizens and political parties, and 3) telephone wiretaps. This illegitimate PASOK surveillance practice was documented and discussed in the Greek Parliament after reports in the Greek press.

1. Military Electronic "Filing"

Despite the official banning of anticommunism in the post-dictatorial period, and the PASOK anti-surveillance preelection promise, nobody could expect that the rise of PASOK to power would have automatically transformed the prolonged authoritarian character of the Greek state and demolished its repressive apparatus. Thus, during the preliminary years of the first PASOK administration, the sporadic authoritarian manifestations of the security, police, and military forces were considered by the press and the left as natural remnants.[6]

According to its preelection promises, the first PASOK public order minister sent a circular to the police departments, ordering them to stop collecting and sending sociopolitical information to the military intelligence for the conscripts' files.[7] This order, however, was never executed, simply because the military chiefs invoking security

---

[6]Pertinent reports for such sporadic accusations on KYP's political surveillance of leftists are found in *Ta Nea*, 23-26 Jan., 1984, and *Anti* #253, 20 Jan., 1984.

[7]PASOK public order minister J. Skoularikis's statement at the Parliament session of September 12, 1989, reported also in *Proti*, 13 September 1989.

issues protested vigorously to President Karamanlis and Prime Minister Papandreou, who both "found their arguments reasonable."[8]

Yet, documents published in the press[9] and also submitted by leftist opposition deputies at several parliamentary sessions, have proved that Greek military surveillance during the entire period of the PASOK administration had been technically and qualitatively modernized; as it was both computerized and used an updated terminology, mainly replacing the words "leftist/communist" by the word "anarchist." This refined military electronic surveillance was widely revealed by the former PASOK Deputy Elias Hazoplakis, in January 1988, when he published in the Athens daily *Eleftherotypia* a great number of military electronic cards of soldiers stigmatized with words and phrases like:

> "Extremist," "his brother is anarchist," "he is associated with individuals of anarchist convictions," "he reads newspapers in the army," "(he has) studied in Italy," "he is married to a Romanian," "his brother (is) a student in Romania for three years," "he is a member of the committee for (democratization) of the Army," "he refused to go to church," etc. (See indicative electronic cards in *Exhibit 9*).

Obviously, this type of surveillance was not just anticommunist stigmatization, as it was in the period before 1981. It also included broader personal information beyond political activities, which were monitored by the pre-PASOK anticommunist surveillance.

Soon after these revelations, the then Greek Communist Party (KKE) deputy, C. Kappos, brought additional documents to the parliament's session of February 5, 1988, exposing the continuing anticommunist electronic surveillance of the army, even after 1981. In one of these documents, dated September 12, 1983, there is a list of soldiers who had visited the Greek Communist Youth (KNE) cultural festival.

[8]This was reported by a usually well-informed journalist, Votsis, G. *Eleftherotypia*, 4 Sept., 1989.

[9]The newspaper *Proti* (July 10, 1989) claimed that, in a document dated May 22, 1985, the PASOK government determined political censorship duties to certain officers.

Kappos also displayed another computerized list, which marked soldiers as: "suspect for terrorist activity," "suspect (as being a member) of the committee (for the democratization) of the army," "anarchist—many accusation reports," "under civilian clothes he read (the communist daily) *Rizospastis*," etc. (Greek Parliament's Records of February 5, 1988, Session O': 3500-3501). To these documented accusations, the PASOK minister of national defence gave a stereotypical answer: "No 'filing' on citizens' political convictions is made by our ministry." This answer was identical to his New Democracy party predecessors', who had repeatedly denied military "filing" during the period of 1974-1981, despite the evidence.[10]

Two additional military secret documents, however, exposed on July 10, 1989, the surveillance activities of the army not only in the camps but also *outside* of them. The first document, dated August 9, 1983, entitled "Report to (Military) Hierarchy for Serious Issues," ordered all military units to report immediately to the General Military Staff, a list of "A" events—not only serious accidents, suicides, and thefts—but also *anarchist* manifestations inside the units and any serious manifestation *outside* them, which is against the army, including political rallies and demonstrations.[11] Three years later, another document dated September 2, 1986, was showing that the order had been renewed to watch for and immediately report "anarchist manifestations in and out of the camps."[12]

Hence, under the pretext of the "threat of anarchism" and the overall security of the army, the military surveillance was continued to monitor all conscripts' activities and beliefs, with two qualitative differences: 1) the surveillance mechanism was computerized to be more effective, and 2) the surveillance target was refined using new labels such as "anarchist," "extremist," and "suspect" instead of the obsolete "leftist," or "communist."

---

[10]To see the similarities, compare the PASOK minister's statement in *Eleftherotypia*, February 6, 1988, with the ND minister's statement in *To Vima*, January 20, 1980.

[11]The photocopy of this draft document was published in *Proti*, 10 July, 1989.

[12]*Ibid.*

This modernization seriously contradicted the official excuse of the
PASOK defense minister that the revealed surveillance order was just a
past and limited remnant. The question then was why were these "filings" so technically and substantially modernized by supreme military
orders, and why did the PASOK government never cancel them, despite
the repeated, documented revelations in the Parliament? One answer is
that the PASOK government was mainly preoccupied with the control
of the rank-and-file military leadership. The Prime Minister Andreas
Papandreou himself was the minister of national defense during the first
years of the PASOK rule, and then was also the president of the Governmental Council for National Defense (KYSEA); he was reluctant to proceed to a substantial democratization of the military apparatus. The
continuation and modernization of the political control "filing" by the
military indicated how difficult its democratic control was. Actually, the
military power status remained as it was before PASOK, a control-proof
enclave (*stegano*) in which only the government could have access,
blocking any control and accountability by the Parliament. (Samatas, M.
1986; Haralambis, D. 1985). Military electronic filing can be considered
as a continuing authoritarian remnant,[13] indicating primarily the
inability of the Greek socialists to take complete control of the armed
forces and democratize their organization. In fact, PASOK came to
power through tremendous popular expectations to put an end to
exactly such authoritarian right-wing surveillance policies. The Greek
sociopolitical control system however perpetuated and even modernized its unconstitutional and undemocratic surveillance mechanisms,
under both conservative and "socialist" governments. Suffice to mention
that all these military surveillance files were not destroyed in August
1989, when the post-PASOK government burned thousands of police
surveillance dossiers. According to pertinent legislation, the military files
were kept and updated by the relevant military-police and security
authorities, who keep an eye on all conscripts even after the end of their
military duty, simply because they belong to the reserves.[14]

[13]For a variety of documents showing the dimensions of the pre-PASOK surveillance system, see Exhibits 1-7 in the Appendix.
[14]Based on the permanent military orders 1-8/1978, and 1-21/1979, that prescribe

2. *"Filing" of individual citizens and political parties*

As it is already mentioned, although on April 19, 1984, Prime Minister Papandreou himself renewed his promise, and three of his ministers declared May 6 as the day of file destruction, the same ministers decided, on May 7, to postpone the date indefinitely, with the excuse that some leftist politicians and intellectuals had demanded the files be delivered to all those marked citizens who had requested them or may request them in the future.[15]

A year later, during the preelection period of 1985, PASOK advertised all over Greece that the files had been destroyed, showing a picture of a burning file on its preelection posters with the slogan:

"Together for the new victory, and now again PASOK, for Democracy without 'filings,' for Freedom without persecutions" *(see Exhibit 10a).*

Yet, the PASOK government not only did not destroy the existing files, but it continued its own selective "filing."

On January 21, 1985, PASOK Secretary General of the Public Order Ministry Constantine Tsimas issued a secret order to the Attica police directorate, cosigned by five high-ranking officers, to "gather, store in file cabinets, in numerical order, and properly classify" the "files of Political Convictions . . . so that their usage *for further exploitation* is made possible" (emphasis added).[16] The document of this order about the PASOK preservation of the past notorious files was revealed by the post-PASOK National Unity government on August 30, 1989.

procedures for a "single system of checking the conduct of military personnel," as well as according to Law PSIST/1878 that "all male Greeks are obliged to accept the checking of their military duty and status by the pertinent military and police authorities from 19 until 50 years old." See Samatas, M.: "Greek Bureaucratism," *op. cit.,* 395-398.

[15]See the pertinent documents of the KKE and the KKE of the Interior by which it was asked to preserve the files, presented at Parliament by the former PASOK minister of public order, Skoularikis. Parliament's Records of Sept. 12, 1989: 1019.

[16]"The whole job is to be completed in a month. Each Monday a report should be made on work progress." This document was presented at Parliament's Session LE' by the post-PASOK National Unity government's public order minister; see Greek Parliament's Records of Sept. 12, 1989: 1016.

Based on fact that the PASOK government preserved the files and intended to establish by law (1599/86) the aforementioned computerized single code register number (EKAM) system for every Greek citizen,[17] the leftist opposition parties argued that most of the important private information had probably already been stored in electronic files.[18] Although the existence of such electronic files was not verified by the post-PASOK National Unity government, its spokesman, Th. Canellopoulos, officially stated on August 26, 1989:

> "... it has been confirmed that files have been kept and updated on political leaders, political personalities, particularly KKE members, during the 1982-1987 period; that is, during the PASOK administration, as the public order minister has already stated. The most important thing is that these files were found within other general files, indicating that they were forgotten there and they were not promptly taken away" (*I Proti*, Aug. 26, 1989).

On August 28, 1989, the public order minister of the post-PASOK National Unity government, Yannis Kefaloyiannis presented official documents to prove that the security services collected detailed information on: 1) the activities of opposition political parties (ND, EDIK, KKE, KODISO, EPEN),[19] 2) specific KKE party officers,[20] 3) the PASOK governmental spokesman as a "terrorist suspect,"[21] and 4) the

[17]As mentioned at note 5 at page 50, the establishment of the EKAM system caused stormy reactions on the part of all of those who, based on the undemocratic past experience, were afraid that EKAM could be the finest electronic totalitarian surveillance system.

[18]Votsis, G. *Eleftherotypia*, September 4, 1989.

[19]See Greek Parliament's Records of Session LE', Sept. 12, 1989: 1007-1040. ND: New Democracy (right); EDIK: Union of Democratic Center; KODISO: Democratic Socialist Party (centrists); KKE: Greek Communist Party (left); EPEN: Greek National Front (far right).

[20]One of the secret surveillance documents on KKE signed by the Attica police chief states that KKE has ordered its illegal mechanism to stay alert, renew its hiding places, dividing Athens into seven districts ... etc. Greek Parliament's Records of Session LE', Sept. 12, 1989: 1022-23.

[21]The then PASOK governmental spokesperson was Yiannis Roubatis, who was

later National Unity government's minister of justice, F. Kouvelis, as the leading figure of the movement for the democratization of the army and several other personalities who supported the same movement.[22]

In fact, selected files of many important personalities belonging to all parties, including PASOK, were regularly updated and kept in the office of the interior affairs minister. Defamatory information, originating from these files, was leaked to the PASOK-friendly populist daily *Avriani*, which occasionally libelled whoever was critical of the government or of that press itself.[23]

The pertinent PASOK minister denied all responsibility for new "filing," saying that those newly revealed files were the outcome of past police habits of the security apparatus.[24] Moreover, defending himself on the subject, he stated that he had even prepared a draft for a law to prohibit and punish any political information collection and processing, electronically or otherwise.[25] Challenged by the refusal of former PASOK ministers to accept the fact that their administration not only

recorded as "terrorist suspect" from 1983 until September 8, 1988. *To Ethnos*, Aug. 29, 1989.

[22]All these files were found to be updated until 1988. In addition to the then Justice Minister F. Kouvelis, V. Filias, X. Peloponisios, A. Mitropoulos, and G. Stamatakis were marked for the same reason. *To Ethnos*, Aug. 29, 1989.

[23]In one case the PASOK-appointed director of the Athenian Press Agency was fired and even dismissed from the party's central committee after *Avriani* libeled him as "homosexual." Also, a journalist, who seriously criticized PASOK, was portrayed by the same paper as an ex-junta informer. In other cases, lists of well-known artists who were critical of PASOK were portrayed as having avoided serving their military duty by being "pseudo-sick," like the case of actor L. Lazopoulos, who, after such accusations, was drafted. For a general analysis, see A. Papanthimos, *Avrianism, The Present Face of Fascism* [in Greek], 1989 and A. Elefantis, *In the Constellation of Populism* [in Greek], 1991, 329-330.

[24]In the Parliament session of Sept. 12, 1989, the PASOK former Public Order Minister Skoularikis, spoke for the continuance of the security service at an "accelerated speed" from the past; see Greek Parliament Records of Session LE" of Sept. 2, 1989: 1020 f.

[25]Although the new draft law was brought to the Parliament three months before the 1985 elections it has never passed, since he was not reappointed as minister. See Mr. Skoularikis' interview in *Ethnos*, Aug. 29, 1989.

preserved but also updated many files, the interior and justice ministers of the post-PASOK National Unity government displayed at the
Parliament's session of September 12, 1989 the following anticommunist surveillance police documents:

1) One proving the close surveillance by paid police informers of
   repatriated political refugees,
2) Another for the "KKE activities" in Macedonia-Thrace, Thessaly,
   etc. during 1983-84,
3) A secret report about an "alert exercise of KKE" allegedly held on
   April 21, 1983, in Thessaloniki,
4) Records about the Communist Youth Organization (KNE), and
5) An information document with surveillance records on social-
   democrat leaders, J. Pesmazoglou and H. Protopappas.[26]

On the basis of the above documents, it seems that there was an
enlargement of the mostly anticommunist "filing" that characterized
the pre-PASOK surveillance, to a "filing" that also included the opponents of the PASOK party and its leader. In fact, the PASOK minister's
argument was that the storage of the past political files was done simply for "historical" reasons; he could not answer why political files were
found to be regularly updated, not only on the active leftists, but also
files on all opposition political parties, eminent political personalities,
and journalists from the entire political spectrum. Most important,
files of several PASOK ministers, deputies, and PASOK party cadres,
were found to be handy at the public order minister's office; the information could have been used against these persons, in several ways, at
any given time.[27]

---

[26]See Greek Parliament's Records of Session LE' of Sept. 12, 1989: 1021-1026.
According to Skoularikis's excuses at the same parliamentary session, these documents
were outcomes of the "event reports" that every police department was to keep. *Ibid.*,
1021, 1027.

[27]The PASOK Interior Affairs Minister Akis Tsochadzopoulos justified the existence of the file of his comrade Costas Simitis in his office, saying that the file was used
to provide data to issue a certificate. See *Ta Nea*, July 8, 1989.

3. *Telephone wiretaps*

The major wiretapping scandal during the PASOK administration broke out in the fall of 1987, when it was discovered that the telephone conversations between the KKE and the new party of the Greek Left (EAR), regarding their political cooperation, were listened to by EYP, the Greek National Intelligence Service , through their tapped telephones.[28] The New Democracy (ND) party, which traditionally had access to EYP, utilized the opportunity to bring more data against illegal wiretaps, and in cooperation with the left to force the PASOK government to accept the formation of a parliamentary investigative committee, albeit excluding EYP from this investigation.[29]

Wiretapping was not the invention of the PASOK administration, but has always been a regular function of the state security apparatus, conducted under all governments in the name of "state security" and "the public interest." Wiretapping under the PASOK administration, however, was scandalous because, as it has been substantiated by the pertinent Parliamentary Investigation Committee, it was irrelevant for national security. It was rather similar to "Nixonian tactics," as Hitchens points out, (Kariotis, Th., ed. 1991: 8), organized to serve the PASOK prime minister's goal to politically control his rivals. As subsequent revelations proved, wiretaps were carried out by a network of EYP and the Greek Telecommunications Organization (OTE), for "public interest" reasons, against such "terrorist suspects," as the then former President C. Karamanlis, the then opposition leaders C. Mitsotakis and E. Averoff, the PASOK ministers who hoped to succeed Papandreou, G. Yennimatas, C. Simitis, and Y. Arsenis, as well as the PASOK ministers E. Yannopoulos and Th. Stathis, almost all the pub-

---

[28]This wiretap was proved by technical experts of the Athens Polytechnic. *Eleftherotypia*, March 1, 1988.

[29]See the parliamentary discussion on the concluding report of this committee in the Greek Parliament's Records of Sept. 20, 1989, Session MA': 1238-1256. During the parliamentary investigation, OTE Director General Th. Tombras leaked to the press an archive of wiretapping cards to prove that it was the ND administration that was actually doing wiretapping, and not PASOK. / *Proti*, Sept. 4, 1989.

lishers of Athens's newspapers, Papandreou's personal security guards, and military and police chiefs[30] (*see Exhibit 11*).

The Inter-party Investigation Committee in the Parliament's session of September 19, 1989, stated that "Machiavellian" wiretaps of this kind were organized especially when, by Law 1645/86, the Greek Central Intelligence (KYP), renamed under PASOK as Greek National Intelligence Service (EYP), was demilitarized—"politicized"—and was placed directly under the prime minister's direction. According to that law, the prime minister could exclusively decide on EYP staffing and structure; Article 5 contains no special qualifications for the EYP director, other than the prime minister's total trust in him; this presumes, of course, the total devotion of the director to the prime minister. It is indicative that the EYP Director C. Tsimas appointed 12 highly paid[31] EYP wiretapping listeners (of which only three knew a foreign language), strictly on the basis of their blind devotion to the PASOK leader. It is interesting to note the interpretation of the term "national security" that one of these listeners related at the committee hearings:

"To make polemic critique against the prime minister and the ministers of the government constitutes a dangerous act for the country's national security."[32]

[30]M. P. Anagnostopoulos Th. presented at Parliament two out of 199 wiretapping cards, that of PASOK Deputy E. Yiannopoulos, and that of the ND party headquarters. See Greek Parliament's Records of Sept. 20, 1989, Session MA': 1247-1248. A detailed list of 193 wiretapped telephone numbers was published in *Ethnos,* July 25, 1989. It is important to mention that during the investigation no evidence was found of wiretaps against the far (extreme) leftists who traditionally are considered as terrorist suspects. It was speculated by the committee members that there were such wiretaps, but they were probably conducted by other unrevealed EYP offices. *Eleftherotypia,* Sept. 20, 1989.

[31]For every two months of 1989, 6-7 million drachmas, i.e. 40 million annually, was spent for fees to the EYP telephone listeners as M.P. Kratsas A. stated in the Parliament. Greek Parliament's Records of Sept. 20, 1989, Session MA': 1243.

[32]A statement by one of the listeners of special hearing rooms 23 and 24 of the EYP building. *I Proti,* Sept. 4, 1989.

EYP closely cooperated on the wiretapping with YETEPA, the special telephone surveillance service of the Greek Telecommunication Organization (OTE), which was responsible, ironically, for the protection of the privacy of telephone conversations.[33] This special surveillance OTE agency was headed, beginning with the summer of 1985, by the PASOK-appointed General Director of OTE Th. Tombras;[34] he "was zealously preoccupied with collecting all sorts of information that would be useful to the PASOK reelection, and enable the PASOK leader to become the master of the political game, through gathering information that could be used against his opponents."[35] Tombras admitted to the Parliament's Investigation Committee that under his direction wiretaps were actually made for the sake of "national security" and "public interest."[36] It is also documented by the report of the same Investigation Committee that out of the 299 EYP-OTE wiretaps, most were " Machiavellian" and only 104 were strictly for national security reasons[37] *(see Exhibits 11 b & c)*.

During a trial against a newspaper that had revealed wiretappings in Thessaloniki, the function of another OTE surveillance service, YESPA—similar to YETEPA—was also unmasked. During that trial it was verified that from September 1984 until February 1989, YESPA was listening in on telephones that belonged to political parties, PASOK dissenters, newspapers, journalists, and unionists.[38]

As the former EYP director, the first appointed by the PASOK gov-

[33]Most of the YETERA employees classified as having top secret access were persons who had been serving there since the dictatorship. *Elejtherotypia*, January 17, 1988.

[34]The appointment of Tombras had caused stormy reactions by the opposition due to his militant activities in OTE, where he was accused of installing his own party state (*Ta Nea*, March 4, 1990).

[35]As stated by the leftist leader, L. Kyrkos, in the Parliament Session of Sept. 20. 1989. See Greek Parliament's Records of same date: 1255.

[36]See report in / *Proti*, Aug. 25, 1989. Since then Tombras was ironically named by the press "The Servant of Public Interest."

[37] See full report with data at newspaper *I Proti*, Sept. 4, 1989.

[38]In the trial against the newspaper *I Proti*, it was found not guilty. Due to the revelations of this trial in the summer of 1989, an inter-party staffing of YESPA was decided by the post-PASOK government. *I Proti*, Aug. 24, 1989.

ernment, Makedos had testified to the investigative committee, that he "wouldn't have thought to do such a thing (wiretaps), without the prime minister's approval."[39]

Thus, based on the investigation committee's resolution, for the first time in Greek history, a former prime minister, A. Papandreou, by parliamentary vote[40] on September 20,1989, was made to stand trial, accused as an ethical perpetrator of wiretapping and of violating the privacy of telephone and verbal conversations for an extended period of time.[41] By the same parliamentery decision, the chiefs of EYP, C. Tsimas, and OTE, T. Tombras, were also made to face a Special Court as accomplices of the prime minister.[42]

PASOK had accused the 1989 coalition government of an anti-PASOK conspiracy that had staged wiretaps and other corruption scandals to politically destroy Andreas Papandreou. The fact is that large-scale wiretapping, used for a long period of time, through a sophisticated surveillance network, mainly against a large number of political adversaries and critics of Prime Minister Papandreou, including the ministers and comrades in his own party, justified the decision made after investigation of the Greek Parliament to officially accuse the former PASOK prime minister and ask him to stand trial before a special court.

[39]Makedos's statement was repeatedly mentioned by the leftist deputies, who accused A. Papandreou personally of the wiretaps at the Parliament's session of September 20, 1989. *Op. cit.*, also *I Proti*, Sept. 21, 1989.

[40]This parliamentary decision was based on 169 yes, 2 no and 2 neutral votes (out of 300, since the PASOK M.P.'s refused to vote). *Eleftherotypia*, Sept. 21. 1989.

[41]This violation is provided for and punished by the Penal Code's Articles 46, paragraph 1A, Articles 98 and 370, paragraphs 1 and 2, combined with the Articles 1 and 5 of the Legislative Decree 802/71 regarding the responsibility of the cabinet members, i.e., ministers and underministers, and the constitutional Article 19 regarding the privacy of mail and freedom of communication.

[42]It was not accidental that the EYP director, C. Tsimas, was rewarded for his EYP services to his leader, by his election as Euro-deputy in the European parliament, where he actually enjoyed immunity from any prosecution. The OTE director, who was expecting to be elected in the Greek Parliament, to ensure immunity missed that chance after reactions of PASOK highranking cadres who had obviously been victims of his "Tombrist" wiretaps.

Whether or not, the parliamentary decision was politically right or wrong is irrelevant to our study. Although PASOK could have claimed in that trial, which has never taken place, that this surveillance was either staged by the opposition or even conducted by over-zealous party officers, without the knowledge and consent of the prime minister, the question is why a socialist leader could have allowed such an anti-democratic practice. An explanation of the reasons for surveillance of the opposition parties' leading politicians, including those of PASOK, was given in the Parliament by a leading deputy of the left:

> The former prime minister aspired to be the best-informed person in order to control the political life of the country. . . . The fact that (PASOK) did not reveal in 1981 the wiretappings made by its predecessor governments of New Democracy (N D), led to their repetition.[43]

Based upon the above documented surveillance practices during the first PASOK administration, we can determine first, the continuation of military surveillance as a remnant of the Greek authoritarian sociopolitical control system, and second and most important, that the political surveillance of specific political opponents of the PASOK leadership was not a past remnant, but an integral "Machiavellian" mechanism of a populist leadership.

---

[43]L. Kyrkos's statement in the Parliament's session of Sept. 20, 1989, when wiretapping was discussed. See Greek Parliament's Records of same date: p. 1255. Deputy P. Skoteniotes, member of the investigation committee, has also answered in the same Parliament's session by asking the following questions: "Who was interested in the surveillance of the political views and the political planning of intra- and out-party rivals? Who cared to systematically cultivate the image of a politician, who always has a rabbit hidden in his hat?" *Ibid.*

B. THE SURVEILLANCE RECORD DURING THE 1989-1993 NEW DEMOCRACY PARENTHESIS

It seems that populist politics and selective "Machiavellian" political surveillance were continued to serve the post-PASOK governmental leadership of the New Democracy "neo-liberal" party, which came to power in 1989 until 1993, after a very brief coalition, and a National Unity government.

On August 30, 1989, the post-PASOK left and the right coalition government destroyed approximately 16.5 million police files, out of the 41.2 million initially gathered by the first PASOK government, putting them on fire throughout Greece.[44] This burning of political files, ordered by both conservative and leftist ministers *(see Exhibit 12b)*, was actually a populist show, because it aimed: first to publicize the fact that PASOK had maintained the files despite its promise to destroy them, and second to persuade the Greek people that the era of political files and state surveillance was over, albeit without the establishment of any anti-surveillance institutional mechanism to guarantee that.

Immediately, many questions came from the press about the millions of files that had still not been destroyed.[45] For example, as press reports had revealed, the files put together by the military dictatorship on the private lives of military personnel were still intact, 19 years after the collapse of the dictatorship.[46]

The PASOK party opposed the burning of files, claiming that it was "a destruction of public record documents on specific individuals

---

[44]7.5 million files were burnt in Athens alone. The Florina district at Greece's northern borders had proportionally the most files in the whole country; 259,945 files were found and burnt, i.e. 5 files for each of the 52,430 inhabitants, including even children. In the same region for a long period the local bishop Candiotis kept his own " religious files" on the private life of his church parishioners, excluding, even excommunicating, those sinful from religious mysteries, like marriage and Christening.

[45]Votsis, G. "They have only burnt the files' trash" in Eleftherotypia, Sept. 4, 1989; "Where have 25 million files been 'lost'?" *Pontiki*, Aug. 31, 1989; "Ten files archives function regularly," *Pontiki*, Sept. 15, 1989; "The files that are not burnt," *Scholiastis* #79, Sept. 1989, pp. 9-11.

[46]See C. Hardavellas's report, "The Files Are in Their Place," *Ta Nea*, Jan. 22, 1992.

(that was) not legally covered."[47] Negative reactions also came from intellectuals, academic historians, and social researchers,[48] as well as from many antidictatorial fighters who demanded their file both as honorary document, even as a record to claim state compensations.[49] The former PASOK ministers claimed that such reactions were the main reason why their government did not proceed with the destruction of the files earlier.[50]

Regarding the surveillance record of the New Democracy administration, there are the following facts:

a) In the parliamentary session of May 15, 1991, Prime Minister C. Mitsotakis stated that:

> "I am very afraid that today telephone wiretaps are carried out and nobody is sure what is going on. I am sorry that as prime minister I am in the sad situation to make such a statement, but we are doing whatever we can to protect the privacy on the telephone."

---

[47]Announcement of PASOK to the press, *Rizospastis,* Aug. 26, 1989.

[48]E.g., see F. Iliou, *The Files* [in Greek], Athens: Themelio, 1990, who claimed the restoration of the files for historians' research. Finally for historical research reasons 2,500 files of well-known resistance personalities were saved.

[49]In a relative case in 1990 in Switzerland it was revealed that " the Political Police had collected files on 900,000 people, two-thirds foreigners, out of a total population of 6.5 million. There were also files on 30,000 organizations. 350,000 people made applications to see their personal files, 39,000 of whom had index cards and files held on them. The 39,000 people and several hundred organizations were given copies of the file index cards on their political activity, which only contained basic information. At the end of June the Swiss parliament decided they would not be allowed to see their files. Only in the city of Zurich were files given to some 3,000 people because these files had never been sent to the Federal Police Department. Records on most people were held at canton (regional) level as well as the federal (state) level. The Military Secret Service also gathered information on more than 7,000 people who were shown their files. The files contained information gathered by the Secret Service and that passed on by the Federal Police. One of the projects undertaken by the political police was to try to find common factors using 25 plus variables—single parent, broken home, students, signing petitions, and attending demonstrations—of "members" of anarchist groups, and concluded there were none." Source *Statewatch* art doc. 1992, Vol. 3 no. 4.

[50]See the statements of Mr. Skoularikis and Mr. Mangakis in *To Ethnos,* Aug. 29, 1989 and *Eleftherotypia,* Aug. 30, 1989.

He had also added:

"We cannot guarantee that wiretaps are not done, since technological means allow any private citizen, organization, or detective to listen to private telephone conversations."[51]

In the same parliamentary session, when the leftist opposition protested the establishment of a second surveillance department at the Greek Telecommunication Organization (OTE), the prime minister justified it as a necessity, in order to cope with terrorism.[52]

b) On the basis of Article 11 of Law 1916/1990 "for the protection of society against organized crime," which was the new anti-terrorist law that the ND government passed, any district attorney could order a telephone wiretap of anybody who was suspected of committing criminal, particularly terrorist, acts. The opposition had accused the Greek National Intelligence Service (EYP) of either giving to district attorneys lists of telephone numbers that included politicians and newspapers' numbers beforehand, or else of falsifying those approved lists, inserting their numbers afterward.

c) On November 8, 1991, the so-called "Evert-gate" broke out, which was about alleged or real surveillance by EYP of the then just resigned minister of the presidency of the government, Miltiades Evert. Given that EYP was directly supervised by the prime minister, who was at odds with Evert, the official excuse that EYP was watching a foreign agent near Evert's office was not persuasive.

The uproar caused by "Evert-gate" and the political role of EYP, brought forth accusations by political parties, opposition newspapers, (*Pontiki*, May 10, 1991; *Rizospastis*, Nov. 23, 1991; *Avriani*, Dec. 8, 1992) and deputies, who claimed that they too had been victims of EYP surveillance during the ND administration. Thus, according to journalistic sources, Evert himself had received a number of tapes with

---

[51]Greek Parliament Records of May 15, 1991 (author's translation) and *Eleftherotypia*, May 16, 1991.
[52]He also added that his government will be absolutely inexorable on issues of protecting telephones' privacy. Ibid.

recorded private conversations of himself and his family members, allegedly wiretapped by ND headquarters.[53] In addition, the KKE Deputy S. Korakas stated that "all KKE activists are still under surveillance," after one of his telephone conversations was published verbatim by a newspaper, which claimed that this was allegedly a wiretapped product of EYP (*Rizospastis*, Nov. 23, 1991). Furthermore, in parliament, 13 PASOK deputies accused the ND government of illegitimate EYP surveillance activities, after a newspaper published the confidential discussions of an entire session of the PASOK party executive office.[54]

While "Evert-gate" once again raised the issue of political surveillance by the governmental security services, it also brought forth a demand by the opposition for a parliamentary committee, comprised of representatives from all parties, to control the surveillance activities of both EYP and the Greek Telecommunication Organization (OTE).

d) The ND government did not pass a bill for the "protection of individuals from the electronic processing of personal information," which had been repeatedly endorsed since 1985. The last time that this draft bill came to parliament was on May 28, 1992, a day before the discussion of a similar bill by the opposition PASOK party, but it was not discussed after all.[55] Thus, despite the ND promise and Greece's obligation to comply with the directives of the Council of Europe Treaty of January 28, 1981 "for the protection of individuals from the electronic processing of personal information," this significant legislation, that could to some degree control state and private electronic surveillance, was again postponed.

e) At the end of February 1992, the ND government ceased prosecuting former Prime Minister A. Papandreou and former EYP and OTE directors C. Tsimas and T. Tombras, respectively, for wiretapping. That decision was a predictable outcome basically due to 1) the fact

---

[53]Quoted by a report titled, "The War of Surveillances," *Kathimerini*, Nov. 10, 1991.

[54]Ibid. See the detailed report.

[55]See *Ta Nea*, May 28, 1992. A summary of this draft bill was published by *Eleftherotypia*, March 15, 1991.

that the European Parliament had not yet decided whether to cancel the immunity of Eurodeputy Tsimas; 2) the prolonged serious illness of Tombras, who later died, and 3) the consequent inability of the ND government to face the political cost of prosecuting only the chief opposition leader and former Prime Minister A. Papandreou, who had just been found innocent of economic misconduct by the Supreme Court (*To Vima,* Feb. 23, 1992).

f) In April 27-29, 1993 the daily newspaper *Eleftherotypia* revealed the so-called wiretap scandal by Prime Minister Mitsotakis's security people, Nicholas Gryllakis and Chris Mavrikis. Former General Nicholas Grylakis, like Oliver North, had taken special secret missions in the Balkans, but his major role was to organize New Democracy's counter-surveillance, mainly against PASOK. Thus, with his assistant telephone wiretap expert, Chris Mavrikis, had created an illegal wiretap ring since 1988. On July 8, 1993, after 12 PASOK deputies had sued 32 individuals for illegal wiretapping, the Parliament formed a new investigative committee. PASOK under Andreas Papandreou came back to power on October 10, 1993 after its victory in the elections. On December 16, 1993, the Parliament announced the conclusions of special investigators Ntafoulis and Dalianis, who made direct and indirect accusations of illegal wiretaps against Prime Minister Constantine Mitsotakis and his minister and daughter Dora Bakoyianni during the period 1988 until 1991, through Gryllakis and Mavrikis's organized wiretap network. Although the Parliament, based on this investigatory conclusion, sentenced Mitsotakis to the Special Supreme Court, Prime Minister A. Papandreou ceased this persecution, putting an end to their political and legal rivalry.

Defending Papandreou's and Mitsotakis's governments, their friendly press has argued that this and other illegal surveillance activities were not approved by the leaders. Simply for PASOK Tombras and Tsimas and for ND Gryllakis and Mavrikis were acting autonomously as over-zealous security prime ministers' people, to collect information for their leaders. Regardless of whether Papandreou and Mitsotakis were personally aware of the illegal surveillance activities of their close associates or not, they were politically responsible for these

"Machiavellian" tactics conducted in their name and for the sake of their political hegemony.

AN EVALUATION

The aforementioned cases of "Machiavellian political surveillance," during and after the PASOK administration, are strictly evaluated here from a sociopolitical control perspective—from the aspect of the deliberate, organized efforts of those in power to acquire, maintain, and impose their authority by all legitimate or illegitimate means (Samatas, M. 1986:36-38). Aside the anticommunist remnants of the first post-dictatorial period, the surveillance of mainly political opponents by populist PASOK[56] leadership was an informal mechanism of a party- and state-organized sociopolitical control system, which was pursuing the protection and continuation of the PASOK leader's hegemonic power. The ND party has done the like during its short administration period, as the "Evert-gate" and the Gryllakis wiretaps ring suggest—the security apparatus was used by an insecure party and state leadership in a similar way to the one used during the PASOK administration, to neutralize the intra-party rivals and the political opponents of the ND leadership, safeguarding prime minister's authority.

Hence, illegitimate governmental surveillance networks to watch real and potential political opponents of the party and state leader were a basic "Machiavellian" mechanism imposed by the sociopoliti-

---

[56]From the growing literature on PASOK populism in Greek, see: Lyrintzis, Ch. "Between Socialism and Populism: The Rise of PASOK" (Ph.D. dissertation, 1983, L.S.E.); Kotzias, N. "The Third Way of PASOK" [in Greek], Synhroni Epochi, 1984; Kapetanyiannis, V. "Populism, Concise Notes for a Critical Reexamination," O Politis, Jan.-March, 1986; Chtouris, S. N. "The PASOK Populism and the Utopia", *Eleftherotypia*, May 8, 1989; Charalambis, D. *Clientilistic Relations and Popoulism*, Athens Exantas 1989A. Liakos, "About Populism," *Istorika* #10, June 1990; Spourdalakis, M., ed. *PASOK: Party, State Society*, Pataki 1998 & Papagaryfalou, P. *Populism in Greece*, Ergo, 2002. In English, see Clogg, R., ed. *Greece, 1981-89: The Populist Decade*, St. Martin, 1993 and Sotiropoulos D. 1991. 1996.

cal control imperative, that is, by the insecure party and state leadership's deliberate efforts to maintain and impose its authority. This type of antidemocratic surveillance by the established populist centralized structures and functions of the party-state apparatus, and especially the institutional "personalized prime-ministerialism" (Manesis, A. 1989: 121f; Makridimitris, A. 1992: 30-37), clearly reflect a poor quality of parliamentary democracy in post-dictatorial Greece, which had remained an underdeveloped surveillance society.

Part II

EURO-SURVEILLANCE AND FOREIGN ANTITERRORIST SURVEILLANCE IN GREECE

Chapter 4

EURO-SURVEILLANCE IN GREECE: THE SCHENGEN INFORMATION SYSTEM

G REECE BECAME A FULL signatory to the Schengen Treaty on March 26, 2000, and from that date on, controls at land, sea, and airport crossings between the then other nine Schengen countries (Belgium, Austria, France, Germany, Spain, Italy, Luxembourg, Holland, and Portugal) were lifted. Freedom of movement in this Schengen passport-free travel zone is based on a central electronic surveillance network, the Schengen Information System (SIS). This system is the basic control apparatus of a potential "Euro-surveilland" for public order and security inside the European Union (EU), as well as a basis for a "fortress Europe" to protect against mainly Third World immigrants and refugees. Whether or not the implementation of the Schengen Agreement and the SIS will produce a "fortress Europe" against undesirable foreigners and a "Schengenland" or a "dataland" as a zone of freedom, or horror, for European citizens and immigrants, is a prospect depending not only on the common Schengen inter-border policy, but also on a plethora of real and perceived domestic contingent conditions in each of the EU member nation states.

Greece, which has gradually joined the passport-free Schengen travel zone since 1992, has a negative human rights record due to the country's authoritarian tradition of mass surveillance, mistreatment of foreigners by police, especially non-EU-citizens, and the frequently "cruel, inhuman, and degrading" treatment of asylum-seekers.[1]

---

[1]See Amnesty International 2000 annual report, and *Statewatch*, (18042), EU: "Asylum: Harmony at a price," *Artdoc*, March, 1995.

73

For the Greek governments, the challenge was therefore to examine all aspects of the Schengen Agreement, i.e., the negative implications of the Greek integration into the European surveillance system, without ignoring any positive impact on free passport movement for European integration. Also to be considered was the serious border control of illegal immigration in Greece, and the modernization/Europeanization of state and security apparatus, which could be confronted at the expense of civil liberties and human rights' protection of Greek citizens and foreigners, immigrants, and refugees, who have proved to be so valuable to the Greek economy (Samatas 2003a).

THE FORMATION OF "SCHENGENLAND" AND THE GREEK MEMBERSHIP

Officially beginning March 26, 1995, the Schengen Treaty took effect, opening up borders in the EU and allowing for cross border flows of information to prevent crime and illegal immigration. Under this treaty, seven of the fifteen European Union member states agreed to lift their border restrictions. The official aim was to eventually create a borderless European Union, through the development of the computer surveillance system of SIS that will help freedom of movement within the EU, while also tracking criminals and illegal immigrants, who might normally be stopped by border guards. The first Schengen Agreement originated in July 1984 as an intergovernmental border agreement between France and Germany to lift many of their frontier controls. It was also signed in the village of Schengen by the Benelux countries in June 1985, "when it became clear at meetings of the Council of Ministers that there was little chance of an EC-wide agreement on internal border controls."[2] Since 1990, the original five EC countries—Germany, France, The Netherlands, Belgium, and Luxembourg—have been joined by Italy (1990), Spain, Portugal (1991), and Greece (1992).[3] The United Kingdom and Ireland still remain

[2]EU: Background to Schengen Agreement, taken from the handbook: "Statewatching the new Europe," 1993.
[3]Besides Greece, Austria has also completed the required legal procedures and has

out.[4] Sweden, Finland, and Denmark were included in 1996, while the non-EU members Iceland and Norway have participated since 1999. Although Schengen I was an administrative agreement requiring no parliamentary involvement, the Schengen Agreement II, agreed to by the governments in 1990, has been subject to parliamentary ratification in each member state.

Since June 1977 the Schengen Agreement has become the Schengen Acquis, after it was officially integrated into the framework of the European Union by the Amsterdam Treaty, which declared that its "over-arching objectives" (are):

> "to maintain and develop the Union as an area of freedom, security and justice, in which the free movement of persons is assured in conjunction with appropriate measures with respect to external borders controls, immigration, asylum and the prevention and combating of crime."[5]

The Schengen Information System (SIS), which will eventually be the European Information System (EIS), is a computerized surveillance information exchange system based in Strasbourg, that finally began operations in Jan. 1995. The first nine Schengen countries in the EU have set up the SIS as part of their agreement to remove internal borders and to institute *"compensatory measures"* covering policing, the law, immigration, and asylum.[6]

become a full member of the Schengen Agreement in the fall 1997.

[4]Although the United Kingdom has not joined the Schengen Agreement, and on present evidence is unlikely to do so, it does want to ensure maximum cooperation with EU police and security forces, including those within Schengen. The British Police National Computer, known as PNC2, has software thatmakes it compatible with the Schengen Information System. Statewatch "The UK and the Schengen Accord," *Statewatch Bulletin*, 2(4) July-Aug. 1992 and Wiener, A. 1999.

[5]Chapter 2: Progressive establishment of an area of Freedom, Security and Justice (Chapter Amend Article B, fourth indent, in the TEU).

[6]Between April-July 1995 the total was 7,556 cases and was attributed to intensive identity checks by the Dutch and French. Around 9,000 of the 30,000 entry points to the Schengen Information System were in Germany . . . In mid-summer, Germany

A valuable assistant of the SIS in combatting crime, illegal immigration, and refugee influx is the TREVI Group, which stands for "Terrorism, Radicalism, Extremism and Violence." The TREVI Group, like Schengen, has a list of "Third World" countries whose nationals require visas to enter and a common list of "undesirables" from non-EU countries.

The official purpose of the SIS is: "to maintain public order and security, including state security, and to apply provisions of this Convention relating to the movement of persons, in the territories of the Contracting Parties, using information transmitted by the system." The data to be stored can include nationality, "any particular objective and permanent physical features" (i.e. a person's race), and the "reason for the report" (which can include information relating to *political beliefs*) (Article 93).[7] (Papakonstantis, G. 1998; Sakelariou, N. 1995 & Toumasatos, K. 2000).

Hence, the most important role of the SIS is to identify individuals to be refused entry, and therefore it can be significant in the police cooperation network for crime prevention and immigration control, narcotic drug trafficking, terrorism, etc.[8] It can, therefore, contribute to the establishment of a borderless European space of freedom, security, and justice, with free and safe movement of persons, goods, capital and services (Papayiannis, 2001; Perakis, 1998).

On the other hand, the SIS, besides the fact that it criminalizes non-documented immigrants and refugees, can also create new problems regarding mass electronic surveillance and violation of citizens' civil liberties and aliens' human rights. There are many reservations and fears regarding: personal privacy laws, which can be violated by the national and centralized computer databases, including the technical implementation by each state apparatus and its judicial and

had provided 2.3 million of the 3.4 million entries on the SIS and France 1 million. *Statewatch Bulletin*, vol 5 no. 6, November-December 1995.

[7]The categories of information are discussed in the next section.

[8]Between 26 March and 8 September 1995, 4,261 people were refused entry: to France 80 percent, Benelux 20 percent, as a result of information provided by Germany. Ten percent concerned asylum seekers who had obtained temporary or permanent documents. *Statewatch Bulletin*, vol 5 no. 6, November-December 1995.

political control; the access to the data, the correction of false data, and transparency for the decisions of its Executive Committee. Further, the SIS entails possible discriminations against non-EU citizens, alien residents, and refugee-seekers in the EU. It also curtails political asylum for EU citizens, who are all considered as coming from safe, democratic countries, and drastically reduces asylum-granting in general. All these issues have been of great concern in the European Parliament. The Van Outrive Report, for instance, underlines the thorny issues of the protection of personal data, political refugees' asylum, legal protection of stigmatized citizens, the destigmatization/correction procedure, and the extensive use of vague key concepts like "public order" and "national security," which, despite the integration of the Schengen Agreement into the European Union Treaty, have not yet been adequately clarified and articulated.[9]

THE SCHENGEN INFORMATION SYSTEM (SIS) AND THE FEAR OF ITS PANOPTIC USE

The SIS constitutes the basic EU surveillance electronic network of collecting and processing various data, fighting criminality, terrorism, and illegal immigration in the European Union (EU), contributing also in the protection of the public order and safety of EU memberstates. The SIS is constituted of a central electronic database (central SIS) in Strasbourg and a network of national SIS data banks (national SIS) in the Schengen's offices (SIRENE) in each memberstate. Each national section of the SIS is directed by the data file managing authority, and a national supervisory authority provided for in Article 114. Further, a joint supervisory authority has been set up, with responsibility for supervising the technical support function of the Schengen Information System. Central SIS is also connected with the national entry points, as with the system VISION, for the exchange of information with regard to the issuing visas to third countries' nationals.

[9]See "Schengen: Teething Problems and First Report," *Statewatch Bulletin*, vol. 6 no. 3, May-June 1996, and Samatas, 2003b.

The SIS operation is regulated by Articles 92-101 of the Schengen Treaty. It contains only the categories of data that are supplied by each of the Contracting Parties. Article 94 prescribes the categories of this data as follows: (a) persons reported, including categories like persons wanted for arrest for extradition purposes, aliens who are reported for the purposes of being refused entry, persons who have disappeared, or persons who need to be protected, as well as those who may be a threat) data relating to witnesses and to persons summoned to appear before the judicial authorities, and (b) objects referred to in Article 100 and vehicles referred to in Article 99.3.

The items included in respect to persons, shall be no more than the following: (a) name and forename, any aliases possibly registered separately; (b) any particular objective and permanent physical features; (c) first letter of second forename; (d) date and place of birth; (e) sex; (f) nationality; (g) whether the persons concerned are armed; (h) whether the persons concerned are violent; (i) reason for the report; (j) action to be taken.

The most controversial and contentious article regarding Euro-surveillance is Article 99, because it prescribes discrete preventive surveillance on the basis of supposed evidence and future intentions. Article 99 actually states:

1. Data relating to persons or vehicles shall be included, in compliance with the national law of the reporting Contracting Party, for the purposes of *discreet surveillance* or specific checks, in accordance with paragraph 5.

2. Such a report may be made for the purposes of prosecuting criminal offences and for the *prevention of threats to public safety:*

> (a) where there are real indications to suggest that the person concerned *intends to commit* or is committing numerous and extremely serious offences, or
> (b) where an overall evaluation of the person concerned, in particular on the basis of offences committed hitherto, *gives reason to suppose that he will also commit extremely serious offences in future.*

3. In addition, a report may be made in accordance with national law, at the request of the authorities responsible for State security, where *concrete evidence gives reason to suppose that the information referred to in paragraph 4 is necessary for the prevention of a serious threat by the person concerned* or other serious threats to internal or external State security. The reporting Contracting Party shall be required to consult the other Contracting Parties beforehand.

4. *For the purposes of discreet surveillance,* the following information may in whole or in part be collected and transmitted to the reporting authority when border checks or other police and customs checks are carried out within the country:

(a) the fact that the person reported or the vehicle reported has been found; (b) the place, time or reason for the check; (c) the route and destination of. the journey; (d) persons accompanying the person concerned or occupants of the vehicle; (e) the vehicle used; (f) objects carried; (g) the circumstances under which the person or the vehicle was found.

When such information is collected, steps must be taken to ensure that *the discreet nature of the surveillance* is not jeopardized.

5. In the context of the specific checks referred to in paragraph 1, persons, vehicles and objects carried may be searched in accordance with national law, in order to achieve the purpose referred to in paragraphs 2 and 3. If the specific check is not authorized in accordance with the law of a Contracting Party, it shall automatically be converted, for that Contracting Party, *into discreet surveillance* (emphasis added).

Under these provisions a common preventive security policy is legitimized in the Schengen zone, accepting a penal law of criminalizing intentions based on suspicions, replacing the assumption of innocence by the assumption of guilt, and prohibiting the movement of suspects throughout the EU.

Articles 102-118 prescribe the protection of personal data and security of data under the Schengen Information System, the right of any person to have access to data relating to him and its limits (Article

109), to correct and delete inaccurate data (Article 110), to bring before the courts or the authority, competent under national law, an action to correct, delete, or provide information or obtain compensation in connection with a report concerning him (Article 111), and to know how long the data (pending each case) will be kept in the SIS databank.

Thus, beyond any ideological conspiracy theory, the Schengen Acquis is formally a crime prevention and immigration control system, justified by the internally borderless Schengen group of EU member states and the protection of its external EU borders. For Euro-enthusiasts, it is necessary for a wonderful, passport-free and crime-free Europe; but for human rights activists, it can be a horrible, anti-democratic exclusionary system for creating a maximum-security "fortress Europe."

THE ADVENTURE OF THE GREEK MEMBERSHIP IN THE SCHENGEN AGREEMENT

Greece was first admitted as an observer in the Schengen group in December 1991 and became a signatory of the Schengen Treaty on November 6, 1992, under the government of the conservative New Democracy party. In 1991 a new law, on Aliens, Immigrants, and Refugees (Law 1975/1991) had also been passed, which brought Greece into line with the Schengen states on the grounds for issuing and refusing visas and setting up "anti-clandestine immigration patrols" and lists of undesirable aliens.[10] Similar to the Greek entrance into the European Monetary Union (EMU) in 1999, the successful application of Greece to join the Schengen group had also been the subject of very little discussion or parliamentary debate (Samatas 2003a).

After repeated delays and postponements, the newly elected PASOK government of modernizer Costas Simitis quietly decided to ratify the Schengen Treaty, "*as a necessary crime prevention apparatus,*"

[10]This law on aliens and immigrants in Greece was characterized as: "a draconian (Greek) contribution to Europe's unification," (Sitaropoulos, N. 1992, pp. 89-96).

according to a statement of the new minister of public order in September 1996.[11]

The real incentive for the ratification of the Treaty, however, came out of the "Imia Crisis," at the end of January 1996, when Greece and Turkey came close to military confrontation over contested Greek sovereign rights in the Aegean Sea.[12] The speculation that the Greek national borders would be recognized as European borders by the Schengen Agreement's contracting parties pushed the Simitis government to ratify the treaty, arguing that the pact would shield Greece's borders against Turkish territorial claims in the Aegean Sea (*Eleftherotypia*, 10 June 1997: 7). Actually, the growing feeling of disappointment in the Greek government after that crisis, due to the fact that NATO and the EU avoided supporting the Greek legal deeds over the sea borders and air space between the Aegean islands and the coast of Turkey, urged Athens to accept the Schengen Agreement as an instrument to a de facto recognition of all Greek borders as external borders of the European Union. That is why the main governmental argument in favor of the Schengen Agreement was that it would first shield Greece's borders against Turkish territorial claims in the Aegean, and only secondarily would it be a crime prevention apparatus against foreigners.[13]

[11]Based on a well-documented report against the Schengen Treaty, the previous PASOK government of Andreas Papandreou, (drafted by Justice Minister G. Kouvelakis, published by the weekly *Pontiki*, 12 June 1997:14), was very reluctant to ratify the Schengen Agreement, fearing that "national sovereignty will be diluted and personal privacy laws would be violated by SIS." Based on that negative evaluation, then Greek Justice Minister Evangelos Venizelos had stated officially at the Greek Parliament's session of 14 March 1995 that Greece would not ratify it, "because of fears that personal privacy laws will be violated by a centralized computer database." (*Athens News* 15 March 1996).

[12]The two countries had deployed warships in the Eastern Aegean sea after Turkey claimed the Greek islet of Imia, and landed troops on an other islet near the one guarded by Greeks—a military engagement was only averted at the last moment after the United States convinced both sides to withdraw their forces (*Athens News*, 1 February 1996).

[13]Both George Papandreou, the then foreign undersecretary, and Justice Minister E. Yiannopoulos defended the treaty using these arguments. *Athens News*, June 11, 1997.

82 SURVEILLANCE IN GREECE

On March 13, 1997, the Greek Parliament approved the Privacy
Bill 2472/97, as a legal precondition for Greece's entry into the Schengen Agreement, and it also ratified the treaty on June 11, 1997, five
years after Greece had signed it, despite small-party opposition and
big-party defection.[14] The leftist opposition warned that the treaty
will: a) violate the constitutional rights and personal freedoms of
Greek citizens and b) help "hand over Greek sovereignty to Brussels."[15]

Besides the mass ignorance of the "what's-its-name" European
border treaty by ordinary Greek citizens,[16] lack of serious political
debate in the Greek Parliament and the media over the impact of the
Schengen ratification reflected a consensus of the Greek power elites
toward the European integration of Greece without any serious nego-

[14]The vote was 142-80 in favor of the Schengen Treaty: 53 MPs from the New
Democracy party and 4 from the ruling PASOK broke party lines and voted against
Schengen. They joined opponents from the Greek Communist Party (KKE), DIKKI,
and the Left Coalition. Seventy-eight MPs failed to show up for the roll call vote in the
300-member parliament. Foreign Minister Theodoros Pangalos accused defecting
MPs of trying to court the superstition vote. KKE said it would seek to have the act of
Parliament annulled, maintaining that 151 votes are needed to ratify the treaty. *Athens
News*, 12 June 1997.

[15]The opposition arguments against the Schengen Treaty ranged from reference
to specific articles that can violate civil rights and personal freedoms, despite Greek
constitutional protections, and characterizations like "the Schengen Treaty equals the
electronic Middle Ages" by the Communist daily *Rizospastis* in 9 June 1997. See also
Toumasatos, K. 2000.

[16]"Schengen" as either a geographical place or as a treaty, doesn' t really mean
anything to most ordinary people of the EU, particularly so for the vast majority of
the lower classes and the poor, marginal groups. This is the case also in Greece, where
despite the stormy furor that was caused in June 1997 over its ratification, 64 percent
of the interviewees in an Athens area poll admitted that they knew little or nothing of
its content, while 47.6 percent were against the Schengen Treaty. Generally, a trend,
that most likely characterizes all EU was verified also for Greece; the lower the inter-
viewee's income, the less they knew about the treaty, and the more they did not accept
it. People belonging to the higher social classes, who potentially can afford to travel
abroad, were generally better informed than those who belonged to the lower social
strata. Yet, the lack of awareness of the Schengen Treaty's implications was almost
complete for those hundreds of thousand of "aliens," Albanians, Polish, and Pakista-
nis, etc., all legal and illegal immigrants and refugees, whose everyday lives and future,
will be greatly affected by the border control in the near future. The poll carried out
by PRC end of July 1997. *Ta Nea*, 14 July 1997.

tiation resistance. In fact, the political debate over the ratification of the Schengen Treaty was almost completely overshadowed by the media coverage of the Orthodox Christian zealots' heated protests against "satanic Schengen," insisting that this pact is nothing but a "Euro-Zionist conspiracy against Orthodox Christianity."[17]

The Greek government defended the treaty against the so called "unholy alliance," of leftists and the religious ultra-right, stating that "only citizens with a criminal record would be included in the SIS." What the Greek government failed to mention were two serious contradictory facts: first, that the Schengen partners would have supported Greece's pursuit to participate in the European Monetary Union, provided that Greece would be an efficient Schengen member protecting EU external borders from illegal immigrants and "Third World" refugees; second, that although Schengen significantly curbs illegal immigration flows from both northern Balkan and eastern Turkey borders, Greece could have unofficially encouraged illegal labor as a means of keeping wages and inflation down and boosting economic growth to achieve EMU criteria.[18]

Finally, despite the implementation problems and partners' fears of inefficiency, Greece became a full signatory to the Schengen Treaty, and the SIS has been implemented in Greece since March 26, 2000.[19] Thus, national insecurity over border disputes, EMU and European integration economic imperatives, plus border security and immigra-

[17]The Orthodox Christians zealots had made a "blacklist" against MPs who voted for Schengen, to be used against their reelection, and a campaign of civil disobedience was prepared to persuade Greeks not to accept the new I.D. cards, along the lines of EU/ Schengen regulations, saying the I.D. cards will carry a bar code concealing the satanic number 666, according to the Book of Revelation. See detailed reports in the Greek press and *Athens News*, 12 June 1997.

[18]See "Greece's migrant policy: Progress at last?" by John F.L. Ross, *Athens News*, 8 Sept. 97.

[19]Although Greece was expected to become a full Schengen member since January 1993, it was delayed for technical, legal, and political reasons until the fall of 1997;a new postponement to early 1998 was caused by the Schengen partners of Greece, who had expressed very serious reservations on the SIS implementation in the Greek airports and harbors (*Kathimerini*, 12 Oct. 1997: 26).

tion control prevailed in Greece over ideological, political, and even religious and superstitious concerns against the Schengen.

SCHENGEN'S IMPLEMENTATION PROBLEMS AND INADEQUATE SAFEGUARDS IN GREECE

In Greece, a total of 100 border crossing points have been modernized to meet Schengen requirements. After an initial investment of 5,5 billion drachmas, 27 airports, 59 sea harbors, and 14 land border controls have been electronically linked with the national N.SIS and the central C.SIS (*Eleftherotypia's* Infotech,16.3.99: 9).

The implementation problems of the SIS in a country like Greece are both technical, due to the extended border line and island geography, and also financial, because of the very expensive ongoing cost,[20] and the sharing of costs has not been clarified (Article 119). For Greece the annual cost of SIS implementation was estimated in 1997 to be approximately 200 million USD or 153 million euros (*Eleftherotypia*, 27 May 1997).

The SIS uses advanced surveillance technology (biometrics, facial thermographs, etc., and soon a DNA databank). This surveillance security technology brings tremendous profits to the corporations that produce and implement it, increasing also the autonomous powers of Euro-techno-bureaucrats[21] and Euro-police, which uses it. An alternative to this investment for a "fortress Europe" could be if this significant amount of money could finance a social policy for the weak European classes and minority groups, and also provide generous aid

[20]For instance, for France, implementing the computerized Schengen Information System (SIS) had already cost 30.5 million French Francs and the operating budget had risen from 1.7 million FF in 1992 to nearly 6 million FF in 1993 (*State-watch*, vol 3 no 4 July-August 1993).

[21]It is amazing how many techno-bureaucratic groups have been organized and work in a public and secret way around the Schengen Agreement: Besides TREVI, there is SIRENE, k4 Committee, CIREA, CIREFI, the Central Group, CNG, Working Group 1-4, and more. This long list is a clear evidence of a growing Euro-bureaucratism. See Samatas (1997).

to the EU poor neighbors and "Third World" countries. By such an EU welfare and development policy, immigration could be controlled through development and not by policing.

Aside from the economic problems, the real technical implementation problems due to the chaotic Greek border landscape, combined with an inefficient civil service, have caused serious fears among the Schengen partners, regarding the ability of Greece, already years behind schedule, to manage the immigration flows; moreover, their mistrust was increasing, first due to their own experience with implementing SIS,[22] and second by their belief that Greece's inability to control illegal immigration was due to the Greek economy's needs to exploit cheap immigrant labor to achieve EMU criteria. As a result, SIS implementation in Greece was postponed until 1998, (*Kathimerini*, 12 Oct. 1997: 26), and finally it was effected in March 2000.

The more serious implementation problems of the SIS are the legal problems, regarding the real protection of citizens' privacy and civil liberties, as well as aliens' human rights. Greek Law 2472 of 1997 on the protection of individual(s) with regard to the processing of (personal) data, adapting the EU Data Protection Directive of 1995, was issued as a precondition for Greece's participation in the Schengen Treaty. Although it defines as "sensitive" the personal data revealing racial or ethnic origin, political opinions, religious or philosophical beliefs, trade-union membership, and the handling of data concerning health, welfare, penal record, even sex life, (Article 2), and prohibits their processing (Article 7, paragraph1) it actually legislates the right of their processing for a host of reasons including *national security, defense and public order* (Article 7 paragraph e). The

---

[22]E.g., in The Netherlands, "after the two week trial period, the Dutch cabinet decided on 21 April 1995 to put an end to the border control regime with magnetic cards at Schiphol airport.. The system's vulnerability to fraud committed by non-Schengen travelers who could easily obtain the non-personalized magnetic cards, appeared to be unsolvable. From 1 May, all passengers once again had to show their passports to enter The Netherlands at Schiphol. Members of parliament expressed surprise and irritation over the "flop" which caused some international embarrassment and left Schiphol with a useless access control system worth 10 million guilders." *Statewatch Bulletin*, May-June 1995, vol 5 no 3.

provisions of this law, combined with those of the Schengen Treaty, actually legitimize preventive police surveillance of all the usual police targets, who can potentially be suspects or could be *violent* or have *future intention* of threatening national security and public safety.[23] Given the Greek authoritarian past, the police surveillance record to date, and its tendency to invent new internal enemies, as it is documented further below, the potential misuse of national and public security interests against human rights and civil liberties is very high.

The Hellenic Data Protection Authority (HDPA), a new institution founded as a requirement of Greece's membership in the Schengen Agreement, staffed by distinguished academics, jurists, and judges, strives not to be a decorative legitimating board, but a serious deterrent and safeguarding authority against any exploitation of sensitive personal data. In fact, having the authority to check the blacklists of the Greek Schengen Bureau, and to cross out Greek citizens' and aliens' names who are listed as "suspects" without adequate evidence, they erased 100 such names of suspect aliens in 1999. Also for 500 blacklisted aliens, who could not get legal status in Greece, based on other Schengen states' lists, HDPA has suggested their reexamination by a special committee, applying the provisions of Article 25 for humanitarian reasons.[24]

Unfortunately, however, the prospects for a truly successful mission of such a board alone cannot not be very optimistic, considering: a. the overall democratic deficit around the functioning of the Schengen Treaty, despite its inclusion in the EU, i.e. its communitarization;[25] b. the aforementioned exemptions and legislative loopholes of Greek law; c. the suffocating governmental controls over all formally

---

[23]Schengen's Article 99 allows information to be held where a person, for the purpose of the "prevention of threats to public safety" is intending to commit "extremely serious offenses" or " Where an overall evaluation of the person concerned, in particular on the basis of offenses committed hitherto, gives reason to suppose that he will commit extremely serious offenses in the future"(Article 99.2).

[24]See "Schengen without safeguards," Sunday *Eleftherotypia*, 28.2.1999.

[25]See in the *Statewatch*'s websites, "Essays for an Open Europe" & "Secret Europe."

autonomous boards;[26] and d. the ongoing "securitization" of Greek society in light of the 2004 Olympics, as it is already reflected by the new antiterrorist legislation based on the primacy of the "right for security" over human rights and civil liberties.[27] All these reflect the absence of a powerful Greek civil society and truly independent, powerful bodies against state violations, as well as the emergence of a neoconservative nationalist culture against all sorts of objectors, heretics, and minorities (Papademetriou, Z. 2000, pp. 298-309).

Because "the Schengen's problem is that it requires to be constantly watched"[28] more effective in alerting citizens can be truly autonomous anti-state watch bodies like the British *Statewatch*, American *Privacy International*, the *Refugee Forum*, etc., which organize citizens' vigilance and counter surveillance of all state, suprastate and corporate violations. That implies, however, an active citizens' movement for a more democratic European society and an all-inclusive, "open EU."[29]

SCHENGEN'S NEGATIVE IMPLICATIONS FOR GREEK AND OTHER EU CITIZENS' RIGHTS & CIVIL LIBERTIES

For Euro-enthusiasts, the Schengen passport-free zone as the realization of the four freedoms of movement of goods, services, capital, and persons has become particularly important for a "People's Europe,"

[26]Although Costas Simitis's PASOK government formally supported the independence of such boards like the Supreme Council for Public Personnel Selection (ASEP), the Ombudsmen against civil service corruption and the Radio-TV Council, still all these boards are in many ways substantially dependent upon the government policy and funding.

[27]See the provisions of the new antiterrorist draft law in *To Vima*, Sunday 4 March 2001: A16.

[28]A statement by Prof. Spyros Simitis, an informatics specialist working in Germany, *Ta Nea*, 10 June 1997.

[29]By the term "open Europe" we do not only mean here a more democratic and accountable Europe versus a secret EU, as *Statewatch* and the European Federation of Journalists strive for, but also a more hospitable and humane to immigrants and refugees Europe.

creating a feeling of belonging, or a stronger bond between the EU and
its citizens (Wiener, A. 1999, p. 2). Greek and European citizens are
given particular advantages, enjoying passport-free travel within the
Schengen zone.[30]
On the other hand, for Euro-sceptics and human rights activists a
serious concern of the SIS is whether its function will deteriorate the
protection of civil liberties and human rights in countries like Greece,
which have an authoritarian state culture and a traditional negative
record on human rights.

One can easily predict a serious negative impact of the SIS on
human rights in Greece, considering the long list of violations of freedom of expression,[31] minority rights,[32] and political asylum refusal,
reflecting in recent years authoritarian remnants of the Greek security
apparatus, 20 years after the end of the military dictatorship. As the US
Department of State's "Country Reports on Human Rights Practices

[30]The removing of border controls for Greek citizens among Schengen memberstates also lifted the ban on thousands of Greeks in debt, who owe small and large
amounts of money to the Greek state, and are now free to travel. (*Kathimerini*, 23 Sept.
2000). Also the Greek draft-dodgers, who are living in EU countries are now able to
visit Greece and travel in the Schengen zone without sanctions (*To Vima* 24.12.00).
Following Greece's adherence to the Schengen Treaty, representatives of foreign
authorities may ask to be present at all judicial proceedings of both witnesses and
accused, improving Greece's judicial image abroad. (*Kathimerini*, 22 February 2000).

[31]E.g., in April 1994, Michael Papadakis, a 17-year-old schoolboy, was sentenced
to a year in prison for distributing anti-nationalist leaflets at a rally over the Macedon-
ian issue. In Dec. 1995, a professor, George Roussis, and a well-known actor, Vassilis
Diamantopoulos, were prosecuted for siding with young "anarchists" by expressing in
a TV talk show views deemed as "praising criminal activities." This issue had been seen
by many as the biggest blow to freedom of speech since the military dictatorship
(1967-74). *Athens News*, Dec. 7 1995. In September 1997, police arrested and sentenced immediately several citizens to two months of jail, who peacefully demonstrated their opposition to the Greek organization of the Olympic Games, by
distributing leaflets under the pretext that they had gathered inside the area of the
Acropolis, and "they polluted the environment." Kiaos, N. "New 'miasma' in Olympic
wrapping," *Eleftherotypia*, 18 September 1997: 9.

[32]In the 1997 citizenship law, the notorious article 19 gave (until the end of 1999
when it was finally cancelled) the right to bureaucrats to strip Greek citizenship from
those Greek citizens, who are of different race or religion, regularly visit Turkey and
stay there for a long period, targeting mainly the Muslim minority.

for 1996" (Privacy Sections, January 1997, excerpted by Privacy International), regarding Greece, states: "(Although) the (Greek) Constitution prohibits the invasion of privacy and searches without warrants, and the law permits the monitoring of personal communications only under strict judicial controls, *the number of persons and groups subjected to government surveillance in recent years raises questions about safeguards.* The security services continued to target human rights activists, non-Orthodox religious groups,[33] and minority group representatives[34] and to monitor foreign diplomats who met with such individuals."[35]

Indicative cases that could be listed in the SIS are the following:

- In December 1995, a secret list of the anti-terrorist police was revealed, comprised of 251 names, including well-known politicians, MPs, actors, journalists, etc., who had resisted the military junta. They were listed as "suspects of involvement in terrorist activities."[36]

---

[33]In August 1993 the existence of a report by the Greek National Intelligence Service (EYP) entitled "Contemporary Heretics and para-religious Organizations in Greece," was revealed by the press. Based on police surveillance of all non-Orthodox Christian organizations, targeting especially the Jehovah's Witnesses, and including the Catholics; this confidential report suggested control measures against all them, seen as a threat to national security. This report dated Jan. 19. 1993 was canceled after wide publicity in the Greek press. *Eleftherotypia,* 4 & 5 Aug. 1993.

[34]E.g. also Sotiris Bletsas in 2.2.2001 was sentenced to 15 months in jail for distributing a leaflet stating that in Greece, besides Greek several other ethnic languages are spoken, causing by this "false rumor fear to the Greek citizens." See "The black list of racism," *Epohi,* 27.5.01.

[35]The report continues stating that: "On several occasions, information about such private meetings, including official government documents, was published by the press. Human rights activists also reported the continuation of suspicious opening and diversion of mail, some of which was never delivered but was subsequently published in newspapers with apparent links to security services. As far as is known, the Government took no steps to stop such practices or to prosecute those involved."

[36]A parliamentary investigation concluded that this list was drafted during the 1979-1980 period, and then in 1995 contained only 20 names with data of their arrivals and departures abroad. *Eleftherotypia* 6 Dec. 1995 and *Ethnos,* 12 Dec. 1995.

- A "cumulative" effect of the Schengen Agreement is illustrated by the example of a foreign correspondent from a non-EU newspaper, who was expelled from Greece in 1993 for criticizing the Greek government's decision not to recognize the state of FYROM (Skopia-Macedonia). Through the SIS he would be registered as an "undesirable" alien in all Schengen memberstates and could only be admitted to another EU country if it served a humanitarian purpose or the national interest; and this state would have to guarantee that the person would not damage Greek interests. By the same token it could be, for example, that any non-EU journalist or academic, who after criticizing Germany's or Austria's toleration of neo-nazism, could be expelled out of these states and be listed as undesirable in the whole Schengenland.[37]

- Yet, in 1998, an Italian EU citizen (Enrico Bianco), who was accused by the Italian police as being a member of a terrorist group in the 1970s, was arrested by the Greek police, sentenced to jail, and two years later was deported to Italy, despite the fact that he had applied for political asylum. This case and several similar others prove the fact that under the Schengen there is no political asylum for EU citizens, since all EU member states from which political dissidents are coming from are considered safe democracies respecting human rights and civil liberties (*Eleftherotypia*, 13.1.1998:18).

The aforementioned examples indicate what kinds of data on individuals may be transmitted in the Schengen Information System by the Greek security forces. In fact, the negative legacy of mass political surveillance in Greece, and the authoritarian remnants in the atti-

---

[37]If an individual is considered to be a *threat to public safety, national security, or the international relations of any* of the Contracting Parties, and therefore refused entry to its national territory, s/he automatically will not be admitted to any of the other Member States (Article 5 e). Katrougalos, G. 1995.This particular example was published by the Dutch paper *Kleintje* 17.2.94. to make the point that "Too little attention has been paid to the effects of exchanging information on individuals," and it was quoted by *Statewatch*, vol 4 no 2, March-April 1994.

tude and behavior of the security apparatus against certain political, social, racial, religious, sexual, and other minorities, have made most Greek citizens and political organizations very suspicious against the SIS; consequently, the common attitude is to reject any state or suprastate information system, as it represents a prolonged victimization through mass surveillance.

THE SIS's SORTING IN TERMS OF ASYLUM & IMMIGRATION

Airline companies have undertaken the role of checking and confirming that migrants carrying a Green Card also have a visa, because in the case of spot-check and a passenger denied entry, the airlines are held responsible, face stiff fines, and must also arrange for the passenger's return to Greece, or to their country of origin. The involvement of major European airlines, such as Lufthansa, KLM, Sabena, Air France, Martin Air, etc., in the cruel deportation-business, which has even caused some deaths of deportees who resisted deportation, has come under attack by the "deportation alliance" activists throughout the EU, who have launched the "outrageous return flight" campaign, and especially in Germany by the "deportation class" campaign, initiated by the slogan, "kein Mensch ist illegal" (see www.deportation-alliance.com).

The fact that the SIS until now is primarily working as an antiimmigration system is shown in *Table 2*, which depicts the entry data or "alerts" by each memberstate of the Central Schengen Information System (CSIS) up to January 2000. Although this is not an official list, it is useful to see the national policies evidence in certain sensitive issues regarding immigration, national security, terrorism, etc.

This list, which was unofficially leaked to the press by the Greek Schengen Office, shows the following:

- The total input data until the end of January 2000 was close to only 1.8 million, 50 percent of which is about missing (lost or stolen) objects, mostly vehicles, and around 800,000 about undesirable aliens in the Schengenland. Although this data is unofficial and

TABLE 2

Schengen Information System (S.I.S) : Data Entries until January 27, 2000

CATEGORIES OF DATA	AUSTRIA	BELGIUM	GERMANY	SPAIN	FRANCE	GREECE	ITALY	LOUXEMB.	HOLLAND	PORTUGAL	TOTAL DATA INPUT
Arrest for the purpose of extradition	717	786	3,374	588	2,273	222	1,890	80	357	259	10,546
Refusal of entry to the Schengen Area	27,664	676	381,207	12,744	61,396	46,186	227,650	222	8,044	1,617	767,406
Missing Adults	115	649	836	4,127	3,493	384	3,493	75	404	582	14,153
Missing Minors	68	866	956	2,634	4,663	43	2,272	39	551	336	12,428
Arrest for appearing in Court as a witness or suspect	2,245	647	960	473	21,328	0	9,223	302	11	418	35,607
Discrete surveillance for averting a threat to public safety	281	16	470	3	5,594	0	4,835	0	20	0	11,219
Specific checks for averting a threat to public safety	0	23	0	22	3,240	0	2,894	1	2	0	6,182
Discrete surveillance & specific checks for averting terrorism and a threat to national security	0	0	0	0	0	0	0	0	0	0	0
Objects: vehicles, firearms, documents or banknotes, stolen or lost	7,752	31,164	179,600	139,871	229,526	36,301	281,222	1,629	41,915	20,853	950,000
TOTAL	38,842	34,827	567,403	160,462	331,518	83,136	533,479	2,348	51,304	24,065	1,807,551

Source: Greek Schengen Bureau's unofficial data, by G. Marnellos, "Filling by each state," *Sunday Eleftherotypia*, February 13, 2000

not revealed for all categories, it represents almost 50 percent less than the total active records of "the first annual report" on the operation of the Schengen agreement—with much fewer members then—issued in 1996.[38] Nevertheless, one could argue that this leaked data was purposely of a lesser extent, compared to other previous records, to pacify the Greek public opinion's Euro-surveillance fear and to facilitate the ratification of the Schengen Acquis.[39]

• Interestingly enough, based on all relevant data categories of this and other available sources (see data statistics: Schengen Info. System (SIS), *Statewatch Bulletin*, vol. 9 no.s 3 & 4,May-August 1999), "third country nationals" to be rejected at borders or deported make up 80 percent of SIS person-related data, while real "criminal data" of the SIS is negligible. Based on that, SIS first and foremost is not an anti-crime mechanism but a means of enforcing a "fortress Europe" in terms of immigration.

• Of all the active records over the period, there was a total of about 800,000 concerned aliens to be refused entry and asylum, compared with 507,859 in 1996; the increase was caused mostly by Italy, Austria, and Greece, which joined the SIS on 1 December 1997. While Italy is responsible for 227,650 entry refusals, Greece is responsible for only 46,186, and Germany remains first with 381,207 undesirable aliens, blacklisted in the Schengenland.

• According to the same source, Greece is also responsible for 3,330 aliens' entry refusals in the Schengenland, based on the Greek blacklist of undesired aliens. In addition, Greece "positively

[38]Germany alone in 1996 had 2.4 million and France 1.2 million entries. Also, in 1998 the SIS had reached a total data input of more than 8.8 million entries, of which 7.4 million referred to objects and 1.2 million were wanted persons' records. Out of them only 795,000 were about real people, because the rest, 430,000, were about the so-called "Alias Group," that is people who have a second identity. (See *Statewatch Bulletin*, vol.6 no 3, May-June 1996).

[39]The journalist concluded that the Schengen zero records prove that central SIS is not a surveillance threat for Greek and EU citizens and aliens; they are still threatened by the special state police and national security office in each memberstate (Marnellos, G. "Filing by each state" *Sunday Eleftherotypia,*13 Feb. 2000).

responded" to refused entry and asylum on 3,799 persons, based on information blacklists supplied by other Schengen states.

- The Greek zero record for subjects like "arrests of witnesses or suspects," "discreet surveillance and specific checks for public safety threats," indicates that either Greece has not "responded positively" to other Schengen states' information to place persons under "discreet surveillance" (Article 99), or Greek records were missing or not disclosed (Perakis, St. 1998).

- Undisclosed records is most likely the case for the subject regarding "discreet surveillance for terrorism and national security suspects," since all memberstates give a zero record. Since there is no enforcement apparatus to make obligatory the announcement of national records, the zero record either means nation states' secrecy or Schengen's expedient, coordinated secrecy. Yet, one interpretation of the fact that all memberstates have refused to publish records on this sensitive subject could be the existence of the national authorities for the protection of personal data, in which anyone could ask information on whether s/he is listed as a terrorist suspect. On the other hand, it seems that "national security" still predominates in any European interstate cooperation. The issues of national security and national sovereignty are really causing serious problems for interstate cooperation and Schengen's efficiency. Inadequate information exchange, as well as refusal to allow cross-border chases, have always posed the serious question of how Schengen is going to work if member nation states are concerned with their own national priorities.

- Regarding the record of the Greek Schengen Bureau depicted by *Table 2,* when compared to other member Schengen states like Belgium, Austria, and Spain, the Greek effort, based on its population and geography, cannot yet be considered successful. Considering, however, the inefficient Greek border control system, and the Greek economy's needs for cheap, unskilled foreign labor, the *Table 2* results are satisfactory. It is also more than certain that without Schengen cooperation even these poor results would not have been produced.

An assessment of SIS's surveillance in Greece

Greek geopolitical and sociopolitical control imperatives have actually affected the surveillance efficiency of SIS in Greece. In particular, two basic factors have supported Greece's participation in the Schengen Agreement. First, national (in)security interests regarding the recognition of Greek borders as EU external borders, after the relative Greek-Turkish dispute; second, the geopolitical situation of Greece in the southern and eastern EU borders, neighboring with very high migratory pressure areas, i.e., the Balkans and Turkey, emphasized the need for border control. On the other hand, the needs of Greek economy for cheap foreign labor, ideological reservations against external suprastate controls versus national sovereignty, (e.g. police crossing borders without permit, etc.), and the negative authoritarian legacy of mass political surveillance, have caused reactions against the Schengen Information System, as preventing economic exchanges with the Balkans and for its potential to violate citizens' civil liberties and aliens' human rights.

Thus, although the implementation of the SIS in 100 border entries to Greece, and the enforced police cooperation in common Schengen structures and policies, raises hopes for the modernization-Europeanization of Greek policing and more efficient Greek border control, it also raises serious fears about strengthening authoritarian tendencies toward a maximum security Greek society within a "fortress Europe."

Based on the above analysis and documented evidence we can conclude that up to the present, while the Schengen's impact is a mixed blessing for Greek and European citizens, considering both the freedom of movement but also the potential violations of privacy and civil liberties, it is clearly an immigration anathema by building a "fortress Europe," particularly having to do with "Third World" immigrants' and refugees' rights and life chances in the EU. It is a mixed blessing for Greek and EU citizens, because what is gained in free movement, mainly for the European middle/business classes, and the enormous symbolic progress by tearing down some of the former border controls between European states, is probably lost in the tendency to build a maximum security EU. Especially after the 9/11 impact and the primacy of security in the EU, like in the United States, for non-Western foreigners, Schengen definitely means a "fortress Europe." Although this "fortress Europe" does not necessarily safeguard the EU from terrorism and organized crime, it entails new control zones between European states, more powers to border officials, draconian control of immigration and asylum; privatization of border control to airline companies with the notorious "deportation class," and so on. In the name of an efficient control of the EU's external borders, "fortress Europe," like a closed and secret Europe, is promoted by specific Euro-techno-bureaucratic elites, unaccountable Europolice, and electronic surveillance networkers, and by the interests of the industry of high-tech security systems (Samatas 2003a&b).

Finally, the contradictions of the Greek Schengen case are not isolated, but reflect wider implications allover the EU, especially on the security issue. Thus, it seems that under the antiterrorism impact, the strengthening of a comprehensive system of internal surveillance combined with tightening of strict external border controls *securitization prevails over human rights and civil liberties in Schengenland.* As both Greek available data and other independent organizations' data prove, the SIS has substantially shifted from freedom of movement to control of movement, reflecting national and supranational fears of migration, as similar to crime and terrorism. The question is how the anti-crime efficiency of the SIS will be increased and not be focused only on the easy target of "Third World" immigrants and refugees and anti-globalization activists. If the real aim of the Schengen Information System is the free movement of people and goods, and the protection of Europe against organized crime, then its serious implementation problems and negative implications call for more openness and accountability and interstate and civil society cooperation to avert any authoritarian tendency and possible expedient interests promoted by the Schengen's Acquis. Unfortunately, the end of the Cold War helps the formation of a "*people's Europe,*" and instead under the terrorist threat a techno-bureaucratic European fortress prevails.

Therefore there always is a need for a constant and vigilant watch of all national and supranational policies and records, protecting citizens' and foreigners' traditional and new rights.

Chapter 5

American and British Antiterrorist Surveillance in Greece

A S MUCH AS THE POST-GREEK Civil War anticommunist police was efficient in its surveillance of communists and leftist activists, the post-dictatorial police proved to be extremely inefficient in arresting terrorists. This inability of the police to enforce an efficient surveillance system, and the prolonged victimization of several foreign citizens by the terrorist group November 17, invited foreign interference and foreign surveillance in Greece.[1]

Following we examine first the so-called "Riancourt case," which has proved the inefficiency and possible corruption of post-dictatorial Greek anti-terrorist police, and also three interesting foreign surveillance cases in Greece, namely: the Ocalan, the Vasilikos, and the Saunders case.

The Greek police surveillance fiasco with 17N on Louise Riancourt Street

The embarrassing police operation on Louise Riancourt Street in Athens in March 1992 revealed the incompetence of the Greek police in catching the terrorist group November 17 (17N) (see G. Gilson's report in *Athens News*, May 23, 2003: A08). Terrorists claimed in the

---

[1]Post-dictatorial police inefficiency, attributed to ideological and structural-organizational reasons, especially to party factionalism, is analyzed by Papaconstantis, G. (2003).

17N trial that it was a police conspiracy. "We have seen here moments of the beautiful moral world of this amalgam of stoolies, intelligence services and agents of the police brass involved in the devouring of secret funds. They should not implicate us in their dirty world," declared confessed November 17 (17N) terrorist Dimitris Koufodinas. Also, the accused terrorist Savvas Xiros said that police had found the van abandoned by 17N on March 29 and, when they found a stolen gun, set up a fake sting operation the very next day in order to pocket 13 million drachmas in police funds. The alleged female informer who had received 13 million drachmas for tipping off police on a planned 17N hit says she was framed. The mystery woman, Maria Tsinteri, appeared in TV programs to deny that she was the informant and said that the police was trying to "slander" her. Then Police Chief Stephanos Makris testified that he received a call from an anonymous woman who claimed 17N was planning a strike against a judge for March 27, 1992. In a second call she said that if the hit failed, the terrorists would assemble in front of a certain three-storey building on Riancourt Street.

Thirty counter-terrorism police officers were stationed at the appointed spot with patrol cars nearby. They saw only two individuals—one with a wig—get out of a yellow van. When one officer tried to alert nearby riot police, the suspects took off. One policeman followed the stolen van but inexplicably lost track of it along the way. It was later found abandoned with a pistol stolen earlier by 17N in a raid of the Vyronas police precinct. "*A stable camera was set up [to record the operation] but, alas, it did not record faces,*" (emphasis added) Makris told the court . . . "We sent the most well-trained group of officers but, unfortunately, it proved inadequate. We were unable to pin down the female informant while I served as chief," Makris testified.

Even the chief judge trying the 17N case at Korydallos prison, Mihalis Margaritis, expressed amazement at police. "*I used to wonder for a long time why 17N had not been caught over so many years. Can I wonder any more? Not a single person did their job properly? What can I say?*" (emphasis added) Margaritis said. . . . "This affair took place while conservative Prime Minister Constantine Mitsotakis of the New

Democracy Party was in power . . . The episode proved utterly embarrassing for the conservatives, who had accused PASOK with everything ranging from incompetence to criminal negligence" (G. Gilson's report. ibid.).

A SUCCESSFUL CASE FOR AMERICAN INTELLIGENCE IN GREECE AND THE REGION

The Greek fiasco of the Kurdish leader Abdullah Ocalan, who had asked for political asylum from Italy, Russia, and then from Greece in January 1999, revealed an extensive US intelligence and political involvement in tracking down Ocalan. After US and Turkish catalytic pressures, all governments had denied Ocalan from settling in their country or being granted asylum. Despite this, however, the Greek government sent Ocalan to the Greek embassy in Nairobi, Kenya, in which the American satellites and ground intelligence, with the assistance of the Israeli intelligence, played a significant surveillance role in tracking him down, arresting, and delivering him to the Turkish government. According to the Sunday *To Vima* report (February 21, 1999) the FBI and the CIA collaborated over six months with Turkey's secret service (MIT) to secure Ocalan's capture, which occurred on February 15, 1999. Turkey received a continuous flow of information from US satellites, as well as by other technical means, and the assistance of US agents on the ground. Athens' choice of Kenya raised serious questions, given the strong US presence in Kenya after the bombing of the US embassy in Nairobi, a year before. Although "the Israeli Mossad has denied involvement in the Nairobi operation, there has been no Israeli denial of close intelligence sharing with Turkey's MIT over two years." (*Athens News*, February 2, 1999: A01). The Ocalan affair, which was a shameful fiasco for the Greek government and diplomacy, and a great success for American intelligence, caused a governmental crisis and a restructuring of the Greek National Intelligence Service (EYP).

The "Vasilikos case": an American dataveillance fiasco

In November 2001 , several months before the arrest of the members of the November 17 terrorist group, the former US ambassador to Greece, Thomas Niles, who served in Athens between 1995-97, revealed in an interview with journalist Alexis Papahelas on the private MEGA TV channel that in 1995 the US Embassy had offered the late Prime Minister Andreas Papandreou's government a list of November 17 suspects, including an individual suspected of being the author of the terrorist group's proclamations. The retired diplomat accused the PASOK government at that time, as well as the following PASOK government of Costas Simitis, of ignoring this list, as well as others given previously. "I told the prime minister (Simitis) in 1997 that I thought the organizers of this group were prominent members of Greek society who in their day jobs were other things than terrorists and had this sort of a vocation. He said that he agreed with me," Niles said . . . (*Athens News*, November 9, 2001: A05). "We told the Greek government who we thought was writing the declarations . . . based on (textual) analysis and comparisons over the years. There was no follow up that I know of," Niles remarked, and added that the evidence was of a kind that could "probably" lead to an indictment in a US court, and that the suspect was not connected to the government "at that time." As Papahelas reaffirms in his book on November 17 with Tasos Telloglou (2003: 179-181, 183), the CIA had actually organized in 1995 a project of dataveillance, electronically analyzing all proclamations of the November 17 group. They had also made a list of key suspects, who could have written these proclamations, based on criteria like their relationship with Paris, their age, their relationship with Jean Paul Sartre, etc. Based on these criteria they selected a couple of intellectuals and electronically compared their writings with the proclamations. The computerized result was to portray as the basic suspect the well-known writer Vasilis Vasilikos, the author of the book "Z." "He was the only one who made reference of Balzac, and used certain words like 'chauffeur,' a word used in the proclamations. Also, the fact that Vasilikos had translated in Greek a book of Regis Dembre's *Learning from*

Toupamaros (1971), was considered very critical to be suspected as the key proclamations writer suspect. American intelligence watched Vasilikos in Paris, where he served as Greek ambassador in UNESCO, and according to Papahelas's sources, they even sneaked into his apartment to look for the November 17 typewriter. French intelligence had also given to the Greek government lists with suspects' names, including philosopher Cornelius Castoriadis. Niles had suggested that "one of the reasons why November 17 has been so impervious to Greece's intelligence service was it never sought to increase their numbers." He continued that "November 17 is comprised of well-known members of Greek society . . ." and further, "The people who carry out the killings I think are hired from the outside and brought in on a one-time basis." Asked why CIA and FBI officials had failed to find solid leads, Niles replied that "It's not the responsibility of the CIA or M15 to do this work. We can help. There's something, some element in the system that does not want this to happen, and has been able to prevent it from succeeding over the years." The Greek government blasted Niles for his bombshell accusations (*Athens News*, November 9, 2001: A05), which after the arrest and trial of most November 17 group members, were proved to be entirely unfounded.

After the first November 17 members' arrests in the summer of 2002, an American Embassy official commented on the "Vasilikos case" to the journalist Alexis Papahelas that this fiasco cost a lot of money to the embassy and took about ten years of investigations. "Unfortunately it was the persistent idea of one CIA agent, who claimed with certainty to know the proclamations writer" (Papahelas and Telloglou, 2003: 181).

This case confirms that dataveillance, like all panoptic high technology, is an efficient instrument only when the hypothesis about the target and the chosen criteria of the documents selected to be matched are correct. Otherwise, as in the Vasilikos case and that of other PASOK politicians, whom occasionally Americans suspected of being linked with 17N, the data can prove to be wrong and lead to a total fiasco.

SURVEILLANCE IN GREECE

104

The British antiterrorist intervention after Saunders's murder

According to a leaked report by G. Gilson in the *Athens News*, (August 16, 2002: A03) " When Scotland Yard arrived in Greece immediately after the murder of British military attaché Stephen Saunders by November 17 (17N), they admittedly experienced police culture shock. Never in the quarter-century history of 17N had the files of nearly two dozen victims been systematically compared. The Greek police's counter-terrorism bureau was not even in the nascent stages of computerization. Forensics facilities also were technologically nowhere close to the British counterpart. In June 2001, the methodical work Scotland Yard conducted in good faith with their Greek colleagues produced a report of several hundred pages. The document reveals that Greek counter-terrorism police "learned methodical analysis and computerization from Scotland Yard," and offered "a systematic overview of the activity of the terrorist group and a plethora of strategic recommendations on how to exploit existing evidence and develop new leads." The report stressed a focus on "re-examination of evidence currently held". "The review team observed that the Hellenic Police (ELAS) did not investigate crime as a linked series, did not have a computerized crime management system and did not use analysis as an aid to investigation," they said, "raising serious questions on what Greek police actually did to probe terrorism for over two decades."

According to the same Scotland Yard report, in many instances, "British recommendations required little more than common sense: adopt standardized serious- and series-crime investigation procedures, introduce computerization to assist in the cross-linking of information gathered during the course of a probe, adopt an analytical approach to the investigation of major crimes." The report proposed that "Greek authorities broaden surveillance in their probes with use of existing private closed-circuit television (CCTV) and the creation of state CCTV networks to monitor the public's movement." For example, the report says, "There are privately owned CCTV systems in Athens, together with other 'official systems,' e.g. 'traffic management.' The Hellenic Police should create a CCTV counter-terrorist database, subject to law, along the same lines as the IRIS Database used in London ... and be directly involved in planning and sitting of CCTV systems to be introduced in Athens for the 2004 Olympic Games," Scotland Yard suggested, focusing on areas where murders had taken place. It also proposed adapting traffic management "automatic number plate readers" (ANPR) for use in counter-terrorism. Finally, broader surveillance of mobile phone communications was advised, with the adoption of cell site analysis, which should be "covered by relevant legislation."

In fact, the murder of Saunders by 17N group surfaced the issue of lifting the confidentiality of the identity of mobile phone subscribers who are suspected of involvement in terrorism. According to the daily newspaper *Ta Nea*, (February 21, 2001) the Greek counter-terrorism authorities had recorded thousands of mobile phone conversations on the day of that murder and had determined that around 100 of those were suspect and destroyed the tapes the next day; but they were unable to exploit the evidence without knowing the identity of the subscribers, whose privacy is protected. The Hellenic Data Protection Authority prevented police from obtaining the identity of the mobile phone subscribers. That problem was resolved by the drafting of the new antiterrorist law, as we discuss later. Furthermore, after British suggestion, Greek police established an anonymous hotline for tips, encouraging citizens' cooperation with police, something that is not easy in Greece following a prolonged authoritarian police state.

In brief, the British police's intervention significantly contributed to the modernization and increased efficiency of the Greek police.

Part III

The Modernization of Greek State Surveillance and the Olympics Panopticism

Chapter 6

THE MODERNIZATION OF GREEK STATE SURVEILLANCE: ELECTRONIC, LEGISLATIVE, AND INSTITUTIONAL

THE MODERNIZATION, DISSEMINATION, AND ROUTINIZATION OF ELECTRONIC PANOPTICISM IN CONTEMPORARY GREECE

IN EARLY 21ST CENTURY contemporary Greece, an open, democratic market society, the "traditional" mass political control state surveillance is superceded by a galaxy of "new surveillance." This new era consists of a multifaceted electronic surveillance of citizens, not only by the modernized state surveillance, data collection, and processing agencies, but also by numerous private data collectors, suprastate organizations, and transnational corporations.

As we have analyzed in the first chapter, under the Greek authoritarian police state, surveillance in Greece was a state and governmental monopoly; even the few private investigators for criminal and family cases were under the strict control of the police. This mass political control state surveillance, a "traditional surveillance," was the basic mechanism of the Greek sociopolitical control system up to the 1980s; it was an efficient surveillance police network, mainly based on human intelligence, and the coercive cooperation of the police and state agencies with private informers all over the country. This mass state surveillance basically monitored citizens' political ideology and behavior, classifying Greeks as clients or non-clients to the state. Hence, traditional state surveillance had a serious impact on the sociopolitical control of the life-chances of the Greek people.

Greece in this century is now experiencing the "new surveillance" of electronic panopticism, since the traditional state has been obsolete under the socioeconomic and political processes that have occurred in the last 15-20 years. Paper police files are replaced by electronic databases, as state agencies and public organizations, but also private firms and corporations, have started to electronically collect and process citizens' data for institutional, marketing and other purposes. Telematics and electronic intelligence are used by the new surveillance, and market, consumer surveillance, biometrics, even biogenetic surveillance can be matched with other personal data, regarding taxes, medical, insurance, and more to produce various information profiles, even simulations forecasting future behavior of individuals.

In the following chapter we report on various private surveillance cases in contemporary Greece. We have tried to include a characteristic sample of the mushrooming variety of surveillance in order to realize its dimensions and interpret its causes.

In fact, the last years in Greece, as in all countries of informational capitalism, citizens' privacy is violated daily by state and private, legal or illegal, surveillors, using the new panoptic technologies (Castells, M. 1997 & Lyon D. 1994, 2001). The problem is summarized by the Hellenic Data Protection Authority (HDPA), which is justifying the necessity of its foundation, but also its weakness to control panopticism in Greece, as it states in its website (*http://www.dpa.gr*):

"The enormous progress of information technology, the growth of new technologies, the new forms of advertisement and electronic transactions, and the electronic organization of state apparatus have as consequence the increased demand of personal information from the private and public sector. The unverifiable storage and processing of personal data in electronic and handwritten files of services, companies and organizations can cause problems in the citizen's private life."

The Hellenic Data Protection Authority's slogan is:

"Each citizen should be in a position to know at every moment who, where, when, how and why processes their personal data."

Former HDPA Chairman Constantine Dafermos had stated that "(Greek) Security Police is a pigeon compared to the surveillance by private individuals" (*Ta Nea*, 20 5.2002: 14-15). This statement should not however cause an underestimation of the modernization of Greek state panopticism, which, as we have already noticed, after the 9/11 attacks and due to the 2004 Athens Olympic Games has been reorganized and reinforced by international cooperation. Moreover, Greeks who have suffered by the repressive mass state surveillance, nowadays enjoy a "sweet" consented and participatory TV surveillance. Like Americans and other Europeans Greeks enjoy daily the new television reality and "Big Brother"-style shows, where the audience is entertained by watching ordinary people who exchange their privacy for temporary fame and profit. Thus, the new television market by the daily TV surveillance entertainment shows, promoting a participatory consented surveillance, causes a deliberate confusion of who is watching and who is watched to the benefit of mass manipulation power centers, that is the mass media, as well as mobile phone companies. Hence the question also in Greece is who is going to watch the watchers?

THE ELECTRONIC AND LEGISLATIVE MODERNIZATION OF THE GREEK STATE: ELECTRONIC POLICE FILES AND THE NEW LAW AGAINST ORGANIZED CRIME AND TERRORISM

Like all nation-states that are currently adopting the applications of new technologies to modernize their panoptic apparatus (Giddens, A. 1985, Webster, Fr. 1995), similarly "Greek bureaucratism," as I have called the structure and function of the Greek state apparatus, which works as a sociopolitical control system (Samatas 1986), is slowly but steadily electronically modernized. If the 1989 populist burning of the political files kept by the anticommunist state symbolized the end of the obsolete and useless anticommunist surveillance, it also meant the beginning of a systematic electronic filing of Greek citizens, not exclusively for political control purposes, but for rationalizing the whole state-citizen relationship. Greek "bureaucratism" is gradually becoming electronic and based on an "e-smart state," i.e. not only using digital technologies to collect citizens' data, but also using computer matching to cross check and verify this data in a very fast and efficient way. Despite the declared electronic modernization of the Greek civil service according to the governmental and EU-funded project "Greece in the Information Society" (www.infosociety.gr, 1998), many Greek public agencies are resisting computerization, still working with the traditional paper-dusted files, due to the low quality of the public personnel in those services. There are, however, computerized agencies like TAXIS, the Greek IRS, that are becoming very efficient in the cross data matching. Thus Greek state agencies are modernized using dataveillance, i.e., to not only collect and store citizens' information from multiple sources in databases, but also to process and very rapidly cross various data, with the possibility of quick identification, profile-making, and even future behavior prognosis, causing new social sorting (Lyon 2003: 20-22).

Greek police (ELAS) and security forces have been electronically modernized to cope with the "anti-terrorist war," using American and British technology and know-how, and equipped with high-tech databases and identification labs for the investigation of personal fingerprints, other biometrics, and DNA. In a central police fingerprint database, personal biometric data is collected, and processed from suspected target groups such as immigrants, hooligans, and anarchists. The databank of those groups is enriching the Automatic Fingerprints Identification System (ASADA), which until the summer of 2002 held the data of 400,000 persons. Police "sweep" operations (*skoupa*) for mass arrests of illegal immigrants or demonstrators result in mandatory fingerprinting under the Decree 342/1977, Article 27, paragraph 1.

The Greek police fingerprinting system ASADA is connected with the Schengen Information System databank, and the EURODAC of EUROPOL, which monitors immigrants and refugees, even anti-globalization and Euro summit protesters who have occasionally been arrested or just spotted by police (Samatas 2003a).

This new electronic police surveillance and electronic dataveillance was legalized under the universal insecure climate of terrorism and the panic it caused after the events of September 11th (Lyon, D. 2003: 17, 24, 81-89). American and British pressure to the Greek government have contributed to the Greek Parliament voting in the so-called "anti-terrorist law," or "terror law" (*tromonomos*), promoting the primacy of security over civil liberties. This controversial law has modernized all surveillance provisions, and has encouraged spying on citizens and police reports providing pecuniary motives for police informers;[1] it introduces non-jury criminal trials, a limited right of appeal, DNA testing without consent, sweeping police powers of infiltration and surveillance, and impose ten-year terms for members of serious crime gangs. In fact, the provisions of this law make no distinction between terrorist groups and criminal gangs.[2]

> Surveillance using cameras and bugging devices, as well as the interception of bank records, letters, emails, mobile phone data, etc. will be sanctioned by a panel of judges and no longer need permission from service providers ... this could speed up access from up to several months to a few days. Judges will also supervise DNA testing. On "serious grounds" of suspicion, suspects will be tested without their consent. The data will be destroyed when their case is concluded. (*Athens News*, February 16, 2001: A04).

The then Justice Minister Michalis Stathopoulos who drafted the bill has vividly defended all controversial provisions of this new law. He pointed out that most of these measures were part of the Greek penal law, including "home searches, body searches, or a prosecutor ordering blood tests for whatever reason. The solution is to ensure that laws are enforced properly. That's what mature societies do. We can be vigilant in fending off abuses. The basic element is to have democratic checks

---

[1]Police received approximately 4,000 telephone calls from various citizens in the summer of 2001, during the police hunting of Dimitris Koufodinas, a confessed terrorist executioner of November 17.

[2]"This effort to try and tackle both drug trafficking and terrorism together has made the provisions vague and therefore dangerous," said criminologist Yiannis Panoussis, who had resigned from the panel of experts created to draw up the new law (*Athens News*, February 16, 2001: A04).

on police." Mr. Stathopoulos has ruled out the bugging of homes and offices, "a provision that would be exploited by opponents." The law allows the consolidation of broad surveillance in public spaces. The former minister indirectly confirmed press reports that thousands of mobile phone calls were indiscriminately recorded in a geographic area of Athens where 17N has often struck, and said that sweeping audio and video monitoring in public places is perfectly legal. He also stated that "we are not living under the conditions of the authoritarian post-Civil War state or the junta, but in a period of the democratic functioning of institutions" (*Athens News* February 20, 2001: A03).

Senior Greek legal experts, civil liberties groups, and left-wing opposition parties have strongly condemned this "terror law," warning that lax control of surveillance and DNA testing could create a "Big Brother" state.

Besides Greek police modernization, Greece's National Intelligence Service (EYP), a traditional "sinful service," has also put on a new face. For the first time a top diplomat was appointed to head and demilitarize it, after the agency's tarnished image due to the aforementioned Ocalan affair. EYP's new operational framework was reinforced by strengthening its electronic surveillance capability, and mainly its civilian scientific personnel, instead of the police and military staff, in order to make it a flexible and efficient service that will cooperate with the other ministries and agencies to safeguard the national security interests. EYP has been placed under direct control of the Parliament and has been radically overhauled to fight terrorism at the 2004 Athens Olympics, ready to deal with "new types of threats to democracy and citizens like organized crime, people smuggling, and drug trafficking" (*Athens News* March 5, 1999: A01).

Similarly, the Greek financial crime squad, SDOE, equipped with high-tech surveillance systems, has in several successful surveillance operations arrested drug traffickers, confiscated arms from smuggling rings, and investigated money laundering.[3]

[3]For a successful arms smuggling surveillance operation by SDOE, see *Athens News*, January 21, 1999: A01; for a crack down of a Greek-Colombian drug cartel with the cooperation of the US Drug Enforcement Agency (DEA), see *Athens News* June 2, 1999: A01).

Chapter 7

THE ATHENIAN OLYMPICS SUPER PANOPTICISM: THE TRANSFORMATION OF ATHENS INTO A "PANOPTIC FORTRESS"

A THENS, AS THE CITY HOSTING the 2004 Olympic Games, has been quickly transformed into a "panoptic fortress" against domestic and international terrorism. This security process, which has already begun since 9/11, and has been strengthened for the security issues of the Greek presidency of the European Union in the first semester of 2003, is now escalating in view of the Olympics. In fact, due to the increasing security needs of the Athens Olympic Games, a "super panopticism" will be inherited to Greece. "Super panopticism" is integrating mass electronic surveillance of the population in public spaces with dataveillance, i.e., qualitative data processing, through data links and cross data matching at network databases, which include even biometric and biogenetic (DNA) personal data (Lyon 2001: 114-115); "super panopticism" provides the electronic possibility of continuing online linking, processing, evaluation, classification, and identification of personal data, and the production, even simulation, of various personal information profiles for a variety of purposes (Norris and Amstrong 1999: 222 & Poster, M. 1996: 184).

The security of the Athens Olympics, based on electronic super panopticism, is not only a Greek police and security operation, but an international endeavor, including American, British, French, German, Spanish, Australian, and Israeli intelligence comprising the "Olympics Advisory Security Team"; all this is connected with the Schengen Information System, Europol, and even NATO sky surveillance. The

115

SAIC-Siemens security consortium of international corporations is the provider of high-tech panoptic technologies. The Olympics security network includes police helicopters, a zeppelin equipped with hyper red radiation panoptic systems, NATO's AWACS surveillance airplanes, underwater sonars, and an expensive C4I surveillance coordination system (*Ta Nea*, Dec. 5, 2003: 1, 8-9).

The major device of the Athenian Olympic panopticism is a network of 1,250-1,600 closed-circuit television cameras (CCTV) installed all over the Athens metropolitan area, running 24-hours a day. Twelve hundred CCTVs, one camera every 50 meters, will scan the whole Olympic installations area; CCTV systems are linked with a whole surveillance network of mobile sets (TETRA), which will receive images and sound in real time by 22,160 security staff members organized in five operation centers and coordinated by a central information, security station (C4I). Besides the Olympic Village and the Olympic Stadium, which are the surveillance focus, in the new Athens airport "Eleftherios Venizelos" alone there will gradually be installed up to 400 CCTV systems; in the Athens Metro system there are already 200 CCTV in 18 stations; in the central area of Athens the 48 CCTV currently in operation will be increased up to 200 until the summer of 2004; also in the major seaport of Piraeus there will be 200 and on the national highway network there will be around 700 installed. The security budget of the Athens Olympics, three times more than that of the previous Olympics held in Sydney, is close to 800 million euros. SAIC, the security consortium that has installed the central security system, will get 255 million euros. Before SAIC, the Australian American BOARTES corporation, specializing in the assessment of the Olympics security requirements in Sydney and Salt Lake City, Utah, and now in Athens, has conducted the security operation planning, implemented by SAIC.[1] Thus the Olympics security,

---

[1]The SAIC consortium includes Honeywell, ITT Industries, SAIC-Telcordia, E Team (US), EADS (France/Germany), ALTEC, Pouliadis Group, DIEKAT Construction, UBM Hellas (Greece), Rafael Armament Development and Elbit Systems (Israel) as suppliers. C4I is standing for command, control, communications, computers and intelligence.

based on high-tech super panopticism, brings about tremendous profits to several transnational corporations.

In brief, due to the Olympics, Athens is becoming a testing ground of the latest anti-terrorist super panoptic technology, to be used from now on throughout the world. The basic question is to what extent this very expensive super panopticism for the Athens Olympic Games will be retained even after the two-week event, and what its post Olympics impact will be, not only on security, but also on civil liberties. Actually, some protest groups are accusing the government of using the Olympics as an excuse to curb frequent dissent on Athens' streets. "It's the same thing as making a video of the demonstrations," said Petros Konstantinou, coordinator of the Greek anti-globalization group Genoa 2001. Like most critics he doesn't believe any cameras will come down when the 16-day Olympics are over. "It's part of suppressive measures taken worldwide after September 11 ... (an excuse) to take measures against democratic rights." In contrast, the PASOK Public Order Minister Chrysohoidis just stopped short of saying the cameras were a necessary assurance to the world. "In the present circumstances, globalized security is likely to be imposed in a rapid and forceful manner" (*Athens News*, February 15, 2002: A07).

One could argue that this extremely expensive[2] security operation is not only for the 2004 Olympics summer, but a long-term security investment for Greece; although such extremely expensive surveillance systems cannot guarantee security 100 percent, while they can easily become a menace to privacy and civil liberties for the Greek people.

---

[2]For the extremely high cost of 2004 Athens Olympic security system ad the C4I system, see:

http://www.ydt.gr/main/Section.jsp?SectionID=10979&LanguageID=2

http://www.athensnews.gr/athweb/nathens.print_unique?e=C&f=13077&m=A 05&aa=1&eidos=S

http://www.athensnews.gr/athweb/nathens.print_unique?e=C&f=12998&m=A 03&aa=1&eidos=S

Part IV

THE GALAXY OF NONSTATE SURVEILLANCE

Chapter 8

INDICATIVE CASES OF PRIVATE SURVEILLANCE: CCTV, "BIG BROTHER" TV SHOWS, AGB, "BIG BROTHER" SCHOOLS, GLOBAL POSITIONING SATELLITES, CONSUMER PROFILES

CLOSED-CIRCUIT TELEVISION (CCTV)

A S IN ALMOST ALL BRITISH CITIES, Athens similarly adopts the surveillance network of CCTV as the new essential security network supplementing the networks of the water, electricity power, communications, and liquid gas (Norton and Amstrong 1999: 206). It seems that progressively due to the 2004 Olympics, following the panoptic security model, Athens will proportionally reach the percentage of CCTV of other western capitals such as London and New York, where the average resident is recorded by police CCTV in public spaces, but also in banks and malls over 20 times a day, unnoticed (NYCLU 1998).

We should note that the essential problem of growing panopticism in Greece, as well, is not the simple presence and dissemination of CCTV, but its connection with databases that match the profiles of suspects, activating the CCTV to focus preventively on a person, whose appearance suits the programmed suspect's digital profile. Thus the technologies of simple recording of images and sound are perfected as digital systems of automatic recording, transmitting, and searching, which can codify and then interrelate the recorded data with enormous databanks, composing specific profiles of suspected

121

persons and behaviors. These data-mining, data-matching, and profiling possibilities, in addition with those of identification and simulation, are transforming simple panopticism into a "super-panopticism" (Poster, M. 1996: 189, Norris and Amstrong 1999: 222, and Lyon 2001: 114-118), which is gradually installed also in Greece with the expensive intervention of foreign services and companies.

"Big Brother" factories, workplaces, even schools and churches

CCTV of all types, as a security panacea, are now placed everywhere in Greece, not only by the police and the various ministries on the streets, in the national highways, in harbors, in airports, in metro stations, and in stadiums, but also in private shopping centers, in banks, in kiosks, and even in certain private schools and churches. Football hooligans who have been identified by CCTV in the football stadium committing violent acts have been arrested by the police. In the name of security, most industrial zones and shipyards are fully monitored by CCTV. According to the Greek Workers General Confederation, the number of blue- and white-collar workers who have been fired in workplaces that are monitored by CCTV has seriously increased (*Sunday Eleftherotypia*, March 17, 2002: 55). In certain private schools, such as the one at Nikaia, teachers and students are under surveillance by the principal, who is watching them during each class by CCTV. In some public schools, CCTV is used to monitor backyards (*Eleftherotypia*, Jan. 15, 2002). Even in certain Greek Orthodox churches, where "holy panopticism" is symbolized by the depiction of God's "eye of justice that watches over everything," placed usually on top of the central gate, the electronic panopticism of CCTV supplements the sacred one. This still however is not adequate deterrence to the burglars, who break into churches for money and old icons.

The rapid dissemination of state and private CCTV, first in the Athens metropolitan area and gradually all over Greece, has been attempted to be harnessed under the control of the Hellenic Data Protection Authority (HDPA). The HDPA, without efficient enforcement power to substantially protect citizens' personal privacy from the use of CCTV systems everywhere in Greece, actually legitimizes their use by the state with its decision on "The personal data processing via closed-circuit TV" (1122-Sept. 26, 2000). While this decision generally prohibits the monitoring and processing of personal data by CCTV as an offence to the personal privacy of individuals, it legalizes its use by state authorities for the protection of persons and property, and for traffic regulation, according to the provisions of Law 2472/1997. Excepting the state CCTV systems, the HDPA's decision requires the destruction of the monitoring recoding material after 15 days, although there is no effective mechanism to control the application of this decision.

So, CCTV surveillance in Greece raises similar privacy questions, as well as the question of its anti-crime efficiency, as other European and American societies do. Mass surveillance of ignorant individuals to prevent potential antisocial or any kind of suspicious behavior raises the question of how such a behavior is defined, and the criteria under which someone is preventatively considered a suspect. Which is the stereotypical profile of the targeted suspect of mass surveillance in Greece, based on age, sex, race, and appearance, compared with the usual young, male, black (African-American) profile in the United States? Without any empirical evidence, we can easily assume that the major suspect profile will be programmed to match the external appearance of a young anarchist-hooligan, even a potential Albanian criminal.

Social research on CCTV use in British cities has pointed out that most of the targeting of surveillance cameras is not made on the basis of actual involvement in antisocial behavior or criminal action, but is constituted of targets based on racial or even class bias, simply because certain personal appearances are assumed to belong to socially stigmatized groups (Norris and Amstrong 1999: 166-170, 188-196). In the case of the United States, the usually suspect targets are young men, mainly African-Americans. Thus the electronic "scanscape" of big cities contributes to the reproduction of social discrimination in the creation of a "discipline society," exploiting fear and insecurity, which brings about profits to the industry of surveillance technology. It should also be noticed that the application of this panoptic technology has not proved to actually contribute to the drastic reduction of criminality or to seriously solve all the security problems in the areas where it has extensive application. What is usually observed is the geographic removal of all those dangerous fellows a little further out of the field of visible video scanning. Without social welfare policy, the use of CCTV as the sole panacea to spot the criminals on a shield from the "dangerous classes" is only causing a vicious cycle of extended panopticism, which is profitable for the companies of panoptic security technology (Strub, X. 1989, Fiske, I. 1998, Lyon 2001: 51-68).

Sky surveillance by Global Positioning Satellites (GPS) is also now working in Greece

A military surveillance system that now has commercial application, even in countries like Greece, is the American Global Positioning Satellite (GPS). First used in the Gulf War, and presently developed by 24 low-orbit satellites, it monitors everything over the earth, and is a valuable tool used in telecommunications, air and sea navigation, weather forecasting, etc. Further, like many wealthy residential areas in most capitalist cities protected by private security companies and transformed into "panoptic fortresses" against criminals and terrorists, similarly in Athens' well-off suburbs, they have started using electronic ground and satellite surveillance technology to enhance customers' security. Therefore, members of the economic and political elite and wealthy residents and entrepreneurs of Athens who can afford it pay for the high cost of sky surveillance protection, as also the industrialists of Thriassion industrial field, who monitor their factories by such satellite services for their protection. Since the last ten years, when GPS first started, its cost is getting lower, and it is now affordable to the middle classes; this means it is even affordable in Greece for mountain climbers, salesmen, fishers, taxi and buses drivers, etc. GALILEO, the European Geostationary Navigation Overlay Service, with 30 satellites, operated exclusively by public agencies, will be the European counterpart to the GPS system, and will be ready in 2008.[1]

The GPS service is also used by Greek state agencies like the police, the merchant marine, the agriculture ministry, the agency against economic crime (SDOE), etc. More and more it is also used by private owners of luxurious cars, pet owners, but also spouses and parents who want to watch their family members by monitoring their movements via satellites. The surveillance works with the placement of a transmitter in vehicles, boats, or objects used by the target persons, and even by implanting electronic devices in the human body, so that they can be monitored and projected onto special websites on the Internet.[2] Implanted electronic chips are already mandatorily to be placed in the bodies of all pets in Greece by a recent law, 3170/2003.

The use of GPS by the new mobile phones that can locate a user's exact position, has raised serious questions of privacy violations. In general, Greece is an open society, eagerly importing new technologies without serious concern for their impact on privacy.

"BIG BROTHER" TV AND REALITY SHOWS

"Big Brother" TV shows which have now arrived in Greece, demythologize and make routine daily surveillance in the perception of the mass TV audience. After the successful and profitable "Big Brother" TV shows on American and European TV channels, Greek private channels have also introduced "Big Brother" television reality games since the year 2000. In these TV surveillance shows, the adult participant players have consented to be monitored by several surveillance cameras, in

---

[1]See the reportage *To Vima*, Aug. 17, 2003: A 22; also, in *Kathimerini*, Dec. 15, 2002: 14.

[2]In 2002, around 4,000 Greek cars had been placed under sky surveillance, 27 stolen cars had been found, and 20 customers had used electronic surveillance to watch vehicles and persons on special websites (*To Vima*, March 23, 2002: 10, 20).

either a closed or an open environment, to entertain the television audiences; viewers watch ordinary persons who have agreed to actually have their privacy exploited for profit and temporary fame. Not only the private life of famous persons, which is always the target of the scandal oriented, yellow press[3] (Alivizatos 2001), but also the personal life and privacy of ordinary people have now become a profitable commodity to lucrative marketeers and TV producers, who persuade ordinary individuals to participate in reality shows. These individuals expect, by exposing their private issues, they will have some economic profit and publicity (Kateb, G. 2001). Indeed, a great number of young people are very eager to exchange their privacy to temporarily become TV celebrities, without realizing the potential humiliation and exploitation that comes with it. Thus we also have in Greece the phenomenon where many viewers watch a few ordinary people, which is called mass media "synopticism" (Mathieson, Th. 1997, Lyon 2001: 92).

The Greek Data Protection Authority has intervened to protect the privacy rights of the participants regardless of their consent. They have prohibited ENA Television and Cinema Production to create a personal databank of all the candidates to play in the "Big Brother" show, and especially of those who are finally selected to participate in the show. The HDPA directive, which is interesting for all such shows in Greece and abroad, points out:

> Under such circumstances, the consent of the individual legitimizing the controller to collect personal data and create a file is anticonstitutional, unlawful and contrary to good morals, since it instigates behavior contrary to the aforementioned constitutional provisions on the respect for and the protection of the human value. These provisions cannot be waived, but, in addition to the participant's consent, the agreement contracted excessively curtails freedom, and is, therefore, void. (HDPA Decision 1346-July 3, 2001)

---

[3]E.g. in 1989 the daily *Avriani* had published a large number of nude photos of Dimitra Liani, wife of the Prime Minister Andreas Papandreou.

The HDPA has also prohibited the constant monitoring, saving, and processing of personal data during the players' sleep, and required one surveillance-free hour a day for all (HDPA Decision 92/2001).

PANOPTIC TV VIEWING METERS BY AGB HELLAS

Greece has not yet seen the digital interactive television that records all the preferences of television viewers and promises to transform the household into a telemarketing shopping center. There is, however, the "panoptic tele-measure" of Greek TV audience data collected and processed by AGB Hellas. According the AGB Hellas's website profile (cf. http://www.agb.gr), it is member of the AGB Group, established in 1987, and has been producing television audience data in Greece using the people meter system since 1988. The beginning of private TV in 1989 and subscription TV are among the developments that AGB has witnessed and monitored minute by minute, every day, 365 days a year. AGB Hellas provides full services in TV audience measurement, i.e. both the data and software of the highest standards for data analysis. The coverage sample of AGB Hellas consists of 1,200 households (roughly 3,500 individuals) representative of the population(?), distributed in mainland Greece and Crete, covering urban, semi-urban, and rural areas. According to AGB, "meters of TV viewing" (people meters) are installed in each television appliance of each household. They record the time, the situation of television (on/off), the choice of television stations, and who watches. The information on the station that watches the household of each day is recorded automatically. The information on who watches what is recorded via a remote control, where each member of the household, declares their presence by pushing their own corresponding button. Coded transmission (e.g. Filmnet, SuperSport) and digital transmission are also incorporated in the AGB system.

The significant, and almost dictatorial, monopoly power of AGB has affected the distribution of television advertising money to only commercial mass culture TV programs, undermining the qualitative ones; based on TV audience measure, commercial private TV uses every cheap and reality show to attract audiences, transforming even TV news into reality shows. Thus, AGB, as the TV "Big Sister," with its own market criteria directs almost the entirety of Greek television programming, with very negative consequences to its quality. The National Council of Greek Radio-Television (ESR), which is responsible for continuously watching radio and television programming 24-hours a day, is still without adequate personnel and infrastructure to watch over all Greek TV programs. Although it regularly announces some penalties, it is still unable to enforce drastic sanctions on TV channels, most of which function illegally without a state license.

ILLEGAL CONSUMER PROFILES AND SMUGGLING OF PERSONAL DATA

The new technologies provide easy and low-cost profit opportunities to private individuals and firms, which systematically collect personal information from various sources, storing it in databases, and processing various personal data ("dataveillance" and "computer matching") (see Kling 1996: 653, & Lyon 2001: 74) to produce consumer lists and profiles for sale.[4] This profitable exploitation of personal data and the industry of consumer profiles is illegally flourishing in Greece. Therefore private profiteers, through a number of legitimate and illegal ways, collect personal data and produce various personal information profiles of consumer groups, television viewers, patients, home and real estate proprietors, vehicle owners, taxpayers, parents, tenants, etc, which they sell to other direct marketing companies, entrepreneurs, and the like. Thus, according to journalist reports, there is a growing profitable market of smuggling personal data in Greece. It is estimated that 4.5 million private individuals and 2.5 million professionals are

---

[4]Choice Point, an American firm that produces and sells such profiles to other marketing firms, even to the police, was symbolically "awarded" (in a negative sense) by the Privacy International 2002 annual awards. See http://www.privacy.org/pi/and http://www.epic.org/privacy/profiling.

recorded in these illegal databanks, which are growing without any real control. As shown in *Exhibits 21, 22, 23*, one can easily and very inexpensively buy CD-ROMS with databases of various consumers groups in Athens' Omonia Square (*Ta Nea*, June 13, 2000: 20).

Particularly in Greece, where several public administration agencies are characterized by corruption (Koutsoukis, Kl. 1997 & Samatas, M. 2003b), legal and illegal provision of personal data for production of information profiles is a relatively easy enterprise. Public agencies and organizations have frequently violated citizens' privacy by disseminating sensitive data among them and, far worse, by providing them to private firms and individuals. For example, in 1998 the General Secretariat of Finance Ministry provided to the OPAP (Organization of Football Pool) around 2.5 million addresses of middle-income taxpayers, so they would receive OPAP's new lottery game Joker's advertisements. The HDPA has administered strict rebukes and warnings to both agencies for such an irresponsible and illegal mishandling of personal data (HDPA's Decisions no.s 59, 60/March 3, 1999).

Further, the HDPA has noted that medical privacy is not respected by certain hospitals, especially maternity clinics, which provide personal data for marketing reasons (Decision 150/December 12, 2001). Similarly, public agencies in Greece, such as some military conscripts' offices, which collect conscripts' personal data, have provided the medical record of those who were exempted to serve their military service for psychological reasons to private psychiatric clinics. This serious negligence against privacy was revealed after some of those who were exempted were targeted for potential therapy by those clinics (*Ta Nea*, June 14, 2000). The HDPA has also declared illegal the Transportation Ministry's data bank holding the names of all those exempted from military service due to psycho-neurotic reasons, which is used to ban them from receiving a driver's license (*Ta Nea*, Sept. 21, 2002). Yet, the HDPA has also placed some restrictions on local municipalities in the processing of their residents' personal data (see www.dpa.gr/decisions).

The HDPA has definitely tried hard to intervene and restrict the ruthless violation of citizens' privacy, either by the negligence of public service or by the profitable exploitation of the market. The former chairman of the HDPA, Constantine Dafermos, who had frequently admitted the ridiculous illegal smuggling of personal data in Greece and the inability of the HDPA to stop that problem, has stated: "As a society we are in front of a chaotic situation, and as citizens we are seriously unprotected . . . from all sort of private initiatives that monitor our private lives and record our personal data" (*To Vima*, Jan.12, 2000: A19).

Part V

INEFFECTIVE LEGAL AND INSTITUTIONAL PRIVACY PROTECTION

Chapter 9

THE PRIVACY PROTECTION LAW, THE WORK OF THE HELLENIC DATA PROTECTION AUTHORITY (HDPA), AND THE REFUGE OF THE EUROPEAN COURT OF HUMAN RIGHTS

A. NEW PRIVACY PROTECTION LEGISLATION AND INSTITUTIONS

A CONSTITUTIONAL AMENDMENT in 2001 added a new provision (Article 9A), stating that "All persons have the right to be protected from the collection, processing, and use, especially by electronic means, of their personal data, as specified by law. The protection of personal data is ensured by an independent authority, which is established and operates as specified by law." Also, constitutional Article 19 protects the privacy of communications, by stating, "Secrecy of letters and all other forms of free correspondence or communication shall be absolutely inviolable. The guaranties under which the judicial authority shall not be bound by this secrecy for reasons of national security or for the purpose of investigating especially serious crimes, shall be specified by law." Two new provisions to this article were also added by the 2001 amendment: a. Article 19(2), which now states, "The matters relating to the establishment, operation, and powers of the independent authority ensuring the secrecy of paragraph 1 shall be specified by law." b. Article 19(3) states, "The use of evidence acquired in violation of the present article and of Articles 9 and 9A is prohibited."[1]

[1]The 1975 Constitution of Greece as amended, available at http://confinder. richmond.edu/greek-2001.htm; also reference at EPIC and PI 2002 Country Reports (Greece).

In addition, Law 2225/1994 provides for the conditions and manner under which it is possible to lift privacy restrictions. Yet, Article 5 of the Greek Code of Administrative Procedure (Law 2690/1999) is the new Freedom of Information Act, which provides Greek citizens the right to access administrative documents created by government agencies. It replaced Law 1599/1986, which regulated the use of the Single Register Code Number (EKAM), that was not enforced.

The Law 2472/97 on the Protection of Individuals with regard to the Processing of Personal Data (Data Protection Act) was approved in 1997, as a requirement for Greece to join the Schengen Agreement. Greece was the last member of the EU to adopt a data protection law, and its law was written to directly adopt the EU Directive.[2]

The problem of the extensive use of panoptic technologies in Greece, not only by state agencies but also by the ruthless private sector, was not resolved by the delayed adoption of European legislation protecting personal privacy and individuals' sensitive data. *Directive 95/45/EK on "the protection of the individual from the processing of personal data,"* which is dictating a common European privacy protection policy in all EU member-states, was imported just a few years ago into the Greek Law N.2472/97. Moreover, for the enactment of this law, but also as a precondition of the operation of the Schengen Information System (SIS), under the Schengen Agreement's implementation in Greece, the aforementioned Hellenic Data Protection Authority (HDPA) was founded in November 1997 as an independent authority to supervise the implementation of the Data Protection Act and all regulations referring to the protection of privacy and personal data in Greece (see the website www.dpa.gr & EPIC & P.I. 2002 Country Reports: Greece). The HDPA is also responsible for: auditing archives; issuing regulatory acts based on data protection legislation and directives to protect personal data from new technologies; drafting codes of conducts; examining complaints and reporting violations; enforcing the right to access information; granting permits for the collection and processing of sensitive personal data; intercon-

[2]For the political and ideological reasons of this delay see Chapter 4, pp. 80-83 and Samatas (1997) & (2003a).

nection of files including sensitive data and the trans-boundary flow of personal data.

According to the report of HDPA to EPIC (June 15, 2002), "in 2001, the HDPA received 944 complaints and inquires. From September 2001 to June 2002 there have been approximately 500 requests referring mainly to unlawful collection and processing of personal data by companies involved in direct marketing, banks and financial institutions, debt recording and telecommunications companies, maternity hospitals, CCTV systems/communication of data to third parties, and entries in the Schengen Information System (SIS). In 2001, the HDPA had also performed 51 audits on privacy policies and standards, 15 audits of files held by general hospitals and clinics, databanks, and debt-recording companies." In 1999, when the HDPA was not well-known, it received 223 complaints, in 2000 the complaints were over three times more, i.e., 729, in 2001 they were 944, and in 2002 there were 1,601. In fact, the HDPA in 2002 received 22 complaints about banks, 41 about TEIRESIAS Ltd. debt recordings, 38 about mobile telephone companies, 21 about general and maternity hospitals, 28 about CCTV, 62 about direct marketing, 326 about entries to the SIS, 366 about private databanks, and 565 various other complaints. During the 1999-2002 period, the HDPA received 143,468 requests for legalizing various data collection and databanks. Out of these, 4,573 were registered as serious data collectors; they belong to public organizations, banks, and various private companies, including advertising, telephone, internet providers, private clinics and medical centers, insurance, pharmaceutical, stock market, weight loss, nutrition, and more (*Eleftherotypia*, Nov.1, 2003: 19).

B. Some important decisions of the Hellenic Data Protection Authority (HDPA)

Some of the basic decisions and directives of the HDPA relate to direct marketing, CCTV, DNA testing, and workplace surveillance.

The most controversial of HDPA's decisions was, however, about the one on the religious affiliation statement on the state identity cards Decision No. 510/17/May 15, 2000. On May 4, 2000, the HDPA ruled that religious affiliations must be removed from the new state identity cards. The decision was opposed by the Greek Orthodox Church and led to massive protests and challenges to the ruling. In March 2001, Greece's highest administrative court upheld the ruling, finding that stating citizens' religious affiliation on the compulsory identity cards was unconstitutional. Prior to the ruling, Greece was the only member of the EU that required citizens to list their religious beliefs on citizen identity cards. The new Greek identity cards do not include religious affiliation, even on voluntary basis; because, according to the HDPA's decision, "religion refers to the inner world of the individual and it is therefore neither appropriate nor necessary in order to prove one's identity."[3]

In addition to the removal of religious affiliation, the HDPA ruled that new identity cards also should no longer include fingerprints, names and surnames of the cardholder's spouse, maiden names, profession, home addresses, or citizenship" (EPIC report: 193) (see *Exhibit 17* of the old and new identity cards). Relative HDPA decisions are: Decision 134/Oct. 31, 2001, prohibiting the statement of religion on any public certificates, and Decision 77a/ June 25, 2002, prohibiting the recording of religion on Graduate Certificates.

The HDPA has also opposed the practice of TEIRESIAS Ltd. of collecting negative credit data in advance, as far as the creditworthiness of a private individual. The HDPA has reserved the right to reexamine the time of data maintenance in the file-classification of TEIRESIAS's databank. (Decision No. 109/Mar. 31, 1999 & Decision No. 523/Oct. 19, 1999).

---

[3]The old identity cards, following article 2, Decree 127/1969, included the following data: 1. photograph, fingerprint, surname, first name, father's name, mother's name, spouse's name, and, in the case of a woman being married, her full maiden name, exact date of birth, place of birth, height (for those over 25 years of age), shape of face, color of eyes, blood type (optional), pensioner status, place of permanent/temporary residence, home address, profession, citizenship, municipality/community of registration and register number, religion.

Regarding the terms for the lawful processing of personal data in respect to the purposes of direct marketing/advertising and the ascertainment of credit worthiness, the HDPA has decided that: "Data collection for the purposes of direct advertising and product or services either by profession or not (in the latter case only for the promotion or advertising of own products or services) is considered to be lawful provided that the data subject has given his/her consent. Consent is necessary in cases of consumer behavior researches where the purpose is the direct or indirect advertising of products or the provision of services" (Decision No. 050/Jan. 20, 2000).

Also, the HDPA has considered to be unlawful:

- the collection, filing, and processing of personal data through taking fingerprints with view to monitoring the presence of workers by employers (Decision 245/9-Mar. 20, 2000);

- the use on a TV program of a certain videotape and a personal diary received by post, which, among others, included sensitive personal data from the sex life of a singer and fashion designer (Decision 100/Jan. 31, 2000). Further, the National Council for Radio and TV has proposed a new ethics code for mass media, prohibiting the product of illegal surveillance to be used;

- processing of personal data of mothers in maternity hospitals for the purposes of direct marketing or advertising without their consent (Decision 523/18-May 25, 2000).[4]

- the Call Management Systems, by which employers verify which one of the employees calls, which individual and if the call is for

[4]"It was discovered that companies collect personal data from mothers by visiting them in the wards of maternity hospitals one or two days after delivery. During these visits, mothers give their data to the company representative, a fact which results in impermissible comments, especially as far as the public sector is concerned. The HDPA has issued a directive so mothers who give their consent shall fill in a form and return it, when leaving the hospital, to the competent department of the maternity hospital. The transfer of personal data is allowed and is set to three (3) months from the date of the mother's departure from the maternity hospital." (Decision 523/18-25 May 2000).

work purposes, for the purpose of monitoring *excessive or costly* calls that are made through work telephone connections (Decision 637/18/June 21, 2000).[5] The HDPA has also dealt with issues relating to monitoring workers' communications, workplace supervision, workers' data transfer to third parties, use of biometric methods for controlling access in the workplace, etc., and has issued a number of decisions.[6]

- Recording and processing of personal data by a closed-circuit television (CCTV) operating on a regular, continuous, or permanent basis is prohibited, because it may infringe on individuals' right to privacy (DIR.CCTV 1122/Sept. 26, 2000). The HDPA has, however, accepted some serious exceptions, such as: the recording (on a regular, continuous, or permanent basis) under the terms and conditions provided for in Law 2472/1997, without prior consent

---

[5]"Since the above means that the controller has to confirm every time *who is the owner* of the telephone connection the employee has contacted and whether it was a call for work purposes or not, this search results in a most serious intervention concerning employees' personal life and blatant violation of their privacy and fundamental liberties ... Since the installation of the said system is considered to be lawful only when data processing does not threaten data subjects' fundamental rights, that is when the management system does not reveal all digits of the number called but conceals the three last digits thereof, because in this way it is not possible to reveal each user's personal data to such an extent that his/her privacy is offended ... The HDPA considers the call management system to be legitimate provided that the said center does not permit the appearance of the last three digits of outcoming calls and data subjects have been informed in advance" (Decision 637/18/21 June 2000).

[6]"While personal data processing in the workplace on the basis of consent or fulfilling obligations arising from the work contract (Articles 5 and 7, Law 2472/97 as is) is lawful, the abstract normative phrasing does not account for the element of dependence within the framework of an employment relationship. The said element reduces the strength of freedom of consent or freedom in shaping the content of the work contract. The availability and use of many new monitoring technical methods raising new issues such as the extent of email monitoring or the use of biometric methods for work organization. It is worth mentioning that similar conclusions and, mainly, the observation that consent is insufficient as an independent basis for workers' personal data processing influences and determines the recent working paper of the European Commission on personal data protection issues within the framework of employment." 'Extract from the Directive on Workers' File' (DIR. 115/18-20 Sept. 2001).

of the data subject, when the purpose of processing is the protection of individuals or goods or the regulation of traffic.[7]

One of the most serious directions of the HDPA is that on DNA analysis for the purpose of criminal investigation and penal prosecution (OPINION No. 15/2001). The following excerpt shows the quality of HDPA's work on this sensitive issue:

The HDPA's authorization is based on the fact that the case of DNA use for the aforementioned purposes pertains to the collection, diffusion, and processing of personal data. The issues raised in relation to DNA analysis do not concentrate on its receipt, which constitutes invasion of privacy in itself, but mostly pertain to the reproduction of genetic information resulting from DNA analysis and the further uses of such information. The HDPA perceives of "genetic data" as any data of any type, which pertains to hereditary traits or the hereditary patterns of these traits within a group of individuals. As

[7]. . . "Data collected by a CCTV shall be adequate, relevant, and not excessive in relation to the purpose for which they are to be used each time. . . . For example, if the closed-circuit television of a store or a bank aims at preventing a theft of goods or a robbery, data collected shall not be such so that it may be used to monitor the behavior or the efficiency of employees. In open spaces, video cameras shall be installed in such locations so that they do not overlook the entrance or the interior of private residences. . . . Data collected shall be accurate. However, the recognition of faces or vehicles shall be possible only whenever necessary to achieve the purpose each time pursued. For example, if the aim of image recording is to control the traffic flow and not to detect traffic offenses, the cameras shall be placed in such locations so that they do not allow for face or vehicle recognition. In the event that the collected data is stored in any way, it shall not be retained for a longer period of time than that required for the purpose pursued and, in any case, no longer than 15 days. In exceptional cases, data may be held for more than 15 days upon special permission of the Data Protection Authority . . . Any individual, or vehicle, about to enter an area monitored by a closed-circuit television must be notified accordingly by the Controller in a comprehensible manner. For this purpose, discernible signs shall be placed in an adequate number and in visible spots, notifying the public of the existence of cameras on the premises. These signs shall also identify the owner/operator of the system, the purpose for which such recording is taking place, the name of the person with whom individuals may communicate in order to exercise their rights under Law 2472/1997, and in particular the "right to access" and the "right to object" (DIR.CCTV1122-26 Sept. 2000).

"genetic data" is equally understood all data pertaining to carriers of genetic information within an individual or genetic line, which relates to any aspect of health or a disease situation, whether the traits are definable/identifiable or not. This is the definition adopted by the Council of Europe in its *Recommendation for the Process of Medical Data of Physical Persons*. We must note that, in theory, there is no unanimity on the issue of the exact categorization of such data. In any case, genetic data relates to individual health, but, at the same time, could be considered as data relating to racial or ethnic descent. It must be mentioned that Law 2472/97 places these categories under so-called sensitive data, and the collection and processing of such data is subject to special circumstances and security terms."[8] Genetic analysis within the frame of the investigation of criminal acts and procedures must be limited to the non-codified section of DNA and the verification of identity. This means that it should constitute exclusively a genetic print. No additional information on the individual should be released. No methods, which could allow conclusions regarding personality traits, such as heredity, character, or disease record, should be applied. Personality profiling through genetic analysis directly violates the value of a human being, a value protected as a constitutional right, and the free development of personality, whose special manifestation is the right to informational self-determination. . . . The Data Protection Authority expresses the conviction that . . . the method of genetic analysis should be reserved for "extremely serious crimes" and, specifically, to those that when analyzed could lead to solving criminal cases (criminal attempts against human life, kidnapping, sexual crimes). . . . Collection and analysis of genetic material for preventive purposes should be

---

[8]"The collection and processing of genetic data embraces—together with unquestionable social benefits—extremely serious risks for the citizens and their rights. The kind of knowledge resulting from such analysis may have disastrous consequences on the individual and his/her family, since, as it has been mentioned above, the information concerned inevitably relates to other individuals, as well. The notification of data resulting from genetic tests may lead to a categorization of individuals and, in the final analysis, to their stigmatization and social exclusion . . . (OPINION No. 15/2001).

excluded. . . . Furthermore, the legal framework must also refer to the obligation to destroy the collected genetic material upon the fulfillment of the intended aim, which is the verification of identity (OPINION No. 15/2001).

As we have already mentioned, the HDPA, despite its operational and infrastructure problems, staffed by limited personnel but recruiting an excellent privacy protection team of experts, has made an appreciable body of work including very useful interventions to regulate the chaotic panopticism in Greece. Despite the HDPA's efforts and numerous decisions on various surveillance and privacy violation cases, a number of which we have already mentioned, it is actually unable to effectively protect Greek citizens' personal life and privacy. Apart from the essential practical inability of the HDPA to identify and intervene in all daily violations of personal life, according to its former chairman Constantine Dafermos:

"the most important fact is the fact that Greek people do not know the violation risks of their personal data nor the ways by which they can be protected. . . . While we have managed to check more or less our state agencies, it is entirely impossible to check which companies keep personal databases and how they use them. . . . The legislation protecting personal data is almost inactive, mainly because as citizens we are very little interested in the protection of this data" (*To Vima*, Jan. 12, 2000: A9).

Yet, the HDPA faces a serious danger of bureaucratization because it must under the law grant permits after accepting all applications to maintain any databases that has personal data, even by all companies' personnel, customers, and providers' databases, as well as their public notification statements that are published in the press (Mitrou, L. 1999). Also, the HDPA has faced additional legitimation problems after its conflict with the Greek Orthodox Church on the issue of stating the religious affiliation in the new police identity cards. The HDPA opposition to the militant persistence of the Greek Church on this issue, and its defamation by Archbishop Christodoulos, deprived the HDPA from wide popular support as a citizens' privacy protector.

Thus, given the weakness of the HDPA but also of the National Committee for the Protection of Telecommunications' Confidentiality, which simply annually reports the growing surveillance problems in Greece to the Parliament, Greek citizens' privacy is not substantially protected. As the existence and interference of the HDPA is becoming more known to the public, citizens' reports and privacy protection requests are increasing. In fact, the violation of secrecy of communications, digital wiretaps, and the violation of privacy on the internet are annually reported by the Greek parliamentary "National Committee for the Protection of Telecommunications' Confidentiality." In all annual reports of this committee, it has repeatedly and emphatically underlined the fact that in Greece there is not any communication type to ensure privacy. Even the prime minister and his cabinet are not safe from the watchful eye of the (domestic or transatlantic) "Big Brother." Even the use of mobile telephones can be intercepted by special wiretap systems that are available in foreign markets, and can be imported for use in Greece. The serious problem with mobile phone use is the ability of mobile companies to locate the place of a caller through the aforementioned GPS system, as well as the retention of data for a period of time for security purposes.

This telecommunications privacy committee has also pointed out:

- the lack of a code of ethics to determine the obligations of public and private telecommunications organizations about the serious issue of privacy protection.
- the violation of Internet privacy and the growing increase of smuggling and the marketing of personal data in the electronic trade (Schneier, Br. & Banisar, D. 1996).
- the awful situation of the Greek Organization of Telecommunications (OTE) outdoor telephone line distributors (KAFAO), which are not safely protected, and actually everyone can have access to wiretaps or can intercept telephone conversations.

- the unauthorized surveillance conducted by all sort of private investigation agencies.
- the uncontrolled surveillance by foreign or international communication satellite systems like Echelon.[9]

The committee's conclusion that no telephone communication whatsoever in Greece is absolutely safe, and its suggestion that even the government lines at the highest level are not safe, has cast a chilling doubt on the privacy of all customers of both state OTE and private telephone service providers (see *Athens News*, February 13, 1998: A01).

C. SOME SIGNIFICANT DECISIONS OF THE EUROPEAN COURT OF HUMAN RIGHTS PROTECTING THE PRIVACY RIGHTS OF GREEK CITIZENS

The European Commission of Human Rights and the European Court of Human Rights has been the refuge of several victims of privacy violation in Greece. Here we mention three of the most characteristic such cases.

a. The case of Gregoriades against Greece[10] *(military surveillance)*

This is a remarkable case of antisurveillance, in the form of the individual resistance of a journalist, Panayiotis Gregoriades, who as a probationary reserve officer actively protested against the traditional

---

[9]Unlike France where in 2000 a state prosecutor had launched a judicial investigation into the US Echelon spy system of satellites, remote sensor surveillance, and listening posts, intercepting millions of telephone, fax, and email messages for economic and other espionage even against the US allies, in Greece aside journalist reports there is a fatal apathy for this super Atlantic "Big Brother".(*Athens News* July 5, 2000: A06, and Simonides, A. 2001 at http://flashfiles.flash.gr/technology/Rid7/article.asp).

[10]The real facts and data of this case have been gathered from two documents: a. the Report of the European Commission of Human Rights of the Council of Europe on the Application No. 24348/94, of P. Gregoriades against Greece, adapted on 25 June 1996, Strasbourg, and b. the Judgment of the European Court of Human Rights (121/1996/740/939), of the same case, Strasbourg, 25 November 1997.

military surveillance in postdictatorial Greece under the first PASOK administration in 1988. It is an adventure of a Greek citizen who dared to condemn the illiberal and oppressing orders of the Greek Army, especially the military political surveillance records, and for the first time to fight in the Greek and European courts against his conviction and sentence for the crime of "insult to the army," defending his and all Greeks' right to freedom of expression in a democratic society, even during their military service.

In fact, in the course of his military service, the journalist Panayiotis Gregoriades, as a probationary reserve officer, had discovered a series of abuses against the conscripts, including a discriminatory electronic database with records of the conscripts' political beliefs. In the spring of 1988 these military surveillance records were leaked out to the press, and Gregoriades came, as a result, in collision with his superiors. Serious criminal and disciplinary proceedings were instituted against him. While after the publicity of his case and political support of various political organizations he was acquitted of the criminal charges, a disciplinary penalty was imposed on him and, as a result, he had to serve 40 additional days in the army. Considering that the extension of his military service was illegal, Gregoriades refused to serve the additional days. On 30 April 1989 he was granted 24 hours' leave, after which he failed to return to his unit; he was declared a deserter on 6 May 1989 and criminal charges were brought against him. These charges were then increased based on the content of a letter he sent to his unit's commander explaining his stance, which was considered to be insulting to the army. Gregoriades presented himself to the Army Judicial Corp and remained in custody for four months; he was tried on 12 May 1989 by the Permanent Army Court of Ioannina for the offense of desertion and insulting the army, and was found guilty on both charges. The army court imposed on him to serve a total sentence of one year and ten months, a sentence that was reduced to three months by the Martial Appeal Court on 5 September 1989. The appeal court quashed the conviction for desertion, but it confirmed, by three votes to two, his conviction for insulting the army. He was immediately liberated, the time spent in detention on remand having counted against his sentence. Mr.

Gregoriades appealed to the Supreme Court (*Areios Pagos*), which on June 26, 1991 upheld the conviction on insulting the army. In a final judgment delivered on September 22, 1993, the Plenary Court of Cassation considered by three votes to two that Article 74 of the Army Criminal Code did not violate the Constitution, and that it had been correctly applied in the applicant's case. Mr. Gregoriades, after he exhausted all Greek court appeals, applied on March 17, 1994 to the European Commission of Human Rights at Strasbourg, which by majority declared his application admissible to the European Court of Human Rights, expressing the opinion that there had been a violation of Article 10 of the European Convention of Human Rights, that guarantees the right to freedom of expression.

The European Court of Human Rights, on 25 November 1997, basing its judgment on a previous similar case of Vogt vs. Germany (1995), stated that "Article 10 does not stop at the gates of army barracks. It applies to military personnel as to other persons within the jurisdiction of the Contracting States . . . The Court accordingly considers that the prosecution and conviction of the applicant cannot be justified as necessary in a democratic society . . ." and it "holds by 12 votes to 8 that there has been a violation of Article 10 of the Convention; . . . and the (Greek) state is to pay to the applicant, within 3 months, 2 million Greek drachmas, plus any value-added tax that may be payable, in respect to costs and expenses. . . ."

Gregoriades's fight against the Greek military's authoritarian political control surveillance and its violations of the human rights of the Greek military personnel has definitely contributed to the democratization and Europeanization of the Greek armed forces (*Eleftherotypia*, O Ios, June 21,1997: 26-27).

b. The case of Gabriel Tsavachidis vs. Greece 21.1.1999 (*religious surveillance*)

The applicant, a Greek citizen and a painter, was a Jehovah's Witness, who complained that his right to respect for his private life and home, guaranteed by Article 8 of the Convention for the Protection of

Human Rights and Fundamental Freedoms, had been violated by the surveillance he was placed under in May 1993, and his prosecution for illegally operating a church in the city of Kilkis. He further complained that he was placed under surveillance due to his religious beliefs, and that the surveillance and the collecting of information concerning the gatherings of Jehovah's Witnesses violates the right of freedom of peaceful assembly under Articles 9 and 11 of the Convention. Tsavachidis also complained that he was a victim of religious discrimination, since persons of Greek Orthodox faith are not placed under surveillance. Finally, Tsavachidis complained that the policy of the Greek National Intelligence Service (EYP) of placing him under surveillance violated his right to security, and was contrary to Article 5, paragraph 1 of the Convention. The applicant recalled that on August 4, 1993 the *Eleftherotypia* newspaper revealed the existence of a strictly confidential report compiled by the EYP, dated January 19, 1993, containing derogatory allegations concerning Greek citizens who are not members of the Greek Orthodox Church. (see page 89 note 33). Tsavachidis's case, as other similar cases, such as *Kokkinakis vs. Greece* (25.5.1993), have been vindicated by the European Court of Human Rights and have contributed to the Jehovah's Witness freedoms in Greece (Pollis, A. 1998 & 1999: 184-6; also Stavros, St. 1999).

c. The case of Donald Peers vs. Greece, 19.4.2001

In April 2001, the European Court of Human Rights (ECHR) found that Donald Peers was entitled to compensation for breach of privacy, under Article 8 of the European Convention, when Greek prison administrators opened his mail while he was incarcerated for drug offenses in Greece in 1994 (EPIC & PI 2002, Report: 195). This case is the only one that Greece has been found guilty by ECHR for violation of communication privacy (letter-opening) and indirectly for the prisoners' rights in a democratic society.

Part VI

SURVEILLANCE AND DEMOCRACY IN GREECE: THE LEGACY OF MASS REPRESSIVE SURVEILLANCE

Chapter 10

Traditional and New Surveillance vis-à-vis Democracy in Greece: Comparisons, Assessments, and Democratic Anti-Surveillance Prospects

A. A comparison of traditional and new surveillance in Greece

TRADITIONALLY, SURVEILLANCE used to be one of the exclusive sociopolitical control methods of each nationstate, which kept the panoptic monopoly in its territory (Giddens 1985). Eventually in high modernity and in informational capitalism the state panoptic monopoly is ended by the growing market surveillance for profit, various types of private surveillance, supranational spy surveillance like *Echelon*, and even commercial satellite surveillance like the Global Positioning Satellite (GPS). Yet, under the impact of the terrorist tragic events of 9/11 and the insecurity it has caused, the state in the United States and in all western societies currently reinforces its antiterrorist panopticism, exploiting also any kind of private surveillance (Lyon 2003; Schulhofer, St. J. 2002).

A pertinent comparison of traditional and new surveillance proposed by G.T. Marx (2002) is based mostly on technological characteristics of the two ideal types of surveillance. In this study, avoiding technological determinism, we argue that the various dimensions of surveillance are not only dependent on technology but mostly on the type of state and society and the sociopolitical control system. Our analysis emphasizes that *surveillance development reflects both modernization and democratization of the state and society and its function, impact, and control reflect the power relations in a society*. Hence, in our following *Table 3* we propose a comparison between the traditional, state surveillance and the new surveillance in Greece, based mostly on qualitative data, directly related to our sociopolitical control approach.

Traditional, state surveillance was a basic sociopolitical control mechanism of the authoritarian Greek state; anticommunist surveillance was an efficient instrument enforcing citizens' loyalty to the Greek anticommunist state, sorting all Greeks according to their loyalty to the regime. New, electronic surveillance by the state, suprastate, and the market is flourishing now in Greece, which is a full EU memberstate and a democratic market society, in global informational capitalism. In our comparison of traditional, "hard," anticommunist surveillance with new, "soft," even "sweet" consumer surveillance, we don't accept the dichotomy that characterizes as "political" the state surveillance and "nonpolitical" the non-state surveillance;" because, as we have already mentioned, we consider that every form of surveillance can have political dimensions and effects. Therefore, political surveillance is not only that which is conducted by the state for directly sociopolitical control purposes, but also the private, commercial, consumer surveillance, which can sort individuals accordingly, by including or excluding them, and affecting their life chances. As a matter of fact, any consumer surveillance can be easily transformed into antiterrorist one, since in our post-9/11 times of insecurity, all sorts of non-state, commercial surveillance can be used by the state and suprastate for the antiterrorist security campaign (Lyon 2003).

We do not accept a simplistic evolutionary model of surveillance, which would begin with a physical, surveillance-free society to an authoritarian state surveillance society, which then would develop into a democratic state surveillance, teleologically resulting in a utopian surveillance-free society. We can, however, observe a surveillance development process reflecting social change. Thus, we observe postwar Greece, with its face-to-face social control, without privacy, an "open-door" society, and the direct dependency of people to the local

TABLE 3
A comparison of traditional with new surveillance in Greece

DIMENSION	TRADITIONAL SURVEILLANCE	THE NEW SURVEILLANCE
SOCIO-POLITICAL SYSTEM	Authoritarian police-state	Democratic market society, European Union member-state
MOST CHARAC-TERISTIC TYPE	Anti-communist surveillance	Consumer surveillance
WHO DOES IT	State monopoly: Basically by the state and dependent informers	By a galaxy of state and supra-state, public and private surveillants and data collectors, even self-monitoring
WHY	Socio-political control for the regime security, loyalty to the regime	Public security and control, supra state espionage or cooperation, marketing influence for profit, self protection
TARGET-OBJECT	Individual and family	Individual, categories of interest
SURVEILLANCE TECHNOLOGY	Human Senses, human intelligence, low technology	Less human, more electronic high-tech, artificial intelligence, even GPS satellite/sky surveillance
INFORMATION DATA	Personal, social, political data, including personal and family sociopolitical beliefs, virtues, voting, etc.	Personal data plus property, (house, cars, boats, etc.) income, credibility, tax-paying status, consumer choices, insurance, medical history
BIO-METRIC DATA	Photographs, fingerprints	Biometric and biogenetic (DNA)
SORTING	Sociopolitical profiles of ethnic-minded and non-loyals	Suspect of anti social conduct, tax payer, drivers, credit, consumer profiles, etc.
CONSENT	No consent	Lack of consent, and consented
ETHOS-CHARACTER	Tough-Coercive	Softer, less coercive, even 'sweat'
PRIVACY CULTURE	Very low, open door society & authoritarian state	Emergent and imposed by EU privacy culture
EMPHASIS	On the working class, intellectuals, ethnic and religious minorities, on political organizations	On middle class, 'dangerous classes', on anonymous individuals, masses
TIME PERIOD	Present	Past, present, future
COLLECTION, STORAGE AND PROCESSING	Bureaucratic in paper dossier-files	High-tech in data banks, dataveillance, data-matching

community power elite—comprised of the priest, teacher, and police-man—socioeconomically developing and producing faceless imper-sonal relations of strangers in mass urban centers. In contemporary Greece, like in all informational capitalist societies, any sense of indi-vidual freedom of communication, expression, or consumption can be undermined by various intruders of one's privacy, with and with-out one's consent. From a period when there were no secrets in urban neighborhoods, nowadays, people live in the same building as strangers. For instance, when neighbors asked by TV reporters about arrested terrorist suspects next door to them, stated that they "fell from the sky" with surprise. Meanwhile, telephone kiosks are disappearing, and mobile phone conversations are conducted out loud in public in a more and more exposing Greek society, merging private with public space. In fact, Greek society, after a prolonged authoritarian rule and a suffocating sociopolitical control in the countryside, is enjoying the liberty in towns and cities where individualism, conservatism, relative political apathy, and anomie are growing.

While "Big Brotherism" by the state was working very efficiently in the traditional postwar Greek authoritarian setting, enforced by a net-work of private informers (hafiedes), nowadays a diffused electronic surveillance by multiple public and private surveillants, "big and little sisters and nephews," are routinely monitoring private life without any serious resistance.

In regards to Greek panopticism and its evolution, and based on the aforementioned indicative cases of state and non-state surveillance in current Greece, we observe that:

a. traditional state—police, military, and intelligence—surveil-lance has been electronically modernized into an electronic panopti-cism, which can use all existing surveillance in the country; although not merely anticommunist as in the authoritarian past, it is maintain-ing its political control function as a key state apparatus, targeting all suspects activists of the far right and extra-parliamentary left groups, who are considered a threat to the public order and security.

b. besides the modernization of the state panopticism, that is now far less repressive and less political-control oriented, we also observe non-state mass applications of public and private electronic surveillance systems in public spaces for security purposes, and multiple data collection and processing, targeting mainly various types of consumers. The violation and exploitation of personal and information privacy for various purposes is perpetrated by a cluster of private data collectors and databanks, without any effective control and limitation.

c. in current Greece, like in all western states, next to governmental-state, institutional panopticism of the masses, there has developed a scandalous "*synopticism*" (Mathieson, Th. 1997, Lyon, D. 2001: 92), i.e. the surveillance of the powerful and famous members of the elite by the masses, via the yellow press and electronic mass media.

d. a new television entertainment oriented "*mazopticism*" is developing, i.e., the surveillance of ordinary persons, who participate in reality, "Big Brother" type of shows, by mass television audiences.

e. yet, a self-monitoring, self-protecting surveillance, or "*autopticism*" is used by the members of the economic, political elite, who buy anti-surveillance security services provided by private agencies for the protection of their privacy (Alivizatos 1998, Samatas 2003c).

In brief, the development of Greek panopticism as it is summarized in Table 3 reflects social, economic, political, and cultural processes in Greece. Traditionally panopticism was identified with the oppressive methods of authoritarian state of the past, now having evolved into a "sweet" television and consumerism manipulation, by a "soft despotism" of "consented" surveillance—a sociologically and psychologically very interesting phenomenon related to the global informational capitalist process, which needs, of course, further theoretical and empirical investigation.

B. THE LEGACY OF MASS REPRESSIVE SURVEILLANCE: CONTRADICTING POPULAR ATTITUDES VIS-À-VIS PRIVACY AND SURVEILLANCE

The problem of controlling the new panopticism in Greece is also reflected in the contradicting attitude and behavior of the average

Greek citizen, who on the one hand bluntly objects to any police and
state surveillance, due to the authoritarian police state in the past, even
if that means legitimate surveillance controls such as traffic and taxes,[1]
while, on the other hand, is either ignorant of new non-state surveillance, very easily accepting consumer and market surveillance. Popular opposition only to the police and state surveillance, which is
directly connected with political control, is a remnant of traditional
anticommunist surveillance; the perception however of the market
and consumer surveillance as nonpolitical, and therefore as harmless,
is fictitious, since its discriminatory effects are deeply political. Marketing, consumer surveillance can violate all inalienable constitutional
guaranteed rights of the protection of personality. This type of new
surveillance allows privacy and dignity to become negotiable, persuad-
ing the consumer or TV player to consent in the trading of his/her privacy and dignity for money, a promising carrier in show business and
temporary publicity.

Libertarians argue that citizens, as consenting adults, should have
the right of free will and choice to trade their privacy, in the role of
consumer or TV viewer or player, in the direct marketing surveillance
and "Big Brother" reality shows, without any interference by the state.[2]
Human rights advocates on the contrary argue that the surveillance
camera use in TV shows, and in many other domestic applications
endorses the "Big Brother" acceptance in everyday life, and it legitimates routine surveillance. In this way, in free market societies a consent is fabricated of selling out inalienable human rights, like the
asylum of home residence, and the human dignity of individual, transforming citizens into a passive consumer, indifferent to any privacy
violation.[3] This attitude is reinforced by the contradictory behavior of
many Greek citizens, who can easily destroy a police camera in a

---

[1]In 2002 in a whole country poll, 65.3% of a total 6,000 interviewees had cate-
gorically rejected any police telephone-wiretapping. *ETHNOS*, Jan. 11, 2002.

[1]Tsakirakis, St." Privacy by force" in *Eleftherotypia* July 5, 2001 (in Greek).

[2]Marios Ploritis (2001), has made a reference to "Mithridatism," the poisoning
practice of the ancient Pontus King Mithridates, who inflicted poison upon himself by
receiving very small poison doses to make his organism resistant in case someone tried
to poison him.

demonstration, because they have learned to be afraid the state political surveillance and the political filing (*fakeloma*); at the same time most ordinary Greeks as consumers are very willing to give up all their personal data to a supermarket or to a travel agency for consumer purposes. Thus, what has been called "the privacy's paradox" (Stalder, F. 2002: 122), the attitude and behavior of current citizens-consumers in most developed countries of informational capitalism, to show a general concern for the violation of their privacy, but not actually taking privacy protection measures, is also valid for Greeks, particularly for the young generation, which has not experienced the oppressive consequences of anticommunist panopticism (Samatas, M. 1999).

We must also point out that, while most Greek political parties and civil society groups formally condemn any state surveillance, they do really nothing against market surveillance. Even the Greek consumers union (INKA) used to be relatively apathetic to direct marketing surveillance. This attitude has changed over the last years, when citizens and consumers have complained to INKA and the HDPA about exploitation of their information and violation of their privacy. The complaints are growing due to the facts that INKA and HDPA are becoming more active and known to the public; civil society is becoming more sensitive to privacy rights, in particular because Greeks have discovered the plastic credit card money, having in the last years taken the most consumer loans ever, and the banks and corporations have frequently abused their credit and consumers privacy. Nevertheless, if general consumers' apathy for their privacy protection is due to the high consuming propensity of Greeks, it needs further empirical research. Also in need of further empirical investigation is to which degree the new very popular television shows of the "Big Brother" type actually contribute in the acceptance of CCTV surveillance, and generally in the demystification of daily routine surveillance by the Greek viewers.

Beyond however the empirical research of attitudes and perceptions, what is certain, is that new electronic panopticism reflects a power relation imbalance against citizens and consumers. It contributes considerably in the reinforcement of the economic, political, and symbolic powers, and in the easier manipulation of citizens. Uninformed ordinary citizens do not realize, do not protest, and often consent to their panoptic—symbolic guidance—manipulation and their subsequent cultural/symbolic exclusion (Bourdieu, P. 1999). Citizens' consent however does not legalize their manipulation. As sociologist Nicos Mouzelis points out:

> If political emancipation is considered the right of citizens to be free from the tyranny that involves an intensely unequal distribution of political power, and if socioeconomic emancipation means the citizen is free from severe poverty that usually involves an intensely unequal distribution of wealth, then the cultural emancipation promotes the right of citizens to be free from what we could call "guided socializations"—or free from what Bourdieu calls symbolic violence. It is the type of violence or guidance that is produced by the intensely unequal distribution of "influence" between the institutions of socialization and socialized, between those that check and those that are checked by the material and symbolic means of configuration of identities and ways of life (Mouzelis, N. 2001: 35) (translation mine).

THE DEMONIZATION OF EVERY TYPE OF STATE SURVEILLANCE

In contemporary democratic market societies, surveillance by public and private institutions is legitimated for security and control. A rational state bureaucracy is counter balanced by powerful civil society, and the rights of sovereign subjects are respected. Therefore "institutional," legal surveillance is not a threat to the individual's rights but a legitimate institutional process (Lianos 2003); it is based on a positive surveillance culture, which characterizes advanced democratic market societies.

In Greece however, a negative legacy of authoritarian mass political surveillance has caused a popular demonization of any state surveillance, even for security, taxes, or traffic control. In general, there is sensitivity and vigilance for any state surveillance due to the prolonged authoritarian surveillance in the past, and at the same time an ignorance of or apathy for private data collection.

After the collapse of the dictatorship, the Greek authoritarian police state has moved to a democratization and European integration process, eliminating gradually but steadily the remnants of state political control surveillance. The problem is that the legacy of this mass political surveillance has produced a negative surveillance culture, which does not allow any positive perception and trust of any legitimate personal data collection. "Filling" of personal data *(fakeloma* in Greek), is always perceived in Greece as a negative term and process due to the authoritarian surveillance culture of the past. Personal data collection and processing is related only to discriminatory inclusion and exclusion of individuals by the sociopolitical control system. Every legitimate "institutional surveillance" presupposes trust to the state/public and private institutions; this institutional trust has never really existed in Greece, since even at the present liberal time, several public administration agencies have often violated the privacy rights of Greek citizens, and especially of the weak minorities. Corruption or negligence characterize several public services, which, as we have already mentioned, provide personal data to private information exploiters. On the other hand, private corporations do not respect the rights of their customers, selling their personal data to other profiteers, without sanctions.

Especially in countries like Greece with a traditional lack of trust between state and citizens (or a mutual mistrust) and a very weak civil society, people are unable to demand and enforce their rights. A balance of power is also missing between individual subjects and institutions; because the Greek subjects, either as citizens or consumers, are still not sovereign but subjugated to the party-state and market powers. Hence, surveillance development reflects the fact that Greece as a newly democratic market society is still characterized by serious democratic deficit, and a negative, however improving, record of respecting the rights of various minorities; meanwhile, the market is not actually controlled by the state nor is it self-regulated.

C. Concluding assessment

Regardless the critical surveillance impact of post 9/11 antiterrorist campaign and that of the Athens 2004 Olympic Games, the growing electronic panopticanization of Greek contemporary society is a complex phenomenon that has to do with the overall modernization and Europeanization of the Greek state and society within the globalization process of informational capitalism. Democratization of the Greek political system has ended the traditional repressive and ideological panoptic role of the state as a sociopolitical control monopoly. Greece, integration in the EU and the Schengen zone, has on the one hand a positive impact against state undemocratic surveillance; Europeanization has contributed to the adaption of privacy protection legislation and to the establishment of the Hellenic Data Protection Agency, which, however, due to bureaucratic and implementation problems, cannot guarantee the control of growing panopticism. Greeks as European Union citizens have more rights, including the right of "information self-determination," which is promoted by the EU; it does not only mean simply to "leave us alone," but also to be guaranteed one's relevant rights in the access and objection to, and correction, or even deletion, of stored personal information in the various databanks. It has to do with the inalienable right of human autonomy, and people's complete control of their own personal data, which they will choose for themselves and only with their consent to reveal (Alivizatos, N. 1998, Mitrou, L. 1999: 31-32). Practically, however, in the everyday routine the individual is unable to practice "information self-determination," and unable to decide which personal information should be revealed and which not, particularly when one is compelled to reveal (Stalder, F. 2002: 122). Because the control and the restriction of illegitimate state and market panopticism cannot be left only in the public policies of the state and the relative legislation, nor in the self-regulation of the market forces; the protection weight falls on the institutional efficiency and independence of the national and European data protection authorities. However, the existence of these authorities should not give a sense of security against privacy violations. These data protection authorities, despite their important anti-surveillance decisions, cannot actually always contradict the state and the market's powerful interests; they are rather functioning as legitimating bodies of the whole surveillance system. Hence, the hopes lie on Greek civil society and its political organizations for a political strategy of vigilance, resistance, and elimination of all forms of illegitimate panopticism, and for a complete control of the legitimate ones.

As we have discussed, Europeanization has entailed a potential negative impact from the function of the Schengen Information System (SIS), which currently works not only against illegal immigration but even against any European real or perceived threats, by monitoring all anti-EU and anti-globalization movements at the expense of European, including Greek, citizens' civil liberties and immigrants' and refugees' human rights (Samatas 2003).

The security of the Athens 2004 Olympic Games has imposed a super panopticism on Greece, as a security investment after the end of the games and unforeseeable effects for civil liberties; also with guaranteed high profits for the surveillance technology providers. In fact the wide application of high-tech surveillance systems in the public and private sector of Greece, like in all western market societies, is related with the globalized informational capitalist market. Concisely the electronic panopticanization of Greece is related to:

a. the promotion of high technology surveillance systems produced by mainly American and British corporations of the military industry, which, after the end of the Cold War, are looking for new markets promoting non-military, market applications of their electronic military surveillance systems, like electronic games and panoptic security systems. With the help of their governments and interrelated mass media these corporations promote their panoptic systems as a technological panacea to the urban problems of the big cities, especially crime, traffic control, buildings security, etc. (Norris & Amstrong 1999: 27-32);

b. the pressing marketing of these companies and their governments, hence western capitals are transformed into fortresses against terrorism, suspected immigrants, and the dangerous lower classes (May, Chr. 2002: 24-28);

   c. the ongoing universal primacy of security, i.e., the "securitization trend" against new or traditional, real or fictitious, internal or exterior enemies, the post-Cold War nation states, which are unable to protect their territory due to globalization; they are coordinating with private security companies, privatizing several domestic security fields, like border controls, passengers entries, etc. (Giddens 1985, McSweeney 1999);

   d. the interrelated interests with the private sector of many state and governmental functionaries, like police officers, customs and border police, who are loosing gradually their competencies and the privileges of their work (Buzan 1991);

   e. the fact that in the information capitalist market all personal information and especially "sensitive private information," not only of the members of the elite but also of the ordinary people, is the most profitable market commodity; hence, privacy is also a commodity, and not an inalienable right (Simitis Sp. 1987; Clarke, R. 1999; Etzioni, A. 1999; Sykes, Ch. 1999; Allen, A. 2001).

   Consequently, under the impact of a globalized informational capitalism, the growing panopticism in Greece, by mass application of new surveillance technologies and the ensuing exploitation of privacy protection, should be considered as a structural feature of the economic, political, and cultural-symbolic power system (Stalder 2002).

   A Greek Canadian painter had stated in November 1997 that she had decided to settle permanently in Greece, because even if she was a law-abiding citizen of Canada she could not bear to live there under surveillance in every one of her step, and the continuing violations of her privacy, not only from police and private CCTV, but also from a generalized panoptic tendency of banks, public services, shopping centers, supermarkets, etc. to electronically record too much of her personal data. (*To Vima*, Nov. 30, 1997). Certainly, six years later this woman could not repeat her statement that "Greece is comparatively a surveillance-free 'paradise' compared to other western countries, particularly if she lives now in the "panoptic fortress" of Athens.

Conclusively, the Greek surveillance reality and the protection of Greek citizens' privacy is much worse than in most EU member states. This is reflected by the sincere admittance of the HDPA former chairman, regarding the inability of this authority to control the daily mass violations of privacy. Similarly this is recognized by the annual reports of the National Committee for Telecommunications and Post Offices as the former pertinent parliamentary committee has been transformed. Also, this is reinforced by the contradictory behavior of most Greek citizens, who while they oppose any police CCTV system and any institutional legitimate surveillance even for security purposes, they are eager to sell out their privacy for consumption purposes.

Contrary to the "Big Brother," Orwelian approach of a technological deterministic and uncontrolled surveillance expansion, which scares and paralyzes ordinary people, in all (post)modern risk-insecure societies, information and education of citizens about the motives and interests of those who gain money and power by personal data collection and processing, raises consciousness and activism on the issue of privacy protection, and calls for control and accountability of all panoptic powers (Stalder 2002). These powers are not only the state and suprastate "Big Brother," but also the corporate "sisters" and many other private surveillance exploiters, which can negatively affect citizens' life chances.

In the United States, the United Kingdom, Canada, and several other European surveillance societies, such as France, where the average citizen accepts legitimate surveillance for mainly security reasons, an emerging anti-surveillance movement has been organized against omnipotent and universalized panopticism. This anti-panopticanization movement is organized by autonomous anti-surveillance watches, using many types of anti-surveillance activism.—for example, city cartography of visible and invisible CCTV and cultural anti-surveillance happenings in front of CCTV, and anti-surveillance privacy protection guides to make consumers, TV viewers, travelers, and generally all people conscious of the pervasiveness of daily surveillance and privacy violations (Schienke 2000).[3] Anti-surveillance and pro-civil liberties

---

[3]The anti-surveillance movement includes a variety of activities like "video-activism," by which activists try to watch the watchers, video recording incidents, such

NGOs like the Institute of Applied Autonomy in NYC, NYCLU, Privacy International, EPIC, Statewatch, etc. are watching the state, suprastate, and corporate surveillance and privacy violations, and by legal and symbolic means pursue their exposure and condemnation.[4]

In Greece, where privacy is not really part of the dominant culture and civil society is not well organized, there is not an anti-surveillance movement yet. There is, however, a popular dissent against state and police surveillance, as a legacy of citizens' fear of state political control of their beliefs and activities. The leftist political parties and unions, and non-parliamentary leftist groups, as prolonged victims of police surveillance[5] frequently express their political protest against police brutal incidents, antiterrorist legislation, and state-police surveillance, including the Olympics zeppelins with cameras. Also, individual activists, usually in mass demonstrations occasionally destroy police CCTV. The Greek press has started over the last years, after the open intervention of American and British antiterrorist intelligence— invited actually as a result of the 17N terrorist activities—to expose the foreign surveillance in Greece. Occasionally, reports are published on electronic surveillance technology and Echelon (see Exhibit 18). Sometimes, due to the HDPA reports and decisions, there are also press reports on ruthless commercial surveillance (see Exhibits 21-23).

Is there a hope that because of the overall Greek anti-state surveillance attitude and the popular reaction against any political control

as police brutality, which are not covered by the official news reports. Illegal actions are e.g. the CCTV vandalism and web hacking by which hackers infiltrate to destroy or falsify the web pages of surveillance centers (see Anastasopooulos, D. 2001, Lazos, G. 2001).

[4]The Privacy International in the United States and in Britain but also with recent annexes in a lot of European countries grant annually the "Big Brother Awards" to the bigger violators per year but also to supporters of privacy. The awards committees, constituted by lawyers, academics, journalists, and human rights' activists, organize a special ceremony where champions of privacy violations and protection receive the Orwell Awards with public participation. (See http://www.privacyinternational.org/bigbrother/index.html).

[5]Since 1998, the KKE has denounced in the Parliament 19 incidents of police officers, who with plain clothes watched trade union meetings; in two incidents taking place in May 27, 1998 and Oct. 20, 1999, secret policemen were using video-surveillance (Rizospastis, April 26, 2002).

surveillance by state and suprastate agencies that the Greek people will be mobilized against the multifaceted profit-oriented panopticism? Hopefully this will happen when citizens eventually realize that like traditional authoritarian state surveillance, all types of new surveillance even direct marketing and consumer profiles can cause new exclusions and discriminations; that every type of surveillance, regardless of its legitimacy, raises political issues, because it can be used to undermine democracy and human autonomy. The current "soft, sweet," entertainment brand of consumer surveillance that is now developing in Greece is becoming an equally serious problem as the "ugly" state surveillance of the past was, given the pervasiveness of new technologies in one's own home and body, and their easy acceptance by the uninformed consumers.

In brief, the problem of controlling panopticism in Greece, like in every contemporary market democratic society, cannot be left to the individual person alone, nor to the self-regulation of the market, nor to the state legislation and the Data Protection Authority. It is a structural problem connected with the nature of informational capitalism, and can be resolved only when all panoptic powers become fully accountable and controlled by the people, who should be constantly vigilant for a real democratic society.

Appendix

LIST OF EXHIBITS AND THEIR SOURCES

1. The civic-mindedness certificate. *Source:* Samatas 1986.

2. KYP (Greek Central Intelligence Agency): Individual information card report. *Source: Ta Nea,* May 7, 1984.

3. Police report to draft board. *Source: Rizospastis,* July 25, 1982.

4. The content of such police report to the military draft board. *Source: To Vima,* January 13, 1980.

5. a. Secret report to armed forces chief about:
   a. communist infiltration in the armed forces (after the fall of dictatorship July 3 &
   b. a similar report in July 19, 1975.
   c. citizens' files from dictatorship maintained in the post-dictatorial period. *Source:* Tzanetakos, B. *Ta Nea,* May 8, 1984.

6. An anthology of "Howevers" in police reports. *Source: To Vima,* March 29, 1981.

7. Two rural police reports, which like similar of many other public agencies during the post-dictatorial period 1974-1981, characterized PASOK as "semi-extreme" array, excluding its followers from its ranks. *Source: Avriani,* Sept. 17, 1981, and Sept. 15, 1986.

8. Two characteristic post-dictatorial cartoons about Greek nationwide filing (*fakeloma*). Source: A. *Rizospastis,* January 27, 1980;

B. *Rizospastis,* January 29. 1984.

9. Electronic military filing during the first PASOK administration. *Source: Eleftherotypia,* February 1, 1988.

10. a. PASOK poster used in the campaign of 1985 elections promising the burning of files "for a Democracy without filings," for "freedom without persecutions" *Source: Rizospastis,* August 27, 1989.
    b. a characteristic cartoon about the expected file burning. *Source:* B. *To Vima,* October 13, 1985.

11. "Machiavellian" surveillance: a. a list of EYP listeners who had wiretapped politicians, journalists and newspapers, the prime minister's guards, etc. presented by the Parliament's Investigation Committee in Sept. 1989. *Source: I Proti,* Sept. 21, 1989.
    b. i & ii. PASOK directed KYP and OTE surveillance cards about telephone wiretapping of PASOK minister G. Arsenis, and the weekly *Pontiki* editor K. Papaioannou. *Source: Eleftheros Typos,* April 3, 1990.

12 a. File storage room in Athens central police headquarters before burning in 1989. *Source: Sunday Eleftherotypia,* August 27, 1989.
   b. The Government Gazette's pertinent issue with the order of the post-PASOK Government of National Unity regarding the destruction of files, signed by the National Unity Government's conservative and leftist ministers together.

13. Two great cartoons by Yiannis Ioannou about the files burning in 1989. *Source:* A. *I Proti,* August 29, 1989; B. *I Proti,* September 1, 1989.

14. Cartoons: Greeks enter now in the period of electronic filing. *Source:* A. *Ta Nea,* October 12, 1985; B. *Eleftherotypia,* March 8, 1982.

15. A. "European electronic filing." *Source: Sunday Eleftherotypia,* Jan. 1, 1995;
B. "Schengen Agreement (imposes) the biggest surveillance in the history of humanity!" *Source: To Pontiki,* Jan. 5, 1995.

16. a. "No to the electronic filing," a slogan against the Schengen in a mass demonstration at Athens by Orthodox Christian demonstrators. *Source: Sunday Eleftherotypia,* March 19, 2000.
b. "No to the electronic filing" a graffiti by anarchists. *Source:* Author's photograph.

17. The old police identity card and the new "Europeanized" one without several items of data, like the fingerprint, occupation, marital status, husband or wife's name, and religion.

18. US and British road and sky surveillance in Athens central streets looking for November 17 terrorist group during 2001. *Source:* A. *Ta Nea,* June 30, 2001. B. *Eleftherotypia,* May 31, 2001.

19. Athens, full of CCTV systems, has become a "Big Brother" city. *Source:* A. *Sunday Eleftherotypia,* March 17, 2002.
B. *Sunday Eleftherotypia,* June 2, 2002.
C. *To Vima,* July 21, 2000.

20. Traffic police CCTV systems almost everywhere in central Athens roads. *Source:* A. *Sunday Eleftherotypia,* Dec. 22, 2002.

21. a. "15,000 commercial firms collect and process our personal data." *Source: Ta Nea* Sept.4, 1999.
b. "In a CDRom they have recorded for sale all our personal data, even those of (former) Prime Minister Simitis!" *Source: Ta Nea* June 12, 2000.

22. a. Illegal CDRom for sale with electronic lists of Athens luxury car owners' names, license plate numbers, addresses, telephone

numbers.
b. professional groups lists and in this one military personnel.
Source: Ta Nea June 12, 2000.

23. In the same CDRom there is specific directions how you can find (former) Prime Minister C. Simitis's car data, address, telephone, even data of his neighbors. *Source: Ta Nea* June 12, 2000.

24. How "Big Brother" watches us: Special military officers explain electronic surveillance and how to protect ourselves. *Source: Eleftherotypia*, Aug. 14, 2002.

25. Audio video surveillance in Athens of various electronic transactions using: a. plastic credit card, b. a bank ATM and c. mobile phone. *Source: Ta Nea*, Sept. 4, 1999.

26. "Multinational 'Big Brother' at Athens airport 'Eleftherios Venizelos': various biometric scanning of *Alitalia* passengers to the USA. *Source: Eleftherotypia*, Sept. 27, 2003.

27. The Athens 2004 Olympic Games super panopticism! *Source: Ta Nea*, Dec. 5, 2003.

28. a. The Hellenic Data Protection Authority's logo & slogan.
b. One of thousands of compulsory statements by a corporation published at Athens daily for legalizing a personal data archive according to Law 2472/1997, Article 11.

29. Artistic anti-surveillance warnings. *Source: Eleftherotypia*, June 4, 2003.

30. A destruction of a CCTV camera. *Source: PATRIS* , April 28, 2001.

Select Bibliography

In English

Ackroyd, C. et. al. (1980) *The Technology of Political Control*, London, Pluto Press.

Agre, Ph., M. Rotenberg, ed. (1997) *Technology and Privacy: The New Landscape*, MIT Press.

Alivizatos, N. (1981) "The Emergency Regime and Civil Liberties," in *Greece in the 1940s. A Nation in Crisis*, ed. Iatrides, J. Hanover, NH, Univ. Press of New England.

Allen, A. (2001) "Is Privacy Now Possible? A Brief History of an Obsession" *Social Research*, vol. 68. no. 1 Spring.

Andersen, S. and Eliassen, K., eds. (1996) *The European Union: How Democratic Is It?* Sage.

Askin, Frank (1972) "Surveillance: The Social Science Perspective," *Columbia Human Rights Law Review* 4.

Barth, A. (1952) *The Loyalty of Free Men*, New York: Pocket Books.

Barth, A. (1955) *Government by Investigation* New York: Viking.

Bontecue, Eleanor (1953) *The Federal Loyalty-Security Program* Ithaca, NY: Cornell Univ. Press.

Buzan, B. (1991) "New Patterns of Global Security in the 21st Century," *International Affairs*, vol. 67, no 3:431-457.

Campbell, J. K. (1983) "Traditional Values and Continuities in Greek Society," in Clogg, R. *Greece in the 1980s*, New York, Saint Martins Press: 184-207.

Castells, M. (1996) *The Rise of the Network Society*. Oxford, Blackwell.

Castells, M.. (1997) *The Power of Identity*, Oxford, Blackwell.

Clarke, R. (1999) "Introduction to Dataveillance and Information Privacy & Definitions of Terms," available at www.anu.edu.au/people/Roger. Clarke/DV/Intro.htm.

Clive, Th. (1984) *The Rise of the Authoritarian State in Peripheral Societies*, NY, Monthly Review Press.

Clogg, R. (1993) *Greece 1981-1989, The Populist Decade*, Saint Martins Press, London.

Collier, D. ed. (1979) *The New Authoritarianism in Latin America* Princeton, NJ, Princeton Univ. Press.

Compton, J. V. (1973) *Anti-Communism in American Life Since the Second World War* St. Charles, Mo.: Forum Press

Dandeker, C. (1990) *Surveillance, Power and Modernity*, Cambridge, Polity Press.

Diamandouros, N. P. (1983) "Greek Political Culture in Transition: Historical Origins, Evolution, Current Trends," in Clogg, R. ed. *Greece in the 1980s* NY, St. Martin's Press.

Diamandouros, N. P. (1983) "Transition to and Consolidation of Democratic Politics in Greece, 1974-1983: A Tentative Assessment," *West European Politics*, Dec.

Emerson, T. J., Hober, D. and Dorsey, N. (1967) *Political and Civil Rights in the United States* Boston: Little Brown.

Etzioni, A. (1999) *The Limits of Privacy* N.Y. Basic Books.

EU The Council (1995) "Common Position (EC) No / 95 "On the protection of individuals with regard to the processing of personal data and on the free movement of such data" 20 February.

European Parliament (1992a) "Resolution on the implementation of the Schengen Agreement" Decree L3-336/92.

European Parliament (1992b) "The Union's policies—Information society, telecommunications: An overview of the Information society and telecommunications policy," DG III-DG XIII-Information Society Project-Office (ISPO).

Fatouros, A. (1981) "Building Formal Structures of Penetration: The U.S. in Greece, 1947-1948," *Greece in the 1940s: A Nation in Crisis*, ed. J. Iatrides (Hanover, N.H.: Univ. Press of New England.

Fijnaut, Cyrille J.C.F.; Marx, Gary T. (ed.) (1996) *Undercover Police Surveillance in Comparative Perspective*, Kluwer Law International.

Fiske, J. (1998) "Surveilling the City: Whiteness, the Black Man & Democratic Totalitarianism" *Theory, Culture & Society*, vol. 15 no. 2.

Flaherty, D. H. (1989) *Protecting Privacy in Surveillance Societies* London, The Univ. of North Carolina Press

Freeland, R. M. (1972) *The Truman Doctrine and the Origins of McCarthyism: Foreign Policy, Domestic Politics and Internal Security, 1946-1948* New York: Alfred A. Knopf.

Gandy Oscar (1989) "The Surveillance Society: Information Technology and Bureaucratic Social Control" *Journal of Communication*, no39(3), 69.

Garfinkel, S. (2000) *Database Nation: The death of privacy in the 21st century* New York, O'Reilly.

Giddens, A. (1985) *The Nation State and Violence*, Cambridge, Polity Press

Gilbert, Paul (1994) *Terrorism, Security and Nationality*, Routledge, London.

Goldfarb, J. C. (1982) *On Cultural Freedom: An Exploration of Public Life in Poland and America* Chicago: Univ. of Chicago Pr.

Goldstein, R. J. (1978) *Political Repression in Modern America from 1870 to the Present* (Boston: G. K. Hall & Co.

Gordon, P. (1989) *Policing Immigration: Britain's Internal Controls.* London: Pluto Press.

Gotlieb, C. (1996) "Privacy: A Concept Whose Time Has Come and Gone," in Lyon & Zuriek, eds. (1996) *Computers, Surveillance and Privacy*, University of Minnesota Press.

Guild, E. and Niessen, J. (1996) *The Developing Immigration and Asylum Policies of the EU.* The Hague: Kluwer Law International.

Hammar, T. (1990) *Democracy and the Nationstate*, Aldershot, Avebury.

Harper, A. D. (1969) *The Politics of Loyalty: The White House and the Communist Issue, 1946-1952* Westport, CT: Greenwood Press.

Iatrides, J. (1980) "American Attitudes Toward the Political System of Postwar Greece," in Couloumbis, T. and Iatrides, J., eds. *Greek-American Relations: A Critical Review*, New York: Pella Publishing Co.

Iatrides J., ed. (1981) *Greece in the 1940s; A Nation in Crisis,* (Hanover, N.H.: Univ. Press of New England.

Joubert, C. and Bevers, H. (1996) *Schengen Investigated:* A Comparative Interpretation of the Schengen Provisions on International Police Cooperation in the Light of the European Convention on Human Rights. The Hague: Kluwer Law International.

Kariotis, Th. (1991) ed. *The Greek Socialist Experiment: Papandreou's Greece*

1981-1989 NY, Pella Publishing Co.

Kateb, G. (2001) "On being Watched and Known" *Social Research*, vol. 68. no. 1 Spring.

Klare, M. and Arnson, C. (1981) *Supplying Repression: U.S. Support for Authoritarian Regimes Abroad* Washington, D.C.: Institute for Policy Studies.

Kling, Rob (1995), *Social Controversies About Computerization, in* Kling, Rob, ed. *Computerization and Controversy: Value Conflicts and Social Choices,* 2nd edition, USA, Academic Press:10-15.

Leon, G. B. (1976) *The Greek Socialist Movement and the First World War: The Road to Unity* (New York: Columbia Univ. Pr.).

Levin, M. B. (1971) *Political Hysteria in America: The Democratic Capacity for Repression* New York: Basic Books.

Lodge, Juliet (1993) "Internal security and judicial cooperation" in Lodge, J., ed. *The European Community and the Challenge of the Future*, London, Pinter Publishers.

Lyon, D. (1988) *The Information Society: Issues and Illusions* Cambridge, Polity Press.

Lyon, D. (1994) *The Electronic Eye: The Rise of Surveillance Society* Cambridge, Polity Press.

Lyon, D. & Zureik, Elia, eds. (1996) *Computers, Surveillance and Privacy* University of Minnesota Press.

Lyon, D. (2001) *Surveillance Society: Monitoring Everyday Life* Open University Press.

Lyon, D., ed. (2003) *Surveillance as Social Sorting* London, Routledge.

Margalit Av. (2001) "Privacy in a Decent Society" *Social Research*, vol. 68.no. 1 spring.

Marx, Gary T. (1985) "The Surveillance Society: The threat of 1984-style techniques" *The Futurist*, June, 21-26.

Marx, Gary T. (2002) "What's New about the 'New Surveillance'? Classifying for Change and Continuity," *Surveillance & Society* 1 (1):9-29, in www.surveillance-and-society.org

McSweeney, B. (1999) *Security, Identity and Interests* Cambridge University Press.

Mathieson, Th. (1997) "The viewer Society: Foucault's Panopticon revisited"

Theoretical Criminology, no 1: 215-234.

Mavrogordatos, G. (1983) *Stillborn Republic: Social Conditions and Party Strategies in Greece, 1922-1936,* Berkeley, CA: Univ. of Calif. Press.

May, Chr. (2002) *The Information Society: A sceptical view,* Polity Press.

McSweeney, B. (1999) *Security, Identity and Interests,* Cambridge University Press.

Millis, W. (1968) "Legacies of the Cold War," in Reitman, A., ed. *The Price of Liberty* New York: W. Norton & Co.

Mouzelis, N. (1978) *Modern Greece: Facets of Underdevelopment,* London: Macmillan.

Mouzelis, N. (1980) "Capitalism and the Development of the Modern State," *The State in Western Europe,* ed. R. Scase New York: St. Martin's Press.

New York Civil Liberties Union (1998) "New York City: A Surveillance Camera Town," NYCLU Special Report 1998, N.Y. December 13.

Norris, Cl. & Armstrong, G. (1999) *The Maximum Surveillance Society: The rise of CCTV* Berg, Oxford & N.Y.

O' Brien, J. L. (1955). *National Security and Individual Freedom* Cambridge, MA: Harvard Univ. Press.

O'Donnel, G. A. (1973) *Modernization and Bureaucratic Authoritarianism* (Berkeley, Univ. of California Press.

Parenti, Chr. (2003) *The Soft Cage, Surveillance in America,* N.Y. Basic Books.

Petras, J. (1982) "Greek Socialism, Walking the Tightrope," *Journal of the Hellenic Diaspora,* vol. X no1, Spring.

Petras, J. (1987) "The Contradictions of Greek Socialism," *New Left Review* no163, May-June.

Pilpel, H. F. (1968) "The Challenge of Privacy," in Reitman, A., ed. *The Price of Liberty* New York: Norton.

Pollis, A. (1965) "Political Implications of the Modern Greek Concept of Self" *The British Journal of Sociology.*

Pollis, A. (1977) "The Impact of Traditional Cultural Patterns on Greek Politics" *The Greek Review of Social Research,* vol.29, Athens.

Pollis, A. (1985) "International and Domestic Constraints on Socialist Transformation in Greece" in Musto, S. and Pinkele, C., eds. *Europe at the Crossroad: Agendas of the Crisis* New York, Praeger.

Poster, M. (1996) "Database as Discourse or Electronic Interpellations" in

Lyon, D. & Zureik, E., eds. *Computers, Surveillance and Privacy*, Univ. of Minnesota Press.

Poulantzas, N. (1978) *State, Power, Socialism* London, NLB and Verso.

Privacy International (1997) "Tapping page:E.U.-FBI Linkup: A Statewatch report" February (http://www.privacy.org/pi/).

Privacy International websites (http:// www.privacy.org/pi/)

Regan, P. M. (1986). "Privacy, Government Information, and Technology," *Public Administration Review*, vol. 46 Nov.-Dec no 6.

Reitman, A., ed.(1968) *The Price of Liberty* New York: Norton.

Roubatis, Y. (1979) "The U.S. and the Operational Responsibilities of the Greek Armed Forces, 1947-1987," *The Journal of the Hellenic Diaspora* 6.1 (Spring 1979).

Rule, J. B. (1974). *Private Lives and Public Surveillance: Social Control in the Computer Age* NY, Schoken Books.

Samatas, M. (1986) "Greek Bureaucratism: A system of Sociopolitical Control" unpublished Ph.D. diss., G.F. New School for Social Research, N.Y.

Samatas, M. (1986b) "Greek McCarthyism: A comparative assessment of Greek post-civil war repressive anticommunism and the US Truman-McCarthy era," *Journal of the Hellenic Diaspora*, vol. XIII, nos.3 & 4 Fall-Winter.

Samatas, M. (1993). "The Populist Phase of an Underdeveloped Surveillance Society: Political Surveillance in Post-Authoritarian Greece" *Journal of the Hellenic Diaspora*, vol.19.1 Jan-Jun.: 31-70.

Samatas, M. (1993b). "Debureaucratization failure in post-dictatorial Greece: a sociopolitical control approach" *Journal of Modern Greek Studies*, vol.11, Oct no. 2: 187-217.

Samatas, M. (1997) "The Participation of Greece in the Schengen Information System (S.I.S) and the Legacy of Mass Political Surveillance" Modern Greek Studies Association Symposium, Kent State University, 6-7 Nov.1997.

Samatas, M. (1999) "Privacy and Democratic Concerns in the Greek Information Society" Modern Greek Studies Association Symposium, Princeton University, 4-7 Nov. 1999.

Samatas, M. (2003a) "Greece in 'Schengenland': Blessing or anathema for citizens and foreigners' rights?" *Journal of Ethnic and Migration Studies*, vol.

29, no. 1: 141-156.

Schengen Agreement: Introduction, bibliography and full text, Statewatch briefing paper no 2. Statewatch website: http://www.staewatch.org.

Schengen: Teething Problems and First Report, *Statewatch Bulletin*, vol. 6 no. 3, May-June 1996

Schienke, E. W. (2002) "On the Outside Looking Out: An Interview with the Institute of the Applied Autonomy (IAA)," *Surveillance & Society* 1 (1):102-119, at www.surveillance-and-society.org.

Schneier, Bruce; Banisar, David (1996) *Electronic Privacy Sourcebook: Documents on the Battle for Privacy,* Wiley.

Schulhofer, St. J. (2002) *The Enemy Within: Intelligence Gathering, Law Enforcement, and Civil Liberties in the Wake of September 11, Twentieth Century Fund.*

Scott James C. (1985) *Weapons of the Weak: Everyday Forms of Peasant Resistance,* New Haven, Yale University Press.

Simitis, Sp. (1987) "Reviewing privacy in an information society," *Univ. of Pennsylvania Law Review* (1987): 707-746.

Sotiropoulos, D. (1991) "State and Party: The Greek State Bureaucracy and the PASOK, 1981-1989," Ph.D. dissertation, Yale University.

Sotiropoulos, D. (1996) *Populism and Bureaucracy, The case of Greece under PASOK, 1981-1989,* Notre Dame, Univ. of Notre Dame Press

Spencer, M. (1995) *States of Injustice: A Guide to Human Rights and Civil Liberties in the E.U.* London: Pluto Press.

Stalder, F. (2002) "Privacy is not the antidote to surveillance," Surveillance & Society 1(1): 120-124, www.surveillance-and-society.org.

Starr, C. G. *Political Intelligence in Classical Greece,* Lugtuni Batavonim, E. J. Brill, Leiden, Netherlands, 1974: 39-48.

Statewatch website: http://www.statewatch.org.

Statewatching the new Europe: A Handbook on the European state London, 1995. *London,* Statewatch Publication.

Stavros, St. (1999) "Human Rights in Greece: Twelve Years of Supervision from Strasbourg," *Journal of Modern Greek Studies,* 1999, Vol. 17.

Stouffer, S. A. (1966) *Communism, Conformity and Civil Liberties* New York: Wiley.

Strub, Harry, (1989) "The Theory of Panoptical Control: Bentham's Panopticon and Orwell's 1984" *The Journal Of the History of the Behavioural Sciences*, 25, 40-59.

Sykes, Ch. (1999) *The End of Privacy* New York, St. Martin Press.

Tanner, W. R. and Griffith, R. (1974) "Legislative Politics and 'McCarthyism': The Internal Security Act of 1950," *The Specter: Original Essays on the Cold War and the Origins of McCarthyism*, Griffith, R. and Theoharis, A., eds. New York: New Viewpoints.

Tsoucalas, C. (1981) in "The Ideological Impact of the Civil War," *Greece in the 1940s: A Nation in Crisis*, Iatrides, J., ed. Hanover, N.H.: Univ. Press of New England.

Vaughn, R. (1972) *Only Victims: A Study of Show Business Blacklistings* New York: G. P. Putnam.

Vergopoulos, C. (1981) "The Emergence of the New Bourgeoisie, 1944-1952" in Iatrides, J., ed *Greece én the 1940s; A Nation in Crisis* Hanover, N.H.: Univ. Press of New England.

Vlanton, E. (1983) "From Grammos to Tet: American Intervention in Greece and Beyond," *Journal of the Hellenic Diaspora* 10.3 (Fall 1983).

Watters, P. and Gillers, S., eds., (1973) *Investigating the F.B.I* New York: Doubleday.

Webster, Fr. (1995) *Theories of the Information Society* Rutledge, London.

Wittner, L. (1982) *American Intervention in Greece, 1943-1949* New York: Columbia Univ. Press.

Working Group of Article 29 of Direction 95/46 EC 2000 (http://europa.eu.int/comm/internalmarket/privacy/wg2000).

In Greek

Alivizatos, N. (1983) *The Political Institutions in Crisis, 1922-1974: Aspects of the Greek Experience* (in Greek) Athens: Themelio,.

Alivizatos, N. (1983b) "The Legal Status of Security Corps," *Nomikon Vima* 31.

Alivizatos, N. (1998) "The conflict of privacy and transparency" *To Vima*, December 6, 1998: B7.

Alivizatos, N. (2001) "The private life of public persons" in his *The Uncertain*

Modernization Athens, Polis.

Association for the Study of New Hellenism, (1991) "Modern Archives, Files and Historical Research," special issue *Mnimon*, no. 6.

Bourdieu, P. (1999) *Language and Symbolic Power*, Athens, Kardamitsa

Catiforis, G. (1975) *The Barbarians' Legislation*, Athens: Themelio.

Charalambis, D. (1985) The Military and Political Authority: The Power Structure in Post-Civil War Greece, Athens, Exantas.

Charalambis, D. (1989) *Clientelist Relations and Populism: The Extrainstitutional Concensus in the Greek Political System* Athens, Exantas.

Charalambis, D. (1998) *Democracy and Globalization* Athens, S. Karagiorgas Foundation.

Chtouris, S. N. (1989) "The PASOK Populism and the Utopia," *Eleftherotypia* May 8, 1989.

Dafermos, C. (2000) "How private life is filed (sorted) by private initiatives," interview in *To Vima*, Jan. 12: A19.

Dafermos, C. (2000) "Innocent as a pigeon the Security services vis-à-vis the private surveillance," interview in *Ta Nea*, May 20, 2000: 14-15.

Dafermos, C. (2002) "Borrowers and the Teiresias' white lists," interview in the *Economic and Industrial Review*, October 2002.

E.U. The Council (1995) Common Position (EC) No / 95 "On the protection of individuals with regard to the processing of personal data and on the free movement of such data" February 20, 1995.

E.U. (1998) "Greece in the Information Society: Strategies and Actions" in www.primeminister.gr & www.infosociety.gr.

Elefantis, A. (1991) *In the Constellation of Populism*, Athens, O Politis

Elefantis, A (1976) *The Promise of the Impossible Revolution*, Athens: Olkos.

Fakinos, Aris (1995) *Stolen life* Athens, Kastaniotis.

Foucault, M. (1976) *Surveillance and Punishment: The Birth of Prison*, Athens, Rappa.

Greek Parliament's Records: Session O', February 5, 1988;

Greek Parliament's Records: Session ΛΕ', Sept. 12, 1989 and Sept. 20, 1989;

Greek Parliament's Records: Session MA', May 15, 1991.

Hardavellas, C. (1992) "The Files Are in Their Place," *Ta Nea*, Jan. 22, 1992.

Iliou, F. (1990) *The Files*, Athens, Themelio.

Kapetanyiannis, V. (1986) "Populism, Concise Notes for a Critical Re-examination," *O Politis,* Jan.-March.

Konidaris, I. M. (1986) "Theory and Nomology for the Jehovah's Witnesses" *Nomiko Vima,* (May 1986); 34.5.

Kotzias, N. (1984) *The "Third Way" of PASOK* Athens, Synchroni Epochi.

Kouloglou, St. (1986) *In the Traces of the Third Way* Athens, Odysseas.

Koundouros, R. (1978) *The Security of the Regime, 1942-1974* Athens: Kastaniotis.

Koutsoukis, Kl. (1997) *The Pathology of politics: Facets of corruption in modern Greek state* Athens, Papazisis.

Kouvelakis, G. (1994) "Report on the Schengen Agreement" published by *Pontiki,* 12 June 1997: 14.

Lampropoulou, E. (2001) "The Schengen Agreements and internal security," *Poiniki Dikaiosyni,* 2001, vol. 4, no 1.

Lazarides, J. (1979) "The 'Idionym Law: The First Anticommunist Law in the History of Greece" *KOMEP 9* (Sept 1979)

Lazos, Gr. (2001) *Informatics and Crime,* Athens, Nomiki Bibliothiki.

Liakos, A. (1990) "About Populism," *Istorika* no10, June.

Linardatos, S. (1965) *How We Arrived at the 4th of August Regime* Athens: Themelio.

Linardatos, S. (1966) *The 4th of August Regime* Athens: Themelio.

Linardatos, S. (1977) *From the Civil War to the Junta* Athens: Papazisis.

Lipovats, Th. (1989) "Populism: An Analysis from the View of Political Psychology," in Mouzelis, N. et. al. *Populism and Politics,* Athens, Gnosi: 55-61.

Lygeros, St. (1990) *The Syndrome of the Big Patient,* Athens, Stohastis.

Lyrintzis, Chr. (1983) "Between Socialism and Populism: The Rise of PASOK," Ph.D. Dissert., L.S.E.

Makridimitris, A. (1992) *The Organization of Government,* Athens, Sakkoulas.

Makridimitris, A. (2002), *State and Civil Society,* Athens, Metamesonykties Ekdoseis.

Manesis, A. (1979) *Civil Liberties,* vol. 1. Thessaloniki, Sakkoulas.

Manesis, A. (1989) *The Constitutional Reform of 1986,* Thessaloniki, Parateretes.

Meynaud, J. (1973) *The Political Forces in Greece,* Athens: Byron.

Meynaud, J. & Karanicolas, G. (1973) *Rigged Elections in Greece* Athens: Epikairotita.

Mitrou, L. (1999) *The Hellenic Data Protection Authority* Athens, Sakkoulas

Moskof, K. (1979) *History of the Working Class Movement*, Thessaloniki.

Mouzelis, N. (1989) "Populism: A New Way of Mass Integration in the Political Processes" in Mouzelis, N. et al. *Populism and Politics*, Athens, Gnosi.

Mouzelis, N. (2001) *For an Alternative Third Way* Athens, Themelio.

Nikolopoulos, G. (2002) *State, Penal Authority and European Integration*, Athens, Kritiki.

Orwell, G. (1981)*1984* New York, New American Library. Also in Greek, Athens, Kaktos 1978.

Panousis, J. (2000) "Big Brother and his own Brothers," *Revmata*, Autumn, no. 6.

Papademetriou, Z. (1988) "The Modernization of Public Administration; The Informatics' Impact on the State-Citizens' Relationship, *Dioikitiki Metarrythmisi* no. 36, October-December: 19-29.

Papademetriou, Z. (2000) *The European Racism*. Athens: Ellinika Grammata.

Papadopoulos, A. M. (1999) *Terms of Personal Data Protection: The case of SIS*, Athens, Sakkoulas A.

Papadopoulou, L. (2001) "The end of privacy," *Eleftherotypia*, August 13th.

Papagaryfalou, P. (2002) *Populism in Greece*, Ergo.

Papahelas A., Telloglou T. *File 17 November*, Athens, Estia

Papakonstantis G. (1998) *The Schengen Agreements*, Athens, Basic Documents.

Papakonstantis G. (2003) *The Greek Police: Organization, Politics and Ideology*, Athens, Sakkoulas A.

Papanthimos, A. (1991) *Avrianism, The Present Face of Fascism*, Athens, O Politis.

Papayiannis D. I. (2001) *The European Space of Liberty, Security and Justice*, Athens, Sakkoulas A.

Pashos, G. (1986) "Towards a 'Security State,'" *O Politis* no. 75, October, pp. 29-31.

Perakis, St., ed. (1998) "A Space for Freedom, Security and Justice in EU" in Stefanou, K., Fatourou, A. et al., eds. *Introduction to European Studies*, Athens, Sideris.

Ploritis, M. (2001) "The Big Brothers and the Biggest" in *To Vima*, June 3: A60.

Pollis, A. (1999) "Greece: A problematic secular state" in Christopoulos, D.

(ed.) *Legal Issues of Religious Otherness in Greece*, KEMO, Kritiki.

Pollis, A. (1988) *State, Law and Human Rights in Greece*, Athens, Foundation for Mediterranean Studies.

Psyroukis, N. (1975) *History of Contemporary Greece*, 1940-1967 Athens.

Robins, K. and Webster, Fr. (2000) *Times of the Technoculture*, Athens, Kastaniotis.

Rowat, D. C. (1984) "The Right of Access to Governmental Information in Modern Democracies," translated in Greek by Spanou, K. *Dioikitiki Metarrythmisi* no. 19, July-Sept.: 5-24.

Sakelariou, N. (1995) *The Schengen Information System*, Sakkkoulas, Athens.

Samatas, M. (2003b) "Security, Freedom and Democracy, under the Schengen Agreement" *Hellenic Review of Political Science*, vol. 22 December 2003: 106-144.

Samatas, M. (2003c) "For a Sociology of Surveillance: From panopticism to an antisurveillance movement," Sociology conference by the "Greek Sociological Association" University of Thessaloniki, Conference Minutes on CDROM.

Samatas, M. (2005) "Surveillance development in Greece: From State to Suprastate and market surveillance," in Maratou-Alimpranti, L.et. all *Social developments in Modern Greece*, Athens, EKKE (in print).

Simitis, Sp. (1999) An interview in *Eleftherotypia*'s special section on The Schengen Agreement, April 3 p. 9.

Simitis, Sp. (1999b) "All of us we are under surveillance," interview with Nasopoulos, D. 21st c. Faces *Ta Nea*, November 20.

Simonidis, A. (2001) "A Terrible Present; A report of privacy violation" http://flashfiles.flash.gr/technology/Rid7/article.asp.

Skiadopoulos, A. (1981) "Files: How and By Whom," *Ta Nea*, 13 April.

Smaili, L. (1986) "Are Firings Occurring for Political Reasons?" (in Greek) *Oikonomikos*, Dec. 4, 1986.

Sotirhou, J., ed. (1999) "The Schengen Agreement" *Eleftherotypia*, Special section, 3 April.

Spourdalakis, M., ed. (1998) *PASOK: Party, State, Society* Athens, Pataki

Spourdalakis, M. (1989) "The Greek Populism in Conditions of Authoritarian Statism," in Mouzelis, N. et. al. *Populism and Politics*, Athens, Gnosi: 74-76.

Toumasatos, K. (2000) *The Schengen Agreement.* Athens: Synhroni Epohi.

Tsakirakis, Sr. (2001) "Privacy by Force," *Eleftherotypia*, July 5.

Tsiantzis, D. (2001) "A market for Privacy," *Eleftherotypia*, May 9.

Tsoucalas, C. (1986) *The State, Society, Work in Postwar Greece* Athens, Themelio.

Velitzelou, G. and Livada, E. (1987) "EKAM, a New Institution in the Greek Reality," *O Politis*, no. 78, April: 23-28.

Votsis, G. (1989) "They Have Only Burnt the (paper) Files" in *Eleftherotypia*, Sept. 4.

Voulgaris, G. (2001) *Post-dictatorial Greece: 1974-1990*, Athens, Themelio.

Vournas, T. (1981) *History of Contemporary Greece: The Civil War* Athens, Tolidis Bros.

Zouvelos, M. (1980) "A Damoclean Sword," *To Vima*, 26 Oct. 1980.

INDEX

Exhibit 1

ΕΛΛΗΝΙΚΗ ΧΩΡΟΦΥΛΑΚΗ
ΣΤΑΘΜΟΣ ΧΩΡΟΦΥΛΑΚΗΣ ....

ΠΕΡ. ΧΡΗΣΕΩΣ

'Εν.......... τῆ   197

'Αριθ. πρωτ. P12 .....

ΠΡΟΣ

ΤΟ ΑΣΤΥΝΟΜΙΚΟΝ ΤΜΗΜΑ............ ......

ΕΙΣ ....

ΘΕΜΑ : "Κοινωνικὰ φρονήματα καὶ ἐν γένει διαγωγὴ τοῦ τ . ...

....•..

. .   ..•.—

ΣΧΕΤ.: 'Υπ' ἀριθ._____ .... ἀπό ..   .. 'Υμετέρα

Λαμβάνω τὴν τιμήν, εἰς ἐκτέλεσιν τῆς ὑπερθεν σχετικῆς διαταγῆς
ὑμῶν, νὰ ἀναφέρω ἐν σχέσει μὲ τὸ ἐν θέματι ἀντικείμενον τὰ κάτωθι :

Α΄ ΠΛΗΡΟΦΟΡΙΑΙ ΠΕΡΙ ΤΟΥ ΙΔΙΟΥ

—Οὗτος κατὰ τὸ ἀπὸ   ἕως   χρονικὸν διάστημα καθ' ὅ διέμενεν
ἐν τῇ περιφερείᾳ ἡμῶν, δὲν ἀπησχόλησεν τὴν Ὑπηρεσίαν μου ἀπὸ ἀντεθνικῆς ἤ ἄλλης
τινός πλευρᾶς, ἐνεφορεῖτο ὑπὸ ὑγιῶν κοινωνικῶν φρονημάτων καὶ ἐτύγχανεν ἄτομον
καλῆς ἐν γένει διαγωγῆς.

Β΄ ΠΛΗΡΟΦΟΡΙΑΙ ΠΕΡΙ ΤΩΝ ΜΕΛΩΝ ΤΗΣ ΟΙΚΟΓΕΝΕΙΑΣ ΤΟΥ

—'Ωσαύτως καὶ τὰ μέλη τῆς οἰκογενείας του δὲν ἀπησχόλησαν μέχρι σήμερον τὴν Ὑ-
πηρεσίαν μου ἀπὸ ἀντεθνικῆς ἤ ἄλλης τινός πλευρᾶς, ἐμφορουμένων ἀπάντων ὑπὸ ὑγιῶν κοινωνικῶν φρονημάτων καὶ καλῆς ἐν γένει διαγωγῆς.

. .   .   .   .   .

....

. . ..

'Ο
Διοικητής τοῦ Σταθμοῦ

This exhibit is the Civic-Mindedness Certificate. It was issued by the chief of the local police station for the superior district police authorities, concerning (literally translated) "The social convictions and the overall behavior" of a citizen. In paragraph A, "Information About Himself," it states "He, from (date) until (date), when he was living in that police station's region, did not bother the authorities through any kind of antinational or other actions, and was inspired by healthy social convictions and was of overall good personal conduct." Also in paragraph B, "Information About His Family Members," it makes the same kind of statement for all of them.

Exhibit 2

Κ.Υ.Π.
Β΄ ΚΛΑΔΟΣ ΑΠΟΡΡΗΤΟΝ

α.α. Δελτίου (4)

α.α.α. 1

ΑΤΟΜΙΚΟΝ ΔΕΛΤΙΟΝ ΠΛΗΡΟΦΟΡΙΩΝ

Τοῦ ~~████████████~~

1 ΒΙΟΓΡΑΦΙΚΑ ΣΤΟΙΧΕΙΑ

Όνομα πατρός ή συζύγου ....,μητ. ός ....

Έτος γεννήσεως   1922

Τόπος γεννήσεως   ..... - .....

Παρούσα διαμονή   .....

2. ΕΠΑΓΓΕΛΜΑΤΙΚΑ ΣΤΟΙΧΕΙΑ

Βαθμός

Θέσις ήν κατέχει   Συνεικαλι..τής - 'Αντι... έ....ς ... Υ.. έντι........

Μόρφωσις

3 ΠΛΗΡΟΦΟΡΙΑΚΑ ΣΤΟΙΧΕΙΑ

(Χαρακτήρ· ήθος. 'Αντεθνική· Πολιτική δράσις. Κοινωνικός· Ιδιωτικός βίος. Επαγγελματική
Ικανότης. ΛΟΙΠΑ ΣΤΟΙΧΕΙΑ):

a. .....

   (1) Κατά τήν κατοχήν ἀνεμίχθη εἰς τήν .....,ἄνευ ἀρί....

   (2) 'Απέσχε τῶν ἐ...ιῶν τοῦ ἔτους 1946.

   (3) Ὑπηρέτησε εἰς τὸ ....ευμα κατά τὰ ἔτη 1947-1948,ἔλαβε
μέρος εἰς τάς ..... τῶν Κ/Σ ἐπι....ρ? εἰς καὶ ἐτιμήθη διά
Πολεμικοῦ Σταυροῦ.

   (4) Τό ἔτος 1950 ἐξεηλώθη ὑπέρ τῆς ".....".

   (5) Ἀπεχαρακτηρίσθη τό ἔτος 1955.

   (6) Μετά τήν 21-4-67,ἐκτελοῦται δι... τῆς 'Γκινα....

b. .....

   (1) 'Επιβεβαιοῦνται τά ἀνωτέρω ἐν ....,3α,πλήν τοῦ ἐδάφ.(4).

   (2) 'Από τοῦ ἀποχαρακτηρισμοῦ του διήγει ἐννομι...ς.

Σελ.1 ἐκ Σελ.2

ΑΠΟΡΡΗΤΟΝ

ΑΠΟΡΡΗΤΟΝ

INDIVIDUAL INFORMATION FORM
GREEK CENTRAL INTELLIGENCE

(Translation on following page)

KYP

INDIVIDUAL INFORMATION CARD

Of . . . . (Name)

1. Biographical Data

2. Occupational Data

3. Informational Data

Character-Ethos, Antinational Political Activity, Social-Private Life,
Occupational Skills, etc.

    a. Information from Official Sources

        1. During the (Nazi) Occupation he got involved in EPON
(leftist organization), took no action.

        2. Abstained from the elections of the year 1946 (like all
leftists)

        3. He served in the military during 1947-1948, participated
in military actions against the K/S (Communist Guerillas)
and he was awarded a military star.

        4. In the year 1950 he declared himself in favor of the
"Democratic Front"

        5. In 1955 he was no longer characterized as leftist (he was
destigmatized)

        6. After 21 April 1967 he declared himself in favor of the
Revolution (i.e. the Military Dictatorship)

    b. Information from Third Sources

        1. The above are confirmed except 3a#4

        2. Since his destigmatization he lives like a nationalist
minded (ethnicofron)

Source: *TA NEA*, May 7, 1984 (parenthetical explanations mine)

Exhibit 3

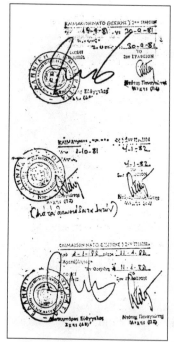

These are copies of the police report to the military information office, regarding a conscript who is described as an "activist in a political party youth organization of ultra-extremist ideologies" during his residence in Saloniki from November 18, 1978 to May 16, 1980. The military information office has sent copies to the NATO division of Saloniki which have been updated from September 19, 1981 to April 11, 1982.

Source: *Rizospastis*, July 25, 1982.

Exhibit 4

POLICE REPORT TO DRAFT BOARD

ΣΤΟΙΧΕΙΑ	
ΠΡΟΤΑΣΕΙΣ	**ΑΠΑΝΤΗΣΕΙΣ**
Α. ΣΤΟΙΧΕΙΑ ΠΕΡΙ ΤΟΥ ΑΤΟΜΟΥ ΤΟΥ	
1. Ποία ἡ οἰκονομική του κατάστασις;	Μετρία
2. Ἀνεμείχθη εἰς Ὀργανώσεις; α. Εἰς ποίας; β. Πότε; γ. Ἐπί πόσον χρόνον; δ. Ποίο ἡ ἀναπτυχθεῖσα ὀρᾶσις του;	Ὄχι
3.α. Ἐξεδηλώθη ἤ ἐκδηλοῦται ὑπέρ ἀνατρεπτικῶν ἤ ἐξτρεμιστικῶν ὀργανώσεων ἤ θεωριῶν; β. Ἀναγιγνώσκει ἔντυπα ἀνατρεπτικοῦ περιεχομένου καί ποῖα; γ. Συναναστρέφεται ἄτομα ἀνατρεπτικῶν ἤ ἐξτρεμιστικῶν πεποιθήσεων;	Ὄχι
4.α. Συναναστρέφεται ἄτομα ὑπόπτου ἤθους; β. Ῥέπει εἰς κακάς ἕξεις; καί ποίας; γ. Ποιεῖται χρῆσιν ναρκωτικῶν ἤ ἡδυνιστικῶν οὐσιῶν ἤ οἰνοπνευματωδῶν ποτῶν; δ. Τυγχάνει ἰσχυροῦ χαρ/ρος;	Ὄχι. Τυγχάνει ἰσχυροῦ χαρακτῆρος
Β. ΠΕΡΙ ΤΗΣ ΟΙΚΟΓΕΝΕΙΑΣ ΤΟΥ	
5. Ποία ἡ οἰκογενειακή κατάστασις;	Τυγχάνει ἄγαμος
6. Ἀνεμείχθησαν οἱ γονεῖς καί ἀδελφοί εἰς ὀργανώσεις; α. Ποίας; β. Πότε; γ. Ἐπί πόσον χρόνον; δ. Ποία ἡ ἀναπτυχθεῖσα ὀρᾶσις των;	Ὄχι
7. Ἀπηυθύνθη κατ' αὐτῶν καμ(μ)ία κατηγορία; Μέ ποίας συνεπείας;	Ὄχι
8α. Ὑπῆρξαν χαρακτηρισμένοι δι' ἀνατρεπτικήν ἤ ἐξτρεμιστικήν δρᾶσιν ἤ θεωρίαν; β. Ἀπεχαρακτηρίσθησαν καί πότε; γ. Ποία ἡ μετά τόν ἀποχ/σμόν διαγωγή των;	Ὄχι
9. Οἱ ἀνωτέρω ἀσκοῦν ἐπιρροήν ἐπί τοῦ ἀνατασσομένου;	Ναί
10. Ὑπάρχουν ἕτερα πρόσωπα ἐπηρεάζοντα τόν ὑποψήφιον; Ἐκ'ον. ἤ... Ὑπὀχον λόγω εἱξειμῶν συνθηκῶν (Ἐφ' ὅσον ἀφορᾶ Ὑποψήφιον' Ἀξκῶν π. Ὑξκῶν)	—
11. Ποῖαι λοιπαί χρήσιμοι πληροφορ. διά τήν διαγωγήν τοῦ ὑ/οσιν ατόμου καί τοῦ ἀμέσου οἰκογ. του περιβάλλοντος;	Ὁ ὑποψήφιος ... ἀνήκει εἰς τάς πλέον ... οἰκογ. του ... καί ... ὑπό τοῦ κόσμου αὐτοῦ.
12. Πόσον τό ἐν λόγῳ ἄτομον ὅσον καί τά μέλη τῆς οἰκ/νείας του εἶναι ἤ ὑπῆρξαν μέλη θρησκευτικῆς τινός αἱρέσεως; (χιλιασταί κλπ.)	Ὄχι

TRANSLATION OF EXHIBIT 4: THE CONTENT OF SUCH POLICE REPORT TO THE MILITARY DRAFT BOARD

A reading of the following translated questionnaire—Exhibit 4—the police report to the draft board for registration of conscripts, speaks for itself. It reveals the spirit of the entire surveillance mechanism and some of the criteria used to stigmatize citizens.

Translation of Questionnaire "Police Report to Draft Board"

INFORMATION — DATA

Questions	Answers
A. INFORMATION ABOUT THE PERSON	
1. What is his economic situation?	Average
2. Has he been involved in organizations? a. Which? b. When? c. How long? d. What are his activities?	No
3a. Has he expressed himself now or in the past in favor of subversive or extremist organizations or theories?	
b. Is he reading subversive publications, and which?	
c. Is he associated (keep company with) with individuals of subversive or extremist beliefs?	
4a. Is he associated with morally suspicious individuals?	No
b. Is he inclined to bad habits? Which?	
c. Is he taking drugs or any kind of stimulants, or alcoholic beverages?	
d. Has he a strong character?	He has a strong character

(continued on next page)

INFORMATION — DATA

Questions	Answers
B. ABOUT HIS FAMILY	
5. What is his family status? (single or married?)	He is unmarried
6. Have his parents and brothers participated in organizations?	No
7. Have they been accused of anything?	No
8. a. Have they been characterized as following extremist action or theory?	No
b. Have they been stigmatized (ideologically) and when?	No
c. What was their behavior after destigmatization?	
9. Are the above parents or brothers influential on the individual under consideration?	Yes
10. Are there any other persons who influence the candidate officer or sub-officer, due to special conditions? (This question is in the case of officer candidates)	
11. What other useful information regarding the conduct of the individual under consideration and his immediate family environment?	He has expressed himself and so have his parents in favor of PASOK and vote in favor of that party
12. Are the mentioned individual and his family members of any religious sect or have they been in the past? (Jehovah's Witnesses, etc.)	No

The following selection of police records published in the Greek press and discussed in Parliament in January 1980 shows that the files were kept not only for those who were stigmatized as communists but also for those who had "healthy social beliefs," but read newspapers supporting the opposition, or they had dead communist relatives, etc.

Exhibit 5

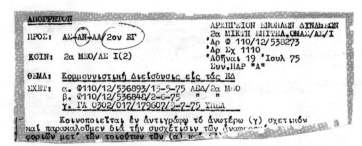

ΑΠΟΡΡΗΤΟΝ

ΑΡΧΗΓΕΙΟΝ ΕΝΟΠΛΩΝ ΔΥΝΑΜΕΩΝ
2α ΜΙΚΤΗ ΕΠΙΤΕΛ.ΟΜΑΣ/ΑΣ/Ι

ΠΡΟΣ: ΑΣ-ΑΝ-ΛΑ/2ον ΕΓ
'Αρ Φ 110/12/538273
'Αρ Σχ 1110

ΚΟΙΝ: 2α ΜΕΟ/ΛΣ Ι(2)
'Αθῆναι 19 'Ιουλ 75
Συν.ΠΑΡ "Α"

ΘΕΜΑ: Κομμουνιστικὴ Διείσδυσις εἰς τὰς ΕΔ

ΣΧΕΤ: α. Φ110/12/536893/15-5-75 ΛΕΑ/2α ΜΕΟ
β. Φ110/12/536848/2-6-75 "   "
γ. ΓΑ 0302/017/179607/3-7-75 ΥΠΕΑ

Κοινοποιεῖται ἐν ἀντιγράφῳ τὸ ἀνωτέρω (γ) σχετικὸν
καὶ παρακαλοῦμεν διὰ τὴν συσχέτισιν τῶν ἀναφο...
φοριῶν μετ' τῶν τοιούτων τῶν (α) κ...

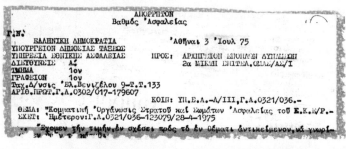

ΑΠΟΡΡΗΤΟΝ
Βαθμὸς 'Ασφαλείας

Γ.Ν.
ΕΛΛΗΝΙΚΗ ΔΗΜΟΚΡΑΤΙΑ   'Αθῆναι 3 'Ιουλ 75
ΥΠΟΥΡΓΕΙΟΝ ΔΗΜΟΣΙΑΣ ΤΑΞΕΩΣ
ΥΠΗΡΕΣΙΑ ΕΘΝΙΚΗΣ ΑΣΦΑΛΕΙΑΣ   ΠΡΟΣ: ΑΡΧΗΓΕΙΟΝ ΕΝΟΠΛΩΝ ΔΥΝΑΜΕΩΝ
ΔΙΕΥΘΥΝΣΙΣ Α   2α ΜΙΚΤΗ ΕΠΙΤΕΛ.ΟΜΑΣ/ΑΣ/Ι
ΤΜΗΜΑ   1ον
ΓΡΑΦΕΙΟΝ   1ον
Ταχ.Δ/νσις Ελ.Βενιζέλου 9-Τ.Τ.133
ΑΡΙΘ.ΠΡΩΤ.Γ.Α.0302/017-179607
                                                       ΚΟΙΝ: ΥΠ.Ε.Α.-Α/ΙΙΙ,Γ.Α.0321/036.-

ΘΕΜΑ: "Κομματικὴ 'Οργάνωσις Στρατοῦ καὶ Σωμάτων 'Ασφαλείας τοῦ Κ.Κ.Ε/Ρ.-
ΣΧΕΤ: Ἡμέτερον:Γ.Α.0321/036-123079/28-4-1975

Ἔχομεν τὴν τιμὴν,ἐν σχέσει πρὸς τὸ ἐν θέματι ἀντικείμενον,νὰ γνωρί-
...

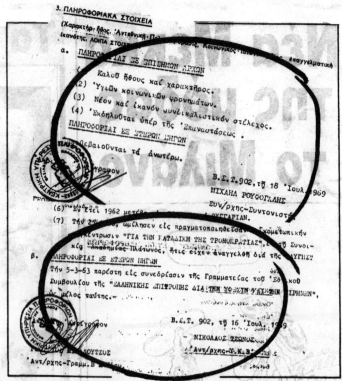

Exhibit 6

An Anthology of "Howevers"

● ● Οὗτος ἐχε· κοινγορηθει
γιὰ παράθαση τοῦ ορθεου 372
τοῦ Π.Κ. (κλοπη) γιὰ δευτερη
φορὰ... Πλὴν ὅμως κατάγεται
από οἰκογενεια ὑγ.ων ἐθνικων
φρονημάτων...ν. (,Από τὸν φα·
κελο Χ. Ν., κατοίκου Θεσσαλο·
νίκης –ἀριθ. πρωτ. 68)224670).

1. "He has been convicted for the violation of the article 372 of the Penal
Code (theft) for the second time. . . .
However he comes from a family of
healthy social virtues. . . ."

● ●... Οὗτος ὁ.ο̣μ̣ἐνει ε.ς Ἀθηνας
ἀπὸ τῆς γεννηςεὡς του μεχ;·
ονμεφον, μετὰ τῆς χηρος μη·
τρος του καὶ τῆς ὁδελφης ιου
Μαρθας, κωρὶς να ἀποσχολησn
την ὑπηρεσιαν ἡμῶν ὁφ· οιοσ·
δηποτε πλευρας. Πλην ομως
ἀπαντες ἀναγιγνωσκουν τὴν ε·
φημεριδα ΕΛΕΥΘΕΡΟΤΥΠΙΑ...ν.
(Από τὸν φακελο του κ. Νικ.
Μπούμπαλη, ὁδὸς Εὐβοιας 37 –
ἀριθ. 642171)Γ)105. Πρόκειται
γιὰ μία μόνο ἐνδεικτικὴ περι·
πτωση – ὅπως θὰ δοῦμε κατό·
πιν – εφακελωματοςο με σια.·
κελο τὴν ἀνάγνωση ἐφημερι·
δων τῆς Ἀντιπολιτεύσεως –
ΤΑ ΝΕΑ, ΑΥΓΗ, ΡΙΖΟΣΠΑΣΤΗΣ,
κλπ.).

2. ". . . He lives since his birth in Athens
with his widow mother and his sister,
without bothering our department
(the police) in any way. However, all
of them read the daily *Eleftherotypia*
. . ." (According to the source, there
are also other police reports regarding readers of the dailies *Ta Nea*,
Aygi, *Rizospastis*, etc.)

● ●Ὁ ἴδιος καὶ ἅπαντα τὰ μέλη
τῆς πατρικῆς του οἰκογενείας
διαμένουν: εἰς Μανδηλιον
Σερρῶν καὶ διαφορούνται παρ'
ὑγιῶν κοινωνικῶν φρονημά·
των. Πλὴν ὅμως ὁ παππούς
του Χρ. Μητσιωτικος, πού ἀ·
πεθιωσε τὸ ἔτος 1975, ἐτύγ·
χανε κομμουνιστὴς ΑΛΦΑ κα·
τηγοριας. (Από τὸ φακελο
του ἐγγονοῦ Νικολάου Σιώπη
του Ἡρακλῆ, ἀριθ. 12.828).

3. "He and all his family members are
living in Mandili of Serres and have
healthy social beliefs. However, their
grandfather H. M. who died in 1975
was a communist Alpha type."

● ●...Ουτος καὶ τὰ μέλη τῆς οἰ·
κογενείας του δὲν μᾶς ἀπα·
σχόλησαν... Πλὴν ὅμως ὁ
θείος του Τσέτογλου Δημή·
τρ.ος τοῦ Ἰωάννου, συναναν·
στρέφεται κατὰ προτίμησιν
ἀριστερούς ὁμοχωρίους τους..
(Από τὸ φακελο του ἀνιψ:οῦ
θεμιστ. Τσέτογλου, κατοίκου
Κρηνιδος).

4. ". . . He and his family members have
not bothered us. . . . However, his
uncle T. D. prefers to associate with
leftist fellow villagers. . . ."

Exhibit 6 (cont.)

AN ANTHOLOGY OF "HOWEVERS"

● «... Εἰς τὸ Ἄργος, οὗτος ἐνυμ-
φεύθη μετὰ γυναικὸς τῆς ὁποί-
ος ὁ πατὴρ τυγχάνει μέλος
κόμματος ἀκραίων πολιτικῶν
τάσεων (ΠΑΣΟΚ) καὶ ἐντεῦθεν
ὁ ἐν θέματι ἐκδηλοῦται ὑπὲρ
τοῦ ἰδίου κόμματος, παρασυρ-
θεὶς ὑπὸ τοῦ πενθεροῦ του...».
('Απὸ τὸν φάκελο τοῦ ὑπαλ-
λήλου τοῦ ΟΤΕ 'Αργους, Χρή-
στου Τσαρούχη).

5. "... In Argos he got married with a woman whose father is a member of an extremist trends party (PASOK), and ever since he expresses himself in favor of the same party, influenced by his father-in-law...."

● «...Οὗτος συναναστρέφεται τὸν
κομμουνιστὴ ΓΑΜΜΑ κατηγορί-
ας Νικόλαο Μπιτζῆλο καὶ πιστεύεται ὅτι εἰς τὰς ἑκάστοτε
βουλευτικὰς ἐκλογας, παρασυ-
ρόμενος παρ' αὐτοῦ ψηφίζει
τὴν ἀριστερὰν παράταξιν...»
(ἀπὸ τὸν φάκελο Κων. Σ.οσιου,
Κρηνίδα).

6. "... He keeps company with a communist, Gamma type ... and it is believed that he is voting in every election for the left, influenced by his friend."

● «...Διὰ τοῦτον οὐδεμίαν συμπε-
ρὴ πληροφορίαν ἔχομεν. 'Ο πα-
τέρας του 'Απόστολος Μοδεμ-
λῆς, κατὰ τὸ παρελθὸν φέρε-
ται ὡς συμπαθῶν τὴν ἀριστερὰν, ἄνευ συγκεκριμένης δρά-
σεως ἢ ἀναμίξεώς του. Εἶναι ἐ-
πιφυλακτικὸς καὶ ἀνεκδήλωτος
διάγει φιλησύχως καὶ νομοτα-
γῶς καὶ δὲν μας ἀπησχόλησε
ἀπὸ οἰασδήποτε πλευρᾶς. Εἰς
τὰς προσφάτους βουλευτικὰς
ἐκλογας, πιστεύεται ὅτι ἐψήφι-
σε ὑπὲρ τῆς ΝΔ ἢ τῆς ΕΔΗΚ... »
(ἀπὸ τὸν φάκελο Θωμᾶ Μοδεμ-
λῆ, κατοίκου Αλ.στεσιας — α-
ριθμ. 12767).

7. "About him we have no information whatsoever. His father A.M. (however) in the past was considered a leftist sympathizer without concrete action or involvement. He is cautious and has not expressed himself; he is living quietly and loyally and he hasn't bothered us. In the recent elections it is believed that he voted either N.D. or EDIK...."

Source: VIMA, March 29, 1981

Exhibit 7

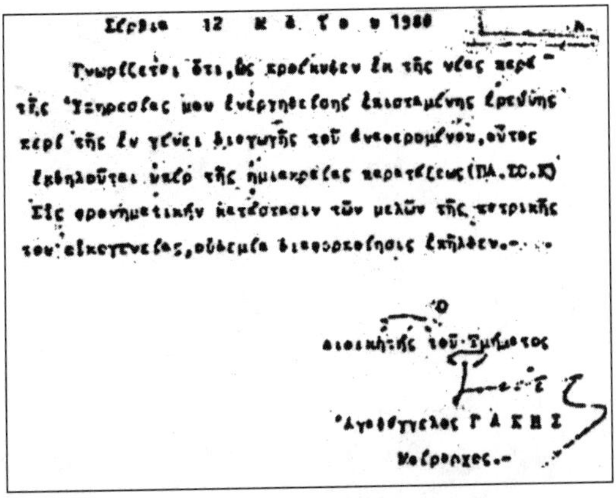

A. Servia 12 May 1980

It is known that, as is shown by the thorough investigation which was conducted by my department regarding the overall conduct of the aforementioned individual, he has declared in favor of the semi-extreme array (PASOK). In his family members' loyalty status, no alteration has occurred.

Source: *Avriani* Sept. 17, 1981

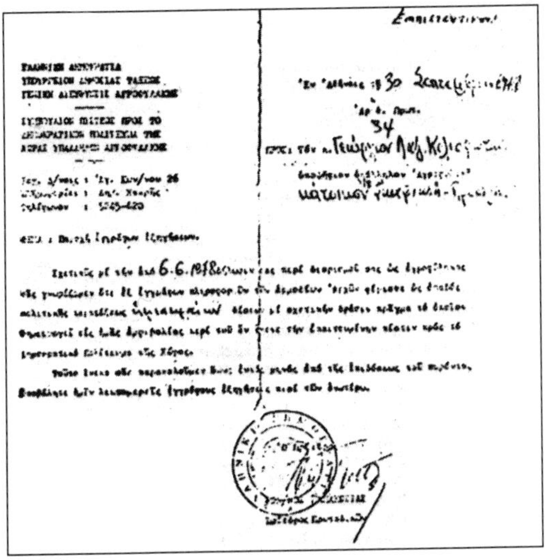

B.   Confidential
      Athens 30 Sept. 1978

(LOYALTY) COUNCIL (CHECKING) THE FAITH
IN THE DEMOCRATIC SYSTEM OF THE COUNTRY
OF THE AGRICULTURAL POLICE PERSONNEL

Regarding your (loyalty) statement on 6.6.1978 for your appointment as an agricultural guard, we inform you that from written information of the pertinent authorities you are considered a follower of a political array of semi-extreme positions and related activity, something which causes us doubts whether you have the required faith in the Democratic System of the Country.

Source: *Avriani* Sept. 15, 1986

Exhibit 8

Exhibit 9

Έτσι φακελώνει το ΓΕΣ

```
ΑΓΜ : 11945990274
ΕΠΩΝΥΜΟΝ : ΑΘΥΒΙΑΚΗΣ        ΓΕΩΡΓΙΟΣ  ΚΩΝΙΤ ΕΥΑ
ΕΤΠΟ : 832                              ΩΒΑΘ : 12      ΒΑΘΜΟΙ : 21
ΠΕΡΙΑΑΛ ΥΠΗΡΕΣ.: ΚΕΥΓ-ΓΟΑ               ΜΑΣΚΑ : 1000001010

Α/Α : Ν Α Σ Κ Α  ΥΠΗΡΣΡΗΜΙΑΣ          Π Α Ρ Α Τ Η Ρ Η Σ Ε Ι Σ
 1  : 1000000010 : 01/06/83 : ΣΧΕΤΙΚΟ : 403241/17-5-83/ΚΥΒ/ΑΙΘ/83
    :           :          : ΠΕΡΙΓΡΑΦΗ: ΕΠΙΤΡΟΠΗ ΓΙΑ ΤΟ ΣΤΡΑΤΟ.
 2  : 1000000000 : 02/06/83 : ΣΧΕΤΙΚΟ : 2201/2-72295/23-5-83/ΥΒΕΑ
    :           :          : ΠΕΡΙΓΡΑΦΗ:
 3  : 1000000310 : 01/08/83 : ΣΧΕΤΙΚΟ : 403241/17-5-83/ΚΥΟ/ΑΙΘ/83
    :           :          : ΠΕΡΙΓΡΑΦΗ: ΣΤΕΛΕΧΟΣ ΤΗΣ ΕΠΙΤΡΟΠΗΣ ΓΙΑ ΤΟ ΣΤΡΑΤΟ.
 4  : 1000001010 : 24/11/83 : ΣΧΕΤΙΚΟ : 408653/19-11-83/ΚΥΣ/ΑΙΘ./83
    :           :          : ΠΕΡΙΓΡΑΦΗ:
```

```
ΑΓΜ : 14714806476
ΕΠΩΝΥΜΟΝ : ΚΑΝΑΠΟΝΚΑΣ      ΤΟΤΗΡΙΟΣ  ΓΕΩΡΓ ΑΡΓ
ΕΤΠΟ : 833                              ΩΒΑΘ : 11      ΒΑΘΜΟΙ : 21
ΠΕΡΙΑΑΛ ΥΠΗΡΕΣ.: 647 ΙΤΣ                ΜΑΣΚΑ : 1110001040

Α/Α : Ν Α Σ Κ Α  ΙΠΤΙΡΟΡΗΜΙΑΣ          Π Α Ρ Α Τ Η Ρ Η Σ Ε Ι Σ
 1  : 1110001000 : 28/06/83 : ΣΧΕΤΙΚΟ : 3201/2-19701/24-6-83/ΥΒΕΑ
    :           :          : ΠΕΡΙΓΡΑΦΗ: ΣΣΤΡΕΜΙΣΤΗΣ.
```

```
ΑΓΜ : 10000802483
ΕΠΩΝΥΜΟΝ : ΜΠΥΚΑΣ          ΚΩΝΣΤΑΝΤΙΝ ΣΥΑΓΓ ΕΡΡ
ΕΤΠΟ : 874                              ΩΒΑΘ : 11      ΒΑΘΜΟΙ : 20
ΠΕΡΙΑΑΛ ΥΠΗΡΕΣ.: 583 ΤΠ                 ΜΑΣΚΑ : 1110000900

Α/Α : Ν Α Σ Κ Α  ΙΠΗΕΡΟΡΗΜΙΑΣ          Π Α Ρ Α Τ Η Ρ Η Σ Ε Ι Σ
 1  : 1000000900 : 12/10/83 : ΣΧΕΤΙΚΟ : Σ ΕΓ/1Α
    :           :          : ΠΕΡΙΓΡΑΦΗ: ΔΗΜΟΣΙΕΥΑΑ ΣΤΟΙΡ'.
 2  : 1110000900 : 23/11/83 : ΣΧΕΤΙΚΟ : 127.41/48/1887/6-10-83/88 ΑΑΙΕ
    :           :          : ΠΕΡΙΓΡΑΦΗ:
```

```
ΑΓΜ : 19912363284
ΕΠΩΝΥΜΟΝ : ΚΑΤΥΛΑΤΗΣ       ΝΙΚΟΛΑΟΣ  ΧΡΗΣΤ ΘΑΣ
ΕΤΠΟ : 733                              ΩΒΑΘ : 11      ΒΑΘΜΟΙ : 21
ΠΕΡΙΑΑΛ ΥΠΗΡΕΣ.:                        ΜΑΣΚΑ : 1000000900

Α/Α : Ν Α Σ Κ Α  ΥΠΗΡΣΡΗΜΙΑΣ          Π Α Ρ Α Τ Η Ρ Η Σ Ε Ι Σ
 1  : 1000000000 : 07/07/83 : ΣΧΕΤΙΚΟ : Σ ΕΓ
    :           :          : ΠΕΡΙΓΡΑΦΗ: ΑΝΑΚΙΝΗΣΙΣ ΚΑΤΑ ΤΗΣΚΟΥ.ΚΡΑΝΟΣ ΜΕ ΣΝ ΠΡΑ
    :           :          : ΣΗ ΕΟΤΕ ΓΙΑ ΓΟΛΕΜΟΣ.
```

```
ΑΓΜ : 10700792276
ΕΠΩΝΥΜΟΝ : ΤΑΣΙΓΙΑΝΝΑΚΟΡΟΥΛΟΣ ΔΗΜΗΤΡΙΟΣ ΠΑΝΑΓ ΠΑΓ
ΕΤΠΟ : 733                              ΩΒΑΘ : 23      ΒΑΘΜΟΙ : 21
ΠΕΡΙΑΑΛ ΥΠΗΡΕΣ.: ΣΤΡΑΤ-Ν ΕΠΙΤΡΕΠΙΙΝ    ΜΑΣΚΑ : 1030000000

Α/Α : Ν Α Σ Κ Α  ΥΠΗΤΡΟΡΗΜΙΑΣ          Π Α Ρ Α Τ Η Ρ Η Σ Ε Ι Σ
 1  : 1000000000 : 13/03/83 : ΣΧΕΤΙΚΟ : 100/67/30006Ο/Σ.196/4-5-83/Σ64
    :           :          : ΠΕΡΙΓΡΑΦΗ: ΑΝΑΓΝΩΣΙΜ ΤΣΤΙΝ ΣΤΟ ΣΤΡΑΤ.
```

```
ΑΓΜ : 14714804301
ΕΠΩΝΥΜΟΝ : ΣΑΚΙΣ           ΜΙΧΑΗΛ  ΚΟΣΤΑ ΑΙΚ
ΕΤΠΟ : 823                              ΩΒΑΘ : 19      ΒΑΘΜΟΙ : 21
ΠΕΡΙΑΑΛ ΥΠΗΡΕΣ.: ΣΣΤΗΜΑ ΣΟΑ             ΜΑΣΚΑ : 1120000000

Α/Α : Ν Α Σ Κ Α  ΙΗΙΕΡΟΡΗΜΙΑΣ          Π Α Ρ Α Τ Η Ρ Η Σ Ε Ι Σ
 1  : 1000000000 : 07/03/83 : ΣΧΕΤΙΚΟ : ***********************
    :           :          : ΠΕΡΙΓΡΑΦΗ: ***********************
 2  : 1120000000 : 07/03/83 : ΣΧΕΤΙΚΟ : Σ ΕΓ/7-3-83
    :           :          : ΠΕΡΙΓΡΑΦΗ: ΣΥΓΥΡΟΣ ΤΟΥ ΒΟΥΛΑΓΑ ΣΗΤΗΣ ΛΑΣΙΑ ΕΠΙΣΚΕΦ
    :           :          :           ΣΣΕ3 446/16/638007335/19-7-83/ΣΨΕ ΘΚ/1 ΕΡ
```

```
ΑΓΜ : 11715742770
ΕΠΩΝΥΜΟΝ : ΜΑΝΟΥΣΑΚΗΣ      ΓΕΩΡΓΙΟΣ  ΜΙΧΑΗ ΠΑΡ
ΕΤΠΟ : 834                              ΩΒΑΘ : 12      ΒΑΘΜΟΙ : 21
ΠΕΡΙΑΑΛ ΥΠΗΡΕΣ.:                        ΜΑΣΚΑ : 1100000000

Α/Α : Ν Α Σ Κ Α  ΥΠΗΕΡΟΡΗΜΙΑΣ          Π Α Ρ Α Τ Η Ρ Η Σ Ε Ι Σ
 1  : 0001000000 : 27/09/83 : ΣΧΕΤΙΚΟ : *********************
    :           :          : ΠΕΡΙΓΡΑΦΗ: *********************
 2  : 1190000000 : 27/09/83 : ΣΧΕΤΙΚΟ : 3201/2-201846/12-9-83/ΥΒΕΑ
    :           :          : ΠΕΡΙΓΡΑΦΗ:
 3  : 1000000000 : 07/10/83 : ΣΧΕΤΙΚΟ : ΠΡΟΑΩΡΙΧΟΣ ΔΠΑ/7=10=83.
    :           :          : ΠΕΡΙΓΡΑΦΗ: ΔΗΜΟΣΙΕΥΤΑ ΤΙΤ 20 ΒΕ83.
```

```
ΑΓΜ : 10000296476
ΕΠΩΝΥΜΟΝ : ΜΑΣΤΟΡΑΣ        ΚΩΝΣΤΑΝΤΙΝ ΙΩΑΝΗ ΕΛΕ
ΕΤΠΟ : 822                              ΩΒΑΘ : 22      ΒΑΘΜΟΙ : 21
ΠΕΡΙΑΑΛ ΥΠΗΡΕΣ.: ΚΕΥΓ-ΓΟΑ               ΜΑΣΚΑ : 1110001000

Α/Α : Ν Α Σ Κ Α  ΙΗΙΕΡΟΡΗΜΙΑΣ          Π Α Ρ Α Τ Η Ρ Η Σ Ε Ι Σ
 1  : 1110001000 : 01/06/83 : ΣΧΕΤΙΚΟ : 82 ΒΥΤΕΑ
    :           :          : ΠΕΡΙΓΡΑΦΗ: ΗΓΕΤ.ΣΤΕΛΕΧΟΣ.
```

```
ΑΓΜ : 12600125505
ΕΠΩΝΥΜΟΝ : ΑΡΑΓΓΕΛΕΤΟΥ     ΔΗΜΗΤΡΙΟΣ ΕΥΑΓΓ ΣΟΥ
ΕΤΠΟ : 835                              ΩΒΑΘ : 11      ΒΑΘΜΟΙ : 21
ΠΕΡΙΑΑΛ ΥΠΗΡΕΣ.: 025 ΤΠ/ΕΟΑ             ΜΑΣΚΑ : 1020000300

Α/Α : Ν Α Σ Κ Α  ΙΗΙΕΡΟΡΗΜΙΑΣ          Π Α Ρ Α Τ Η Ρ Η Σ Ε Ι Σ
 1  : 0001000000 : 05/10/83 : ΣΧΕΤΙΚΟ : *********************
    :           :          : ΠΕΡΙΓΡΑΦΗ: *********************
 2  : 1020000000 : 05/10/83 : ΣΧΕΤΙΚΟ : *********************
    :           :          : ΠΕΡΙΓΡΑΦΗ: Ο ΑΔΕΛΦΟΣ ΤΟΥ ΦΟΙΤΗΤΗΣ ΣΤΗ ΡΟΥΜΑΝΙΑ ΑΠΟ 3ΕΤΙΑΣ
```

```
ΑΓΜ : 14520320324
ΕΠΩΝΥΜΟΝ : ΑΛ ΙΩΑΝΗΣ       ΧΡΙΣΤΟΘΟΥ ΝΙΚΟΛ ΚΑΕ
ΕΤΠΟ : 629                              ΩΒΑΘ : 11      ΒΑΘΜΟΙ : 21
ΠΕΡΙΑΑΛ ΥΠΗΡΕΣ.: 825 ΙΤΣ                ΜΑΣΚΑ : 1032000000

Α/Α : Ν Α Σ Κ Α  ΙΠΗΡΙΙΗΙΑΣ           Π Α Ρ Α Τ Η Ρ Η Σ Ε Ι Σ
 1  : 1000000000 : 22/06/83 : ΣΧΕΤΙΚΟ : 411.6/37/70616/13-6-83/Γ ΣΣ71
    :           :          : ΠΕΡΙΓΡΑΦΗ: ΚΑΝΙ Ο ΠΑΤΕΡΑΣ ΣΙΟΥ ΥΣΙΓΡΑΦΗΣΕ ΚΑΤΑ ΚΥ/ΑΚΟΥ-ΕΙΝ
    :           :          :           ΤΗΣΙ ΝΑ Ν4 ΤΑΡΓΕΤΙΣ 16 ΑΝΕΡΓ.ΑΟΒΙΟΛΑΟΙΑ(ΝΑΟ).
```

Exhibit 10

A.

Η αφίσα του ΠΑΣΟΚ το 1985. Τότε που έκαιγε τους φακέλους . . .

B.

Exhibit 11

A.

A portion of the list made by the Parliament's Investigation Committee on wire-tappings showing the names of some E.Y.P. listeners and the names of the corresponding persons, they were charged to surveille politicians—including Caramanlis—journalists, the Premier's Guards, etc. in *I Proti,* Sept. 21, 1989.

Ακροατές Ε.Υ.Π.	Παρακολουθούμενα πολιτικά στελέχη, Εφημερίδες κλπ.
Σταγάκης	ΕΛΕΥΘΕΡΟΤΥΠΙΑ, Ανδρες προσωπ.φρουράς τ.Πρωθυπουργού.
Μίτζιος	ΒΗΜΑ, ΑΥΡΙΑΝΗ
Μεντζιδάκης	ΕΛΕΥΘΕΡΟΤΥΠΙΑ, Τεγόπουλος; Φρουρά τ.Πρωθυπουργού. Τακτικός.
Τζομάκας	ΑΥΡΙΑΝΗ, ΕΘΝΟΣ, Φρουρά τ.Πρωθυπουργού, Ανωμεριτάκης, Γιαννουλέας.
Βαρδάκης	Καραμανλής, ΕΘΝΟΣ, Μπόμπολας, Γεννηματάς.

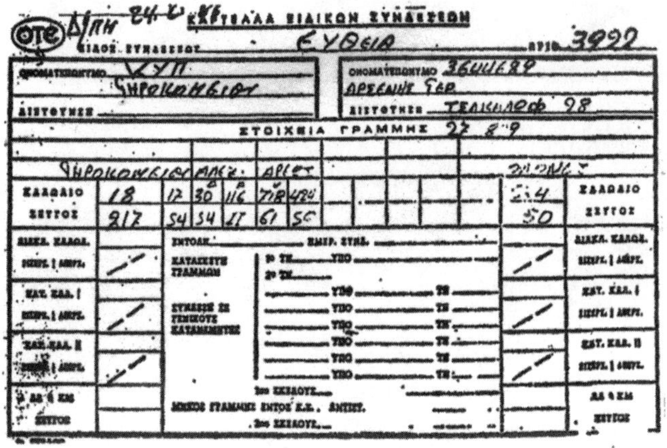

B.

Two of the 300 K.Y.P./O.T.E. cards of "special connections" indicating the wiretapping of the telephones of the PASOK deputy G. Arsenis, and the weekly publisher, K. Papaïoannou, in *Eleftheros Typos* of April 3, 1990.

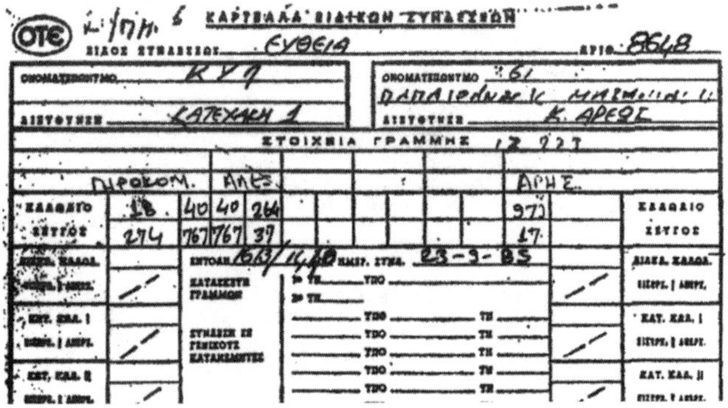

Exhibit 12

φακέλωμα!»

ΕΦΗΜΕΡΙΣ ΤΗΣ ΚΥΒΕΡΝΗΣΕΩΣ
ΤΗΣ ΕΛΛΗΝΙΚΗΣ ΔΗΜΟΚΡΑΤΙΑΣ

ΑΘΗΝΑ 28 ΑΥΓΟΥΣΤΟΥ 1989	ΤΕΥΧΟΣ ΔΕΥΤΕΡΟ	ΑΡΙΘΜΟΣ ΦΥΛΛΟΥ 830

Αριθ. 8504/7-14668   (11)

Καταστροφή των ατομικών φακέλων πολιτικών φρονημάτων των Ελλήνων πολιτών. των φυλασσομένων σε Υπηρεσίες του Υπουργείου Δημόσιας Τάξης.

ΟΙ ΥΠΟΥΡΓΟΙ
ΠΡΟΕΔΡΙΑΣ ΚΥΒΕΡΝΗΣΕΩΣ, ΕΣΩΤΕΡΙΚΩΝ
ΔΙΚΑΙΟΣΥΝΗΣ ΚΑΙ ΔΗΜΟΣΙΑΣ ΤΑΞΗΣ

Έχοντας υπόψη:

1. Τις διατάξεις του Ν.1558/1985 «Κυβέρνηση και Κυβερνητικά Όργανα» (Α-137).

2. Την από 24.8.1989 απόφαση του υπουργικού Συμβουλίου. αποφασίζομε:

1. Την καταστροφή των ατομικών φακέλων των πολιτικών φρονημάτων των Ελλήνων πολιτών. που φυλάσσονται από τις Υπηρεσίες του υπουργείου Δημόσιας Τάξης.

2. Η καταστροφή των ανωτέρω φακέλων για κάθε Νομό ανατίθεται σε Επιτροπή, αποτελούμενη από τους:

α) Νομάρχη, ως Πρόεδρο

β) Εισαγγελέα Πρωτοδικών και

γ) Αστυνομικό Δ/ντή της έδρας της Νομαρχίας. ως μέλη.

3. Ειδικά για το Νομό Αττικής. η Επιτροπή αποτελείται από:

α) Το Γενικό Γραμματέα της Περιφέρειας Αττικής. ως Πρόεδρο.

β) Το Εισαγγελέα Εφετών Αθηνών και

γ) Το Γενικό Αστυνομικό Δ/ντή Αττικής. ως μέλος.

4. Ως ημερομηνία έναρξης της καταστροφής. ορίζεται η 29η Αυγούστου 1989. ημέρα Τρίτη και ώρα 11.00΄ και σε χώρο κατάλληλο και προσιτό στο κοινό.

5. Κατά την καταστροφή των ανωτέρω φακέλων. παρίστανται εκπρόσωποι των κομμάτων. προσκαλούμενοι για το σκοπό αυτόν και το κοινό ελεύθερα.

Η απόφαση αυτή να δημοσιευθεί στην Εφημερίδα της Κυβερνήσεως.

Αθήνα. 28 Αυγούστου 1989

ΟΙ ΥΠΟΥΡΓΟΙ

ΠΡΟΕΔΡΙΑΣ ΤΗΣ ΚΥΒΕΡΝΗΣΕΩΣ	ΕΣΩΤΕΡΙΚΩΝ
ΑΘΑΝ. ΚΑΝΕΛΛΟΠΟΥΛΟΣ	ΝΙΚ. ΚΩΝΣΤΑΝΤΟΠΟΥΛΟΣ
ΔΙΚΑΙΟΣΥΝΗΣ	ΔΗΜΟΣΙΑΣ ΤΑΞΗΣ
ΦΩΤΙΟΣ ΚΟΥΒΕΛΗΣ	ΙΩΑΝ. ΚΕΦΑΛΟΓΙΑΝΝΗΣ

Exhibit 13

YIANNIS IOANNOU'S POLITICAL CARTOONS

A.

"Our government has assured us that only (paper) files will be burnt . . . and not the informers."

Source: *I Proti*, August 29, 1989.

B.

"Oh No the computers! You have burnt the files, If you burn and the tapes, how can we exist as a state?"

Source: *I Proti*, September 1, 1989.

Exhibit 14

«ΤΑ ΝΕΑ», Σάββατο 12 Οκτωβρίου 1985

«φακέλωμα»

Πρέπει να
διαφυλαχτούν
οι ελευθερίες
του ατόμου
από τους
κινδύνους της
πληροφορικής
και κυρίως να
προστατευτεί
το απόρρητο

"The personal freedoms must be preserved by the informatics' threats and especially (communications) privacy must be protected."

Exhibit 15

Κυριακάτικη   1 Ιανουαρίου 1995

Το **ΣΥΜΒΟΥΛΙΟ** *της Ευρωπαϊκής Ενωσης προβαίνει στη δημιουργία*
ΚΕΝΤΡΟΥ ΠΛΗΡΟΦΟΡΙΩΝ

Φακέλωμα ευρωπαϊκό και ηλεκτρονικό

Του ΓΙΩΡΓΟΥ
ΠΕΧΛΙΒΑΝΙΔΗ

Τελικά δεν το
γλιτώνουμε το
ηλεκτρονικό
φακέλωμα. Ύστερα από
κυοφορία ετών και
διαβουλεύσεις, και παρά
τις αντιρρήσεις,
αντιδράσεις και
αμφισβητήσεις, η
Ευρωπαϊκή Ενωση
επιβάλλει στα κράτη-
μέλη της -άρα και στην
Ελλάδα- το ηλεκτρονικό
φακέλωμα των πολιτών
με τα πλέον σύγχρονα
μέσα.

A. "European, Electronic Filing
(surveillance) is enforced by
EU against the citizens of the
member states."
Source: *Sunday Eleftherotypia*,
Jan. 1,1995.

ΣΥΜΦΩΝΙΑ ΣΕΝΓΚΕΝ

Το μεγαλύτερο ηλεκτρο-
νικό φακέλωμα
στην ιστορία
της ανθρωπότητας!

B. "The Schengen
Agreement
(imposes) the
biggest surveillance
in the history of
humanity!"
Source: *To Pontiki*,
Jan. 5, 1995.

Exhibit 16

A.
"No to the electronic filing," "Not to the police (censorship) of our ideas" slogans against the Schengen Agreement by Orthodox Christian demonstrators in a mass demonstration at Athens. Source: *Sunday Eleftherotypia*, March 19, 2000.

B.
"No to the electronic filing" a graffiti by anarchists. Source: Author's photograph.

Exhibit 17

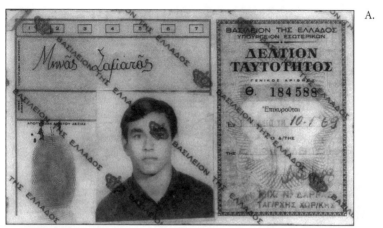

A.

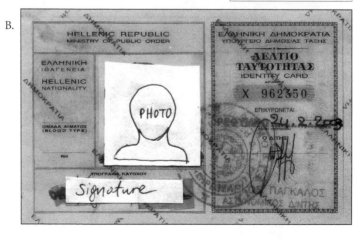

A. The old police identity card and B. the new "Europeanized" one without several items of data, like the fingerprint, occupation, marital status, husband or wife's name, and religion.

Exhibit 18

ΗΠΑ και Βρετανία πιέζουν για 17Ν

«Ομπρέλα» δορυφορικής παρακολούθησης

Στην ΚηφιCIAS...

US and British road and sky surveillance in Athens central streets looking for November 17 terrorist group during 2001. Source: A. *Ta Nea*, June 30, 2001. B. *Eleftherotypia*, May 31, 2001.

«Οι κάμερες του "μεγάλου αδελφού", της CIA, παρακολουθούν τα πάντα στην Αθήνα. Οι υπηρεσίες των ΗΠΑ διενεργούν από μόνες τους παρακολουθήσεις και επιχειρήσεις σε όλη την πρωτεύουσα. Ο "Ε.Τ." ανακάλυψε τους Αμερικανούς στην Κηφισίας, όπου με ειδικά οχήματα-βαν. που φέρουν κάμερες και ειδικά ηλεκτρονικά συστήματα, "σαρώνουν" καθημερινώς τη λεωφόρο»...

Από το ρεπορτάζ του Θανάση Αργυράκη στον «Ελ. Τύπο».

Exhibit 19

A.

Μια πόλη Big Brother

B.

C.

Athens, full of CCTV systems, has become a "Big Brother" city. Source:
A. *Sunday Eleftherotypia*, March 17, 2002
B. *Sunday Eleftherotypia*, June 2, 2002
C. *To Vima*, July 21, 2000.

Exhibit 20

Traffic police CCTV systems almost everywhere on central
Athens roads. Source: *Sunday Eleftherotypia.* Dec. 22, 2002.

Exhibit 21

A.

Οι αρμόδιοι προειδοποιούν:

15.000 εταιρείες μας φακελώνουν

Και άγριο εμπόριο προσωπικών στοιχείων

B.

Σ' ΕΝΑ CD-ROM ΦΑΚΕΛΩΜΕΝΟΙ ΟΛΟΙ ΑΠΟ ΕΤΑΙΡΕΙΕΣ

ΠΩΛΟΥΝΤΑΙ

όλα τα προσωπικά μας στοιχεία

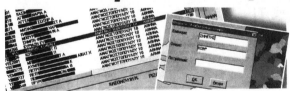

Για 10.000 δρχ.
όλα τα στοιχεία
- και οι γείτονες -
του Πρωθυπουργού!
σελίδες 18-19

A. "15,000 commercial firms collect and process our personal data"
Source: *Ta Nea*, Sept. 4, 1999.
B. "In a CDRom they have recorded for sale all our personal data,
even those of (former) Prime Minister Simitis!"
Source: *Ta Nea*, June 12, 2000.

Exhibit 22

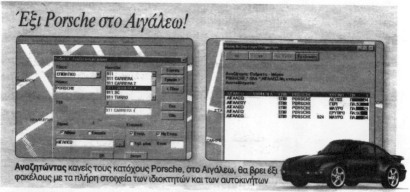

Έξι Porsche στο Αιγάλεω!

Αναζητώντας κανείς τους κατόχους Porsche, στο Αιγάλεω, θα βρει έξι φακέλους με τα πλήρη στοιχεία των ιδιοκτητών και των αυτοκινήτων

A.

«Λαδώνουν» υπαλλήλους για να πάρουν καταλόγους με τα στοιχεία μας

B.

Στις λίστες και όλοι οι αξιωματικοί

Οι αξιωματικοί του Στρατού και της Αστυνομίας καθώς και οι συνταξιούχοι συνάδελφοί τους εντοπίζονται, μέσα σε λίγα λεπτά, σε όποιο σημείο της Ελλάδας και αν διαμένουν

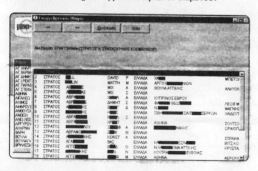

A. Illegal CDRom for sale with electronic lists with Athens luxury car owners' names, license plate numbers, addresses, telephone numbers.

B. Professional groups lists and in this one military personnel.

Source: *Ta Nea*, June 12, 2000.

Exhibit 23

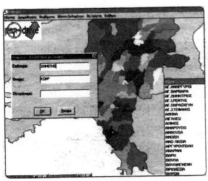 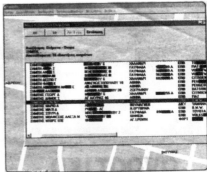

Βρίσκεις τον Σημίτη, το Ι.Χ. του και τους γείτονες

Μια αναζήτηση στο όνομα Σημίτης Κωνσταντίνος στη βάση δεδομένων των σχημάτων θα δώσει τον αριθμό κυκλοφορίας και όλα τα στοιχεία του αυτοκινήτου του, τη διεύθυνση και το τηλέφωνό του. Το σπίτι του θα εντοπιστεί στον χάρτη και μαζί τα στοιχεία των... γειτόνων του

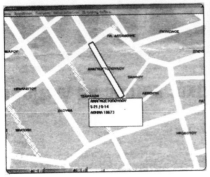 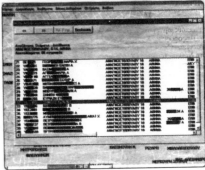

In the same CDRom there are specific directions on how you can find (former) Prime Minister C. Simitis's car data, address, telephone, even his neighbors' data.
Source: *Ta Nea*, June 12, 2000.

Exhibit 24

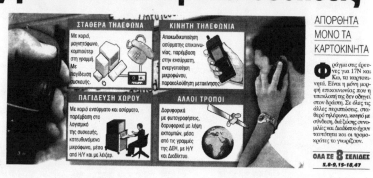

How "Big Brother" watches us: Special military
officers explain electronic surveillance and how
to protect ourselves.
Source: *Eleftherotypia*, Aug. 14, 2002.

Exhibit 25

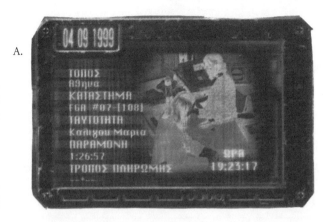

A.

B.

C.

Audio video surveillance in Athens of various electronic transactions using:
A. plastic credit card
B. a bank ATM and
C. mobile phone.
Source: *Ta Nea*, Sept. 4, 1999.

Exhibit 26

"Multinational 'Big Brother' at Athens airport 'Eleftherios Venizelos': various biometric scanning of *Alitalia* passengers to the USA. *Source: Eleftherotypia*, Sept. 27, 2003.

Exhibit 27

The Athens 2004 Olympic Games super panopticism! A zeppelin, helicopters (even NATO's Awacs), and speed boats, radars, and CCTV systems integrated in the expensive C41 security system pacify fears for terrorist attacks during the games. Source: *Ta Nea*, Dec. 5, 2003.

Exhibit 28

A.

Hellenic Data Protection Authority

"Every citizen should be in a position to know at every moment who, where, when, how and why processes their personal data."

Contact the Authority and get informed about your rights.

Copyright 2001 | Hellenic Data Protection Authority

http://www.dpa.gr

B.

ΕΝΗΜΕΡΩΣΗ ΓΙΑ ΤΗΡΗΣΗ ΑΡΧΕΙΟΥ
(ΑΡΘΡΟ 11 ΠΑΡ. 1 Ν. 2472/1997)

Η Ανώνυμη Εταιρεία με την επωνυμία "ΟΛΥΜΠΙΟΣ ΑΝΩΝΥΜΗ ΕΙΣΑΓΩΓΙΚΗ & ΕΜΠΟΡΙΚΗ ΕΤΑΙΡΕΙΑ" που εδρεύει στην Καισαριανή, οδός Τ. Κέννεντυ, αρ. 35 και εκπροσωπείται νόμιμα, σύμφωνα με τις διατάξεις του νόμου 2472/97 και σε εφαρμογή της με αρ. 408/30-11-98 απόφασης του κ. Προέδρου της Αρχής Προστασίας Δεδομένων Προσωπικού Χαρακτήρα, ενημερώνει τους υπαλλήλους, τους πελάτες, τους μετόχους και τους λοιπούς συναλλασσόμενους ότι: Η εταιρεία στο πλαίσιο άσκησης της επιχειρηματικής δραστηριότητάς της και σύμφωνα με τις απαιτήσεις της εκάστοτε ισχύουσας νομοθεσίας καταχωρεί δεδομένα προσωπικού χαρακτήρα του παραπάνω Νόμου για πελάτες, προμηθευτές, μετόχους, προσωπικό και λοιπούς συνεργάτες.

Σκοπός της επεξεργασίας: Η εκπλήρωση υποχρεώσεων που επιβάλλονται από τη φορολογική, εμπορική και εργατική νομοθεσία, η εξυπηρέτηση, υποστήριξη και παρακολούθηση των συναλλαγών της εταιρείας με τους πελάτες της και τους προμηθευτές της, η προάσπιση των συμφερόντων της εμπορικής πίστης και των οικονομικών συναλλαγών.

Αποδέκτες των δεδομένων: Αποδέκτες των δεδομένων δύναται να είναι το Ελληνικό Δημόσιο, οι εποπτικές, φορολογικές και δικαστικές αρχές και οι διάδικοι κάθε δίκης, στην οποία εμπλέκεται η Εταιρεία για την προστασία των εννόμων συμφερόντων της, οι συνεργαζόμενες τράπεζες και τα ασφαλιστικά ταμεία προς εξυπηρέτηση των συναλλακτικών σχέσεων ή των εν γένει θεμάτων προσωπικού.

Χρόνος διατήρησης αρχείου: Είναι ο απαιτούμενος από την φορολογική, εμπορική και εργατική νομοθεσία καθώς και την καλή πορεία των εργασιών της επιχείρησης. Πέραν των παραπάνω χρονικών ορίων, το αρχείο ή τμήμα αυτού δύναται να τηρείται για ιστορικούς ή στατιστικούς λόγους ή για λόγους πρόνοιας, στα πλαίσια προάσπισης των συμφερόντων της Εταιρείας.

Μέσα τήρησης αρχείου: Τα δεδομένα τηρούνται με έγγραφα καθώς και με ηλεκτρονικά και μαγνητικά μέσα.

Ασφάλεια επεξεργασίας: Η επεξεργασία των παραπάνω στοιχείων διεξάγεται από τους εργαζόμενους της εταιρείας στο πρόσωπο των οποίων συντρέχουν οι προϋποθέσεις του άρθρου 10 του ν. 2472/97.

Δικαίωμα πρόσβασης: Έχουν όλοι εκείνοι των οποίων τα ονόματα περιλαμβάνονται στο αρχείο μας. Επίσης πρόσβαση στα αρχεία αυτά έχουν τα όργανα δημοσίων αρχών, κλπ. που έχουν αρμοδιότητα ελέγχου της εφαρμογής της φορολογικής, ασφαλιστικής, εμπορικής και λοιπής νομοθεσίας.

Αθήνα, 25 Φεβρουαρίου 1999
ΟΛΥΜΠΙΟΣ ΑΝΩΝΥΜΗ ΕΙΣΑΓΩΓΙΚΗ & ΕΜΠΟΡΙΚΗ ΕΤΑΙΡΕΙΑ
Τ. Κέννεντυ 35, 16121, Καισαριανή

A. The Hellenic Data Protection Authority's logo & slogan.
B. One of thousands of compulsory statements by a corporation published at Athens daily for legalizing a personal data archive according to Law 2472/1997, Article 11.

Exhibit 29

Artistic anti-surveillance warnings.
"They watch you," "A Zone of monitored daily life."
Source: Eleftherotypia, June 4, 2003

Exhibit 30

A destruction of a CCTV camera, after a demonstration at Heraklion, Crete.
Source: Patris , April 28, 2001.